B 453117

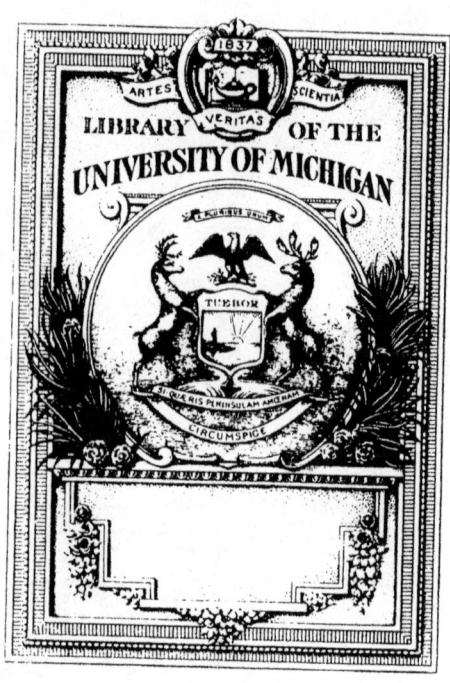

THE GIFT OF
Charities Pub. Committee

RUSSELL SAGE
FOUNDATION

REPORT ON THE DESIRABILITY OF ESTABLISHING AN EMPLOYMENT BUREAU IN THE CITY OF NEW YORK

By EDWARD T. DEVINE

SCHIFF PROFESSOR OF SOCIAL ECONOMY, COLUMBIA UNIVERSITY,
GENERAL SECRETARY OF THE CHARITY ORGANIZATION SOCIETY OF
THE CITY OF NEW YORK

NEW YORK
CHARITIES PUBLICATION
COMMITTEE
MCMIX

COPYRIGHT, 1909, BY
THE RUSSELL SAGE FOUNDATION

PRESS OF
WM. F. FELL COMPANY
PHILADELPHIA

Report on the Desirability of Establishing an Employment Bureau in the City of New York

INTRODUCTORY NOTE

On October 27, 1908, Mr. Jacob H. Schiff, who had previously suggested on several occasions the establishment of an unofficial employment bureau on a business basis, definitely proposed that the Charity Organization Society should invite to a conference several gentlemen who might be interested in the plan, for the purpose of securing their co-operation and the necessary financial support. The President and General Secretary of the Society conferred with Mr. Schiff in regard to the matter on two occasions, Mr. Cyrus L. Sulzberger, President of the United Hebrew Charities, being present at the second conference. Mr. Schiff's proposition submitted in writing at this conference was as follows:

The proposition is to organize in the City of New York an Employment Bureau under a board of trustees composed of experienced men, preferentially from the mercantile and industrial classes.

The Bureau should be placed under a manager of great executive ability, with two or three assistants, the latter to be thoroughly conversant with the classes and their peculiarities which compose New York City's working population.

The Bureau is to establish an organization covering all sections of the United States, so that it shall be in immediate and constant touch with requirements for labor and employment wherever such may exist, but its benefits are to accrue primarily to the unemployed of the City of New York.

The Bureau is to charge a reasonable fee to the employer for the procuring of labor, for which the latter may reimburse himself, gradually, if this is deemed well, from the wages of the employee. It is hoped that by this the Bureau will in time become self-supporting; but to assure its establishment and maintenance for a number of years, until it shall have become self-supporting, a working fund of $100,000 ought to be assured at the outset.

It was the opinion of Mr. de Forest, in which view the others present concurred, that before calling such a meeting there should be a careful examination of the need for such a bureau and inquiry into the reasons for the discontinuance of the Free State Employment Bureau, the Cooper Union Labor Bureau, and other similar agencies which under various auspices have attempted to deal with the same problem, and, if it is found expedient to recommend that a bureau be established, that a somewhat fuller statement should be made of the lines on which the proposed bureau is to be conducted.

Mr. de Forest offered on behalf of the Russell Sage Foundation to meet any necessary expense of such a preliminary inquiry, and the undersigned was requested to undertake the preparation of the report.

Although the Employment Bureau is not intended as an emergency measure to deal with an existing temporary situation, it was thought to be desirable to reach a conclusion in time to permit the undertaking of the enterprise during the present winter, if it is decided that it is to be undertaken at all. For this reason the inquiry has been made in the briefest possible time and has rigidly excluded everything which does not directly bear upon the immediate question in hand, namely, whether it is desirable to establish a bureau substantially on the lines indicated in Mr. Schiff's memorandum.

REPORT ON THE DESIRABILITY OF ESTABLISHING AN EMPLOYMENT BUREAU IN THE CITY OF NEW YORK

That there are in New York City in good times as well as in periods of depression a very considerable number of employable persons who need work who are not actually employed, may be taken for granted. Immigration, migration from other communities, irregularity in building operations and in other industries, and the seasonal character of many trades, are causes which operate in all communities, but in New York City in a wholly extraordinary degree. Besides such causes affecting large masses of people, individuals, of whom there is a large number in the aggregate, lose much, to them, valuable time in finding work after illness, or when from any other cause they have been compelled to give up their work. For our present purpose it has not been thought necessary to make any estimate of the unemployed. Common observation and the testimony of trade unions, charitable societies, and the daily press sufficiently establish the fact that in normal years the total number who lose a substantial part of the working year is very considerable, and that in every depression, however local or temporary, the number is sufficiently large to become a matter of grave concern.

The question which is pertinent and important is whether the unemployed are so (1) because they are unemployable, (2) because there is no work to be had, or (3) because of mal-adjustment, which an efficient employment bureau could at least to some extent overcome. It is obvious that if they are unemployed because they are unemployable, the employment bureau is no remedy. The only adequate remedy for a lack of efficiency would be education and training. If, again, they are unemployed because of a real and permanent surplus of supply over the demand for labor, it is plain that an employment bureau could not remedy the difficulty. The bureau does not directly create opportunities for work, and its success will therefore depend on the possibility of finding it. In so far, however, as the lack of employment is due to mal-adjustment, that is to the inability of people who want work to get quickly into contact with opportunities which exist and to which there are no other equally appropriate means of access, the employment bureau will be justified. This mal-adjustment between labor and opportunities for labor may either be local, *i. e.*, within the community itself, or it may be as between communities. That is, if there is an actual surplus of labor in New York City there may still be a deficiency in other towns or cities, or on farms in New York or other states, and the employment bureau may therefore find a field for usefulness in equalizing these conditions as between communities.

The time at our disposal has not permitted an original investigation of the extent to which there is an unfilled demand for labor, either in New York City or in other communities, nor, even had there been more time, would the present be a favorable period for such an investigation. I have, however, addressed a careful letter of inquiry to about thirty persons who would be in position to give definite information on these points, if it were to be had, and whose opinions at least would be worthy of special consideration. The most striking fact about the replies to these inquiries is the complete demonstration that they give that there is no definite information on these matters and that the views of those who have evidently considered them most carefully are apt to be diametrically opposed. Professor Edward A. Ross, for example, of the University of Wisconsin, has "a growing impression that local labor markets are not sections or provinces of a general labor market, but markets of a considerable individuality," while Professor John R. Commons, of the same institution, referring to present conditions, says that "the depression in industry and resulting unemployment is general throughout the country"; and the only ground on which it appears to him that it would be worth while to establish such an employment bureau is as a model for other employment bureaus, and as a means of driving out the unreliable ones. He assumes "that the existing bureaus are adequate to make the transfers and the interchanges needed for those employers who actually are looking for workmen."

There is, however, a general consensus of opinion among economists and authorities on labor problems that even in periods of active trade there is by no means a complete adjustment between seekers after work and opportunities for employment even within the city. Professor H. R. Seager summarizes the cause of this mal-adjustment as follows:

(1) Irregular employment in many trades:
(2) The rise and fall of particular employing firms causing a constant shifting of employees from employer to employer:
(3) Immigration and the unadjusted immigrant worker resulting from it:
(4) The absence of any satisfactory agency or agencies for properly classifying workmen in search of employment so that employers can be relieved in part of the task of trying out new hands.

The contrary view of Dr. A. F. Weber, chief statistician of the New York Public Service Commission, speaking from an experience gained in part in the New York Labor Department, should be recorded:

"As to local mal-adjustment of demand and supply in the labor market, I should be disposed to say that the existing agencies and methods do on the whole meet the requirements of the situation; that is to say, in a period of normal activity there are relatively few workers without employment at a time when employers are seeking help of the same grade or class. There is much room for improvement in the methods of the private employment offices, which may be obtained through more careful public regulation and possibly through the example of a well endowed bureau, but that the latter could find local situations for the unemployed in any considerable numbers to me seems doubtful."

On the other hand, Mr. Robert A. Woods of South End House, Boston, writes that he has known of many instances in which the evidence of mal-adjustment in the matter of employment was convincing, and he thinks that there cannot be any doubt that employers and workmen both lose a great deal of time and meet with much embarrassment which an employment bureau could remedy if it went at its work with something of the scope and detailed accuracy of the weather and crop reports.

Professor Frank A. Fetter of Cornell University is led by general considerations, in the absence of exact figures, to the belief that unemployment is to a considerable degree due to mal-adjustment.

Professor E. L. Bogart of Princeton holds the same view, and adds that the lack of adjustment differs greatly in different branches of labor.

Professor J. B. Clark of Columbia holds emphatically the view that loss of employment by large bodies of men personally fit for it is invariably due to mal-adjustment, but admits that the re-arrangement may be too extensive to be made within the neighborhood within which the men reside.

Mr. Sidney Webb, the historian of the trade union movement in England, writes that "unemployment in large cities can only in a restricted sense be said to be caused to any great extent by the mere failure of employers to find workmen or of workmen to find employers. They do find each other now, even in the worst of times, though only after some delay. If there were no unemployment, in the sense of there being exactly as many vacancies as there were men to fill them, there would still be a certain proportion of time lost in shifting situations. This, even if no more than one day in each case, would appear in the statistics as a percentage of men unemployed. Experience of the best organized trades in

England, at the very busiest of times, rather points to the fact that minimum of unemployment, if it can be so called, due to time lost in shifting from job to job, and analogous causes, may amount to something like one per cent of the whole of the working-class population, indicating an average loss, from this cause alone, in the best of times, of three days per annum."

Turning to mal-adjustment as between communities, practically all differences of opinion disappear. Even Professor Commons, whose opinion concerning the general character of the present industrial depression is quoted above, admits that if the Bureau had capable agents in the several cities to which surplus labor is sent, and these agents are able to thoroughly master the local situation and get beneath the representations both of employers seeking cheap labor and trade unionists hostile to imported labor, it might be possible to avoid the difficulties to which he refers, although he thinks that the expense of securing this kind of competent help would be so great that it is impracticable.

All others from whom opinions have been obtained, economists, employers, trade unionists, social workers, and government and state officials who have had to deal with labor questions, are firmly convinced that surplus labor is a feature of congested communities and not a general phenomenon, that in ordinary times an urgent demand for both skilled and unskilled labor may exist, and does exist, in many communities at the very moment when the unemployed are congregating in other communities, and especially that labor is needed at remunerative wages on farms at the very time when the already overcrowded cities are increasing in population.

The conclusion to which I am forced to come from a painstaking examination of all of the data on this subject available in print, and from correspondence and personal conference with those whom I have thought most competent to advise on the subject, is that there is a need at all times, and in periods of even slight depression a very urgent need, of an efficient system of bringing together as quickly as possible those who are seeking work and those who are seeking workers. For the reason suggested by Mr. Sidney Webb, I am inclined to think that such an agency would actually increase to an appreciable extent the effective demand for workers. Whether such an agency is the Employment Bureau which we are considering, or the system of labor exchanges advocated for England, we may be equally confident that they would, in Mr. Webb's language, "not only greatly increase the worker's chances of improving his or her position, greatly lessen the time lost between job and job, greatly diminish the wearing anxiety of looking for work, and greatly facilitate the employer's getting all the labor he can profitably employ. It would not only increase the mobility of labor, but would actually increase the aggregate volume of demand, to the extent of the opportunities for profitable employment that the employer now lets slip because he can't get just what he wants when he wants it."

I have dwelt upon this aspect of the inquiry at length because as Dr. J. H. Hollander of Johns Hopkins University pointed out in a personal conversation, it is the crucial and fundamental point to be considered. If it is established, or if there is reason to believe that there is such failure of adjustment resulting in a considerable addition at any one time to the total number of the unemployed, then there is no doubt of the necessity to meet this need, and the only questions are whether it is sufficiently met by other existing agencies, and whether it can be better met by some different type of agency from that which is proposed. It is not necessary to inquire whether the number of the unemployed at present is ten thousand or one hundred thousand. There is no doubt that the number is large enough and the distress and hardship involved are great enough to lead to prompt and energetic action in the establishment of some suitable means of dealing with the problem. It may be pointed out also that the distress and hardship are by no means measured by the number who would register themselves in any public or official way as unemployed. Besides those who would thus appear, there are many who are irregularly employed or who accept employment at lower wages than they are capable of earning or whose particular place and kind of work do not fully utilize their powers and capacities. While some of this is no doubt inevitable, it remains true that an employment bureau could help many individuals to avoid these hardships and could place them in positions where society would get a better return from them.

The proposed Employment Bureau would certainly be one means, and as I shall hereafter show, probably the best means, of meeting this great and permanent need by mediating between work and workers in that large number of instances for which no other especially appropriate means of communication has been established.

IS THE NEED MET BY EXISTING INSTITUTIONS?

Commercial Employment Agencies
I have not thought it necessary to make an independent investigation of the existing commercial agencies for the reason that numerous investigations have been made, and one, which is official and doubtless exceptionally thorough, is in progress at this writing under the direction of the New York State Immigration Commission. Moreover these agencies are now licensed by a municipal License Bureau under authority of state law, so that there is more or less continuous supervision of them, and knowledge of their methods and results is readily obtainable. Unfortunately there is no room for doubt that the grave abuses in these bureaus still prevail, although naturally under official inspection and oversight they are somewhat less serious than in former years.

Without anticipating the findings of the State Commission it is within bounds to say that the private commercial agencies do not meet the need which has been described, that their standards of integrity and efficiency are low, that their real service to employers and employees, except in a few occupations, and in the case of a few well conducted agencies, is exceedingly slight. Operated primarily for profit, they have a constant temptation to over-charge, to misrepresent, and to encourage frequent changes for the sake of the fee. Miss Kellor in her volume "Out of Work" estimated that two-thirds of the 732 employment agencies visited in New York at the time of her study five years ago resorted to these dishonorable practices and fraudulent methods; that a very small proportion conducted an honorable business by efficient methods; and a somewhat larger number, without being open to the unreserved strictures justly made on the lowest class, were still so unsystematic and inefficient as to be practically worthless from the point of view of the community. Probably because of prosecutions, revoked licenses and official scrutiny, these proportions would be somewhat modified at present,* but with the exception of the few agencies constituting Miss Kellor's first class, the whole business is conducted on so low a plane, with so much of extortion, misrepresentation, fraud, and direct affiliation with immorality and vice, as to afford one of the strongest arguments for the establishment of an efficient bureau conducted primarily in the interests of working men who seek its services, even though in the expectation of obtaining a moderate return upon the investment. It is a striking fact that the principal argument for the establishment of free state labor bureaus has always been found in the abuses of the private commercial agencies. In Europe as well as in America there has even been a demand for their suppression by law, and though this demand has come from a minority there has frequently been a sufficient recognition of the evils in them to secure legislation requiring them to be licensed and supervised by the state. The situation is not unlike that which was disclosed by the investigation made by the Charity Organization Society in 1892 regarding the evils of the old-time unregulated pawnshop. It was then decided that in addition to any possible police supervision, there should be brought to bear upon the recognized abuses of the pawnshop system the pressure of competition from an agency which, strictly upon a business basis, would enter their own field and demonstrate that the business could be conducted without either fraud or extortion.

Charitable (Free) Employment Bureaus

The three most important attempts in New York City to conduct a free employment bureau under the auspices of philanthropic agencies are the Cooper Union Labor Bureau, conducted by the New York Asso-

* It is the opinion of the Commissioner of the License Bureau that at present 60 per cent of the private employment agencies do an honorable and straightforward business, but others think this estimate unduly optimistic. It is said that two-thirds of those whose licenses are revoked continue in business under another name, or as nominal employees of other agencies.

ciation for Improving the Condition of the Poor, the Employment Bureau of the United Hebrew Charities, and the Employment Bureau of the Society of St. Vincent de Paul. All of these have been discontinued; and all for this reason, among others, that the maintenance of a general employment bureau is not the proper function of a charitable society, and that from the point of view of the success of the employment bureau the connection with a charitable society is disadvantageous. No one of these three employment bureaus ever had at its command an adequate working capital or a superintendent of the executive capacity suggested in Mr. Schiff's memorandum, and it can hardly be said that the responsible managers of any of them ever seriously proposed to themselves that their employment bureau should fill the large place contemplated in the present plan. If the underlying ideas and policies of these bureaus had been different, if they had had at their disposal a superintendent and staff really qualified to deal with the task in its larger social aspects, and if they had been in position to invest a large capital in creating a mechanism and establishing proper trade relations, it is possible that they might have overcome the handicap of connection with a charitable agency, however serious and embarrassing such an affiliation may be. Their experience, therefore, while instructive and illuminating in many respects, cannot be regarded as conclusive.

Still less importance can be attached to such free agencies as the Free Employment Bureau now maintained at the Barge Office by the German Society and the Irish Emigrant Society. This Bureau deals almost exclusively with immigrants from the British Islands and northwestern Europe. Its patrons are chiefly those who have been accustomed for many years to rely upon the Bureau for occasional laborers, and the volume of work done by the Bureau is not sufficiently great to throw very much light on the need for a bureau which shall seriously attempt to overcome the lack of adjustment between work and workers in the city. Excellent service has been rendered for many years by this Bureau for the particular class for whom it is intended, and there need of course be no attempt to displace it. The same is true of the employment bureaus which deal with immigrants of other nationalities, like the Italians* and Slavs, and those conducted by the various religious organizations, which do in the aggregate a considerable amount of work in finding employment for their beneficiaries, although as a rule in so unsystematic a manner and with such meagre results that it is difficult to draw any conclusions from their experience.

There are no statistics as to the total number of persons who are placed in employment by these free agencies. Although the aggregate number of persons affected and benefited is of course considerable, the fact remains that the work of these bureaus is so fragmenary, so unco-ordinated and so meagre when compared with the number of persons in the city who require such assistance that it could scarcely be seriously maintained that they meet the need. No one of them is conducted on a broad, unsectarian basis with a sufficient clientèle of employers and a staff sufficiently well organized to do the work that is proposed.

Division of Information of the Federal Bureau of Immigration

By authority of act of Congress of February, 1907, dealing with the general subject of immigration, there has been established in the Bureau of Immigration of the Department of Commerce and Labor a special division for collecting and distributing information to aliens and others interested. Mr. T. V. Powderly, the former Commissioner-General of Immigration, is at the head of this Division, and on the theory that the only information which is of interest to aliens or others interested is information concerning a particular job suitable to their own individual needs, the Government has established at 17 Pearl Street what is virtually, though not in name, an employment bureau. In co-operation with the Post Office Department and the Department of Agriculture,

---

* Of these the most important is the Labor Information Office for Italians, 9 Lafayette Street, which is subsidized by the Italian Government.

the Division of Information has undertaken a very comprehensive plan for obtaining information from farmers and others concerning their need for workers, and places this information at the disposal of the superintendent of the local bureau for the benefit of aliens or others who may call at the office. Having the franking privilege and the advantage of co-operation with other Federal bureaus, it would naturally be expected that such an employment bureau might develop large proportions and to a measurable extent supply the need for such service as we have been considering. There are, however, grave reasons to doubt whether such a Federal bureau can, unaided, appropriately supply the need. It requires a liberal construction of the act to justify the maintenance of a thoroughly equipped employment bureau, and although the act may be modified to meet any possible obstacles on this score, it is difficult to see on what grounds the Bureau of Immigration could properly conduct an employment bureau which would equally be at the service of citizens and aliens. If it should become a general labor bureau for all alike it should logically be transferred to the Bureau of Labor or conducted as an independent bureau within the Department of Commerce and Labor. Independently, however, of these considerations, which might be met by supplementary legislation, there are objections to the assumption of this duty by any branch of the Federal Government. It is impracticable for the Government to distinguish between citizens who would seek to use the bureau as employers, and yet such discrimination is necessary if applicants are not to be sent at unreasonably low wages or to positions where the conditions are unsatisfactory. Questions arise as to calls from employers on the occasion of strikes or lockouts, and even when there are not such acute disturbances, there would often be reason to anticipate that labor was being engaged in anticipation of a lowering of wages or other changes adverse to the interests of labor. A voluntary agency could properly insist upon full and accurate knowledge on all such questions before undertaking to supply a demand. For the Government to do so would be to invite friction and antagonism which might have very regrettable consequences. It is an open question how much of the demand for agricultural labor is a bona fide demand for efficient labor at sufficient wages, and how much is merely a demand for cheap labor at low wages, or under other very unfavorable conditions. The same is true of a part of the demand for labor in railway construction, and other similar occupations. No Government official should ever be placed in a position where it is necessary to discriminate between citizens, who, apparently in good faith, are demanding a service which the Government has undertaken to supply. Without such discrimination, however, an employment bureau operating on a large scale over a large territory would inevitably become merely a factor in reducing wages and lowering standards of living. If a generous response to inquiries on behalf of the general Government means that employers are seeking immigrant labor because it is cheap labor, and if the Government by advising immigrants to accept such offers or by facilitating their acceptance becomes a party to such lowering of standards, it may easily do harm which would vastly outweigh the services given in finding employment for a given number of people. This is a danger against which any employment bureau should take ample precautions, but it will be easier and more practicable for a voluntary, unofficial agency to take such measures than for any branch of the Federal Government.

If, however, the actual work of acting as intermediary is assumed by a voluntary agency properly equipped for the purpose, it is quite possible that co-operation between such an agency and the Federal Government might be mutually advantageous. If the Federal Government with the resources at its command, acting in the interests of employers and employees alike, and in the interests of citizens and aliens whose labor is really in demand, would collect such information as is apparently contemplated by the Immigration Law, and would place such information at the disposal of reputable voluntary agencies or make it available in some suitable way to the general public, this would enormously increase the usefulness of the voluntary bureau, and of course precautions could be taken to see that this advantage did not accrue to any one who might exploit it merely for selfish business purposes, but on the contrary to the workers and thus indirectly to employers and to the community.

After conference with the Secretary of the Department of Commerce and Labor and with the Chief and Assistant Chief of the Division of Information, and with the Superintendent of the local bureau, as well as with the Commissioner of Labor and many others who have given attention to the subject, I am convinced that while there is a great field of usefulness for the Division of Information, it is not and cannot wisely become an effective intermediary between workers and employment to an extent that will make unnecessary such an employment bureau as is under consideration.

The Labor Bureau of the State Department of Agriculture The State Department of Agriculture conducts in its branch office at 23 Park Row, New York City, a special Labor Bureau for the purpose of supplying farmers of the State with farm hands and transplanting families as tenants on New York farms. The Assistant Commissioner in charge of this office will report to the Department that in the past fiscal year 90 families have thus been sent to the country, and about 900 single men as farm laborers.

The Department learns of these opportunities through the Farmers' Granges, Institutes, advertising and news notices in the daily papers, and by correspondence. The primary purpose is to help the farmers of the state to find the labor of which, especially for certain portions of the year, they are in urgent need. The limitation in the usefulness of this plan from the point of view of the unemployed in New York City is that comparatively few of the opportunities are for work during the entire year, the wages are as a rule comparatively low, and the Bureau naturally restricts its activities to this state. Nevertheless the principle which the Bureau represents is sound, and in connection with a general

IS THE NEED MET?

Employment Bureau its services could be greatly extended. It is possible that this Labor Bureau of the Department of Agriculture might be expanded into a comprehensive and effective plan for transplanting individuals and families from New York City to the country. Whether, if it is developed in this way, it should remain a branch of the Department of Agriculture may be a question, but certainly as long as it is so conducted it represents only one aspect, although a very important aspect, of the problem with which the Employment Bureau would attempt to deal. Neither the Division of Information conducted by the Federal Government nor the Agricultural Labor Bureau of the State Government would be in any way hampered or displaced by the Employment Bureau, but both could and doubtless would co-operate with it to the mutual advantage of all concerned.

Want Advertisements
It is sometimes thought that the cheapening of daily newspapers, and the development of the want advertisements, afford a means of supplying the need in question. Such advertisements have, of course, a distinct field of usefulness, although one perhaps more restricted than is ordinarily supposed. The most superficial examination of the want columns of any newspaper which has developed this feature on a large scale discloses the fact that many of those which are nominally for help are "fake" advertisements, that is, that they do not represent a bona fide opportunity for employment of the kind indicated in the heading. Many others are intentionally vague and misleading, and frequently, after eliminating such padding, an exceedingly small remnant of bona fide requests for help remains. The system at best throws entirely upon the advertiser the responsibility of sifting out from among the replies to advertisements the one which suits his needs. To ascertain whether advertisements by employers and by applicants for work respectively vary in accordance with well known conditions of trade activities and depression, and to get some idea of the nature of the "wants" thus advertised, I have had a careful examination made of the want columns of two news-

papers in New York City on selected days in 1902 and 1905, representing what may be considered normal conditions of trade, and in the winter of 1907–08, covering the transitional period from the activity of the early autumn to the depression of the winter. The sharp change that occurred between October and November in 1907 in all kinds of positions and especially in the skilled trades, is very clearly reflected in the advertising columns.

Detailed tables with diagrams and a full report covering nearly 40,000 classified want advertisements from New York papers are to be found in an Appendix. This study of New York newspapers is supplemented by a similar examination on a slightly different plan of the files of Chicago newspapers.

My conclusion, based upon personal examination of want columns, upon this detailed examination of the files of New York and Chicago newspapers on certain selected days, and on conference with others who have been in the habit of following such advertisements in connection with the work of the Free State Employment Bureaus, is that the want columns, although a factor in the general mediation between employers and employees in clerical occupations, in certain kinds of miscellaneous odd jobs, and in some of the skilled trades, do not by any means meet the entire need, and that the question of their usefulness is by no means to be ascertained merely by measuring the space which they occupy on the padded page of many newspapers.*

* It is possible that the successful operation of an employment bureau which has a national organization for securing positions might have an appreciable effect on the policy of publishing articles which seriously misrepresent local demands for labor. The cruelty involved in the glowing and exaggerated accounts of industrial expansion, the re-opening of mills, the demand for harvest hands, can be appreciated only by those who are compelled to turn away applicants for work attracted from a distance by such articles at a time when working men are idle in the very locality thus misrepresented. Although such stories have no direct connection with want advertisements, they are closely akin to the "fake" advertisements which similarly mislead. The motive may be entirely different, but the hardships which they inflict upon those whom they mislead are similar. In this connection see the letter in the Appendix (p. 91) from Frederick L. Smith, of Lansing, Mich.

IS THE NEED MET? 21

Trade Unions At my request the Director of the Bureau of Social Research in the New York School of Philanthropy assigned one of the Fellows of the Bureau to the task of interviewing the secretaries of a number of representative trade unions to ascertain what are their methods for finding work for their unemployed members, and incidentally to obtain their views as to the desirability of establishing an employment bureau so far as concerns its possible usefulness to their own members. This inquiry was supplemented by similar interviews with representative employers, with the officers of associations of manufacturers and other employers and with representatives of the important railways.

It appears that in those trades which are completely organized and in which there is practically no non-union labor, the union is itself the ordinary means of communication between employer and employee. The business agent or walking delegate, on being notified that a certain number of men are wanted for any particular job, in turn notifies the unemployed members of the union in order of priority. This applies, however, only to the building trades, the newspaper pressmen, the pattern-makers, and a few other highly organized trades. In general the system of finding work for unemployed members of trade unions is exceedingly haphazard. An out-of-work list or book is usually kept, with the help of which men are sent to any job which happens to be reported to them. Sometimes the men who happen to be at the union headquarters at the time when a call is received are sent. In other cases the men are notified in order from the list, or in some instances in accordance with their fitness for the position which is to be filled. Sometimes information regarding possible employment is placed on a blackboard and any one who sees the notice and wishes to do so may respond.

The general opinion of the representatives of trade unions interviewed in the course of this inquiry appeared to be that their mechanism was not sufficient to deal with the situation as a whole or even within their own trades, so far as it is a matter of distributing labor to other communities. There is no doubt that the cooperation of union labor can be secured in carrying out the plan for an employment bureau, if that is desired, and it would seem on many accounts to be very desirable. The state and municipal Employment Bureaus of Germany and other European countries which are most successful are conducted by boards of managers on which both employers and employees are represented. Suspicion and hostility are thus disarmed, and the use of the Bureau either to injure or unfairly to promote the interests of either class is prevented. While there may not in the present instance be the same reasons for anticipating such hostility or actual injury to either party in the labor contract, there are obvious reasons why a favorable attitude from both employers and employees would be most advantageous.

Interviews with employers were on the whole rather unsatisfactory because of the indefinite and tentative manner in which the proposition could be explained, but the two interesting results of such interviews are first that there would be no lack of disposition to use the services of the Bureau as soon as it was shown that it was in position to do its work, and second that even among the few whom we visited there were some who had reasons of their own for instant hostility to any plan which would by arrangement with higher officials deprive them of their present prerogatives of hiring labor. One service which the Employment Bureau would be led to undertake, though perhaps not at the beginning, would be the investigation of conditions under which contract labor is engaged and managed on some of the railway systems.

By Individual Responsibility There are no doubt still to be found some who look with misgiving on any plan for helping people to find work, even though they are expected directly or indirectly to pay for the service, lest the feeling of personal responsibility should thereby be undermined. Valid objections may indeed be urged to the establishment of a labor colony or of relief work on this ground, and, as we have already seen, the free services of an employment bureau conducted by a charitable society does in practice encounter difficulties of this kind. A bureau, however, conducted on a business basis, expecting eventually to pay reasonable dividends on the capital invested in it, would scarcely be open to this objection, whether fees were charged to employers only, to employees only, or to both. If employers are in such need of help that they feel warranted in engaging the services of the Bureau to find workers, certainly the latter in responding to such calls from the Bureau are in no danger of deterioration of character merely because they make such response. If, on the other hand, the workers themselves pay a fee, which I believe on the whole to be advisable, and if they learn to insist upon getting a return worth the fee which they pay, they have not only avoided the danger but may easily in the process have developed a higher degree of personal responsibility. What is proposed is not a paternalistic assumption of responsibility for employees, but the rendering of definite economic service in return for suitable compensation. Workingmen out of a job may now look to their unions or advertise in a want column, or register in a commercial employment agency, or tramp about from place to place applying personally for work. It is the last method that is ordinarily in the mind of those who favor "throwing persons upon their own responsibility" in the matter of finding work. It is the time-honored method of finding something to do, but it requires no argument to show that it is expensive, time consuming, physically laborious, and mentally depressing. Any man out of work should of course be willing to resort to it in case of necessity, but it would be difficult to show that it is in any superior or more praiseworthy degree meeting "one's personal responsibility" than to seek work in any one of the three other methods. To patronize a well conducted employment bureau which gave a full equivalent for the fee charged—though the collection of the fee might be postponed until wages should be received—would be only a very sensible and commendable manner of meeting this responsibility. The dearth of such agencies and the lack of any conducted with the motives and on the plans under consideration is, then, only an obstacle in the way of educating workingmen to meet their responsibility.

CAN THE NEED BE MET ON ANY OTHER PLAN THAN THAT PROPOSED?

Free State Employ- It would perhaps be sufficient to recite
ment Bureau the bald fact that New York State has within three years discontinued a Free Employment Bureau "on the ground that it has not become a reliance of or indispensable to any particular group of unemployed, that such discontinuance can be effected without detriment to the interests of any individual or group of individuals, and that the functions it now performs can be as well performed by private agencies."

As, however, it has been suggested that the Free State Employment Bureau might advantageously be re-established, and as it is generally believed that the experiment has been more successful in several other states, I have thought it expedient to visit personally the Free State Employment Bureaus in Boston, Columbus, Cleveland, Chicago, Milwaukee and Minneapolis, and have obtained such information concerning these and other state and municipal bureaus as is contained in their annual reports and is available in the United States Labor Bureau and elsewhere. While some of these Bureaus are of course better than others, I regret to report that so far as I can ascertain they are everywhere in politics, and are too perfunctory and inefficient in their methods to become factors in bringing about any real adjustment between work and workers. I have visited one private commercial agency in a western city which has obviously done more work in finding remunerative and permanent, although largely seasonal employment, than all of the Free State Employment Bureaus put together; and it seems actually to have done more free work, *i. e.*, free to employees, than the three branches of the State Employment

Bureau in the state in which it is located. It has, moreover, an equipment and system by the side of which the best managed of the State Bureaus makes a sorry showing. Purely for business reasons its statistics are better kept, its information concerning contracts more accurate and reliable, and the interest of its managers and employees in its beneficiaries more in evidence than in the case of the best managed State Bureaus which I had the pleasure to visit. I have no reason to consider that this private agency is greatly superior to others which can be found in New York and elsewhere. The difference is primarily one of efficient administration and of adequacy of compensation for the head of the Bureau. The salary paid to the Superintendent of a Free State Bureau is $1200 or less—usually less. He has often only one assistant, and sometimes none. No funds are ordinarily available for advertising, for the sending of agents into the field, for interpreters to look after the interests of special groups of immigrants who do not speak English, or even, as a rule, for the keeping of adequate records. Judging from the experience of New York and other states, these fundamental defects are not easily to be overcome. The peculiar relation between organized labor and the State Employment Bureau and the temptation to utilize the Bureau merely to make it appear that the administration of the day is "doing something for labor" are apparently ineradicable obstacles in the way of efficient service. The Municipal Bureaus in Duluth and Seattle appear to be free from the defects of the State Bureaus, and it would be easy to make favorable comment on particular features of certain of the Bureaus, especially those in Massachusetts and Wisconsin, but I have been unable to find in any of these State Bureaus as now conducted warrant for the belief that the re-establishment of the New York State Bureau would be advisable in itself or that it would in any appreciable degree serve the purpose of giving substantial and practical aid to the community in solving the problem which we have in mind.

Further Regulation of Commercial Agencies

Every step in advance in the elimination of fraud and extortion in the ordinary commercial agencies only increases the need of a general agency which shall be in position to command public confidence and shall unquestionably be free from the abuses which state regulation is intended to prevent. At however high a price and with whatever fraudulent practices, these agencies, even the disreputable ones, do to some extent serve the purpose of an intermediary. To deprive them of their license or to maintain over them such an oversight as puts them practically out of business, is to impose some injury along with the undoubted benefit. The high-grade agencies already in existence might conceivably fill the gap thus created except that for the most part they have an entirely different kind of patronage, and have not developed the mechanism for dealing with the people who have been the patrons and too often the victims of the less reputable agencies. Stricter regulation and supervision, therefore, while desirable on their own account, do not lessen the increasing need for an agency which will be conducted primarily for the good that it will do rather than for the profits that it can earn.

Labor Colonies and Public Relief Works

Fortunately there is no general agitation in this country at present for the establishment of labor colonies or relief works for the unemployed. The proposed penal colony for the open-air custodial care of vagrants, inebriates, and others who require such special treatment, has of course nothing to do with our present problem. The objections to the establishment of relief work organized not because the undertaking is justified on its own account, but for the sake of giving employment, are so obvious and so familiar that they need not here be recapitulated. Even those who advocate them would certainly prefer that as an earlier intermediate step employment should be found in ordinary occupations under ordinary economic conditions for as many as possible. To use a forcible figure originally applied to a different proposition, the opening of public relief works as a means of helping the unemployed is like tying on the flowers, while the opening of an employment bureau on a business basis is like watering the plant.

RECOMMENDATIONS

I have approached this inquiry with an entirely open mind, with no prejudice against a State Bureau or in favor of any Bureau at all if it were found not to be needed. The plan for distributing immigrants by the Federal Government and of transferring city residents to the farms of New York through the State Department of Agriculture have both been considered, with every inclination to recommend that they are sufficient for the purpose if this were found to be the fact.

As a result of a month's careful study of the whole subject, involving a considerable amount of reading, visits to several states and to the national capital, and extended correspondence, the co-operation of the Bureau of Social Research, and numerous personal interviews, especially in regard to the reasons for the failure of experiments which have been made in New York City, I am of the opinion that the establishment of an Employment Bureau substantially on the lines indicated in Mr. Schiff's memorandum is desirable, that the need for such a Bureau is very great, that it is not met by other existing agencies, and cannot be met by other plans more effectively or economically than by that proposed.

The only serious modification which I would recommend is that a fee should be charged to employees rather than to employers, unless it is found practicable and advisable to charge a fee to both. I believe that eventually the Bureau could make such a position for itself that large employers would be willing to make contracts with it, perhaps on an annual basis, which would be mutually advantageous, but I doubt the wisdom of charging a specific fee for each employee furnished, especially in the initial stages of the experiment. I have no doubt, however, that from the very beginning it could be made apparent to employees that in paying a reasonable fee for the services of the Bureau they would be making a good investment. I am much impressed by the reasons given for this view by Mr. Herbert S. Brown in his communication included in Appendix II. If employers were charged and not employees, my fear would be that the tendency of the Bureau would be to serve the interests of employers, rather than those of employees. It is of course our desire that it should serve both, and primarily the community.

There is complete unanimity of opinion that the success of the whole enterprise will depend upon the capacity of its executive officer, although it is also conceivable that a board of trustees or managers might be created that would contribute very materially to its success. My suggestion would be that the board should consist of not more than nine members, and that among them there should be at least one labor representative, and one social worker or university instructor interested in the problem on the scientific side. This suggestion is made simply in the interest of efficiency and public usefulness, but if those who provide the capital feel that they should exercise exclusive control over the Bureau, some part of the advantage which I have in mind might be secured by creating an advisory board with an even larger representation of such elements as I have proposed for the board of managers.

The general plan on which the Bureau should be conducted has perhaps already been sufficiently indicated. Recapitulating, however, for the sake of clearness, I would recommend:

That there be organized in the City of New York an Employment Bureau under a board of trustees composed of experienced men representing the mercantile, academic, philanthropic and industrial classes, each member of the board, however, being selected not so much in his representative capacity as because of his probable usefulness as an active working member of the board. The control should of course remain with those who furnish the working funds, but need not be exclusively limited to them.

The Bureau should be placed under a manager of great executive ability, with the necessary number of assistants, and the staff should be thoroughly conversant with the peculiarities of the various groups that compose New York City's working population. Herein lies the special strength of the small and often badly conducted employment agencies, that those who manage them really know their people. The Employment Bureau cannot be expected to succeed unless it can secure similar intimate knowledge of the peculiarities, and especially of the valuable qualities of particular groups. It would be necessary to have interpreters, men to take charge of gangs in transit, and to perform virtually the functions now exercised by the padroni—although without the abuses of that system.

The Bureau should establish an organization covering all sections of the United States, so that it shall be in immediate and constant touch with requirements for labor and employment wherever such may exist, but its benefits should accrue primarily to the unemployed of the City of New York. It may not be necessary to maintain agencies permanently in particular localities outside of New York, although it might be advisable to have one or two branch headquarters. For the most part the agents in the field would be moving from place to place, establishing relations with employers, looking after the interests of men who had been sent to work, and ascertaining when they would be free from particular engagements, so that there would be little loss of time in transferring them to other places where they were needed.

The Bureau should charge a reasonable fee to employees, although waiving this, as private employment agencies do, whenever it is necessary in order to supply particular demands, and postponing it, whenever employees are entirely without funds, until it can be paid from wages. Eventually the Bureau might make contracts with employers on the basis of compensation to the Bureau for its services, but my suggestion would be that the service be free to employers until it had been demonstrated that the Bureau is in position to do this work as well as other agencies or better.

On account of the general dissatisfaction with all existing systems—free employment bureaus, ordinary private commercial agencies, want advertisements, employers' exchanges, trade union registers, etc., and for other reasons already indicated, I am of the opinion that an Employment Bureau conducted as has been proposed, with a working capital of $100,000, would eventually become self-supporting, and would pay a reasonable, or even, if that were desired, a very substantial dividend on the capital invested. As the motives of those who would establish the Bureau are not, however, pecuniary, but public-spirited, I would recommend that the Bureau be incorporated on a plan similar to that of the Provident Loan Society, limiting dividends to six per cent and providing that the surplus, if any should be accumulated, be devoted to some appropriate public purpose.

Aside from the main purpose of helping the unemployed to get work, I would expect that a Bureau of the kind that is under consideration would have three indirect and incidental but exceedingly important functions:

(1) By competition it would help to eliminate the evils of the ordinary commercial agencies.

(2) By opening up opportunities for employment in other communities, both urban and rural, it would contribute to the solution of the overshadowing and increasingly serious problem of congestion of population in New York City.

(3) It would gradually establish standards of work which might eventually, if the establishment of a State Bureau or even a National Bureau is found expedient, be taken over in the management of such official bureaus. Conditions in this country do not at present seem favorable for establishing high standards in official bodies of this kind. This is greatly to be deplored, and it is doubtful whether voluntary agencies in the field of social work can render a better service than by working out at private expense and under the more favorable conditions of private initiative, standards of work which will subsequently modify the work of public agencies if they become desirable. Without attempting to anticipate whether social legislation in this country will follow the course which it has taken in all European countries, including Great Britain, we may at least feel it to be a patriotic duty to do anything

that is possible to be prepared for such legislation by unhampered experiment with the problems which elsewhere have already become governmental functions. If on the other hand it is found that recent tendencies in these directions are modified or reversed and that such activities are to remain indefinitely in private hands, then nothing is lost but everything is gained by such pioneer work as is now proposed.

(4) It would help to decasualize labor, if we may use a phrase which has become more familiar in England than in this country, but which implies a lamentable condition towards which a large part of our unskilled labor is unfortunately tending. Any employer in undertaking a new job would prefer, other things being equal, to secure laborers who have been at work, rather than men who have been demoralized by idleness or underemployment.

(5) Eventually the Employment Bureau might exert an important influence on the critical period in the lives of boys and young men when they first begin work. We have child labor committees and a widespread interest in protective legislation, but not enough attention has been given to the kind of work in which working boys from fourteen to twenty years of age are engaged. It is largely lost time, paying relatively high wages at the start but leading nowhere. While it could not become the main function of the Employment Bureau to deal with the problem, it might incidentally contribute materially to its solution.

The strongest, and to my mind conclusive, argument in favor of the establishment of an Employment Bureau is to be found in the very dearth of information and even of views which this brief and necessarily superficial inquiry has disclosed. There appears to be no way of finding out how much mal-adjustment actually exists either in our own city or between this and other communities, or of discovering remedies except by trying the experiment. At the end of a year or two of actual work by such an Employment Bureau as has been proposed we would have a body of experience and information from which conclusions could be drawn in regard to many important questions of public policy and of private social effort. It may seem extravagant to say that the mere collection of such information and its proper interpretation would be worth all that it is proposed to spend in the experiment even if it should prove to be an utter failure, but I believe this to be a moderate and reasonable estimate. I do not believe that it will be a failure, and have indicated what appear to me to be convincing reasons for believing that it will be a success.

I have thought it advisable to incorporate in Appendices several special reports on particular aspects of the inquiry and other material which will repay examination by those who desire to be in position to form their own conclusions.

All of which is respectfully submitted.

EDWARD T. DEVINE.

Appendices

Appendices

	PAGE
APPENDIX I. LETTER OF INQUIRY CONCERNING NEED FOR AN EMPLOYMENT BUREAU....................	39
APPENDIX II. REPLIES TO LETTER OF INQUIRY:	
Reply from Mr. William H. Baldwin, Washington, D. C.....	41
Reply from Mr. Frank L. Baldwin, Attorney-at-law, Youngstown, Ohio...	43
Reply from Prof. Ernest L. Bogart, Princeton University	45
Reply from Mr. Herbert S. Brown, New York City.......	50
Reply from Mr. H. L. Cargill, New York City............	56
Reply from Prof. John B. Clark, Columbia University.....	58
Reply from Prof. John R. Commons, University of Wisconsin	60
Reply from Prof. H. J. Davenport, University of Missouri..	62
Reply from Prof. Henry W. Farnam, Yale University......	68
Reply from Prof. Frank A. Fetter, Cornell University......	69
Reply from Prof. (Emeritus) Wm. W. Folwell, University of Minnesota...	74
Reply from Prof. J. E. Hagerty, Ohio State University.....	76
Reply from Mr. James Mullenbach, Superintendent of the Municipal Lodging House of Chicago.................	78
Reply from Prof. E. A. Ross, University of Wisconsin......	84
Reply from Prof. Henry R. Seager, Columbia University....	86
Reply from Mr. James B. Seager, General Manager of the Olds Gas Power Company, Lansing, Michigan........	89
Reply from Mr. Frederick L. Smith, Vice-president and General Manager of the Olds Motor Works, Lansing, Michigan..	91
Reply from Mr. Sidney Webb, London...................	96
Reply from Mr. Adna F. Weber, Chief Statistician of the New York Public Service Commission.....................	104
Reply from Mr. Robert A. Woods, South End House, Boston	106
Letter from Mr. James W. Van Cleave, President of the National Association of Manufacturers..............	107
APPENDIX III. PLAN FOR AN EMPLOYMENT BUREAU FOR MEN UNFAMILIAR WITH THE ENGLISH LANGUAGE. BY MR. CYRUS L. SULZBERGER............	109
APPENDIX IV. STATEMENTS IN REGARD TO THREE FREE PHILANTHROPIC BUREAUS CONDUCTED IN NEW YORK CITY......................	112
Cooper Union Labor Bureau. Extract from the Report of the New York Association for Improving the Condition of the Poor.......................................	112
Bureau of the United Hebrew Charities. Statement by Dr. Lee K. Frankel.....................................	113

APPENDICES

	PAGE
Bureau conducted by the Society of St. Vincent de Paul. Statement by Mr. Thomas M. Mulry	117
APPENDIX V. EXPERIENCES OF MR. BENJAMIN C. MARSH IN TRYING TO GET WORK IN NEW YORK CITY ON DECEMBER 17 AND 18, 1908	119
APPENDIX VI. STUDY OF NEWSPAPER ADVERTISEMENTS AS A MEDIUM FOR SECURING WORK AND HELP	130
Report by Mr. H. G. Paine on New York papers	130
Report by Mr. Arthur I. Street, editor of Street's Pandex of the News, on Chicago papers	157
APPENDIX VII. REPORTS PREPARED IN THE BUREAU OF SOCIAL RESEARCH OF THE NEW YORK SCHOOL OF PHILANTHROPY, UNDER THE DIRECTION OF DR. R. C. MCCREA	159
On Trade Unions as Employment Agencies	159
Notes on Interviews with Trade Union Officials	164
On the Attitude of Employers toward a General Employment Bureau	181
On Unemployed Men at the Municipal Lodging House of New York. By Mr. E. E. Pratt	186
Character of Lodgers in Municipal Lodging House. By Hon. Robert W. Hebberd	201
On the Mobility of Workers. By Dr. R. Brodsky	202
APPENDIX VIII. STATEMENT IN REGARD TO AN EXPERIMENT BY THE JOINT APPLICATION BUREAU IN FINDING WORK FOR MEN IN THE COUNTRY. BY MR. CHARLES K. BLATCHLY, SUPERINTENDENT OF THE BUREAU	216
APPENDIX IX. EXTRACT FROM THE SIXTH ANNUAL REPORT (FOR 1908) OF HON. OSCAR S. STRAUS, SECRETARY OF COMMERCE AND LABOR, IN REGARD TO THE WORK OF THE DIVISION OF INFORMATION IN THE BUREAU OF IMMIGRATION	218
APPENDIX X. THE VALUE OF LABOR EXCHANGES. EXTRACT FROM A PAMPHLET BY MR. W. H. BEVERIDGE, OF LONDON	221
APPENDIX XI. EXTRACTS FROM AN ADDRESS BY THE RT. HON. WINSTON CHURCHILL, M. P., PRESIDENT OF THE BRITISH BOARD OF TRADE	224
APPENDIX XII. EXTRACTS FROM A LETTER BY MR. CYRUS L. SULZBERGER TO THE CHAIRMAN OF THE NEW YORK STATE COMMISSION OF IMMIGRATION, IN REGARD TO THE WORK OF THE INDUSTRIAL REMOVAL OFFICE	227
APPENDIX XIII. A PARTIAL BIBLIOGRAPHY ON THE SUBJECT OF EMPLOYMENT BUREAUS	232

APPENDIX I
Letter of Inquiry Concerning Need for Employment Bureau

---

105 East 22d Street, New York City,
November 20, 1908.

It has become my duty to make a somewhat comprehensive report on the advisability of establishing an Employment Bureau in New York City, substantially on the lines indicated in the accompanying memorandum.* A sufficient sum of money has been placed at my disposal for this purpose to enable me to offer modest payment—such as would ordinarily be made for a magazine article—for such statements from competent authorities on the labor situation as will be of special aid in making this report. If, therefore, you will submit your views on the following questions, together with any information, statistical or other, that you think would be serviceable, I shall be very glad to have them and will at once send you in payment therefor not less than ten dollars, and in case of exceptionally valuable communications, or in case much time is expended in collecting new information, some reasonable additional compensation.†

Time is, however, an important element in this inquiry, and unless by special arrangement, I would not be able to use any reply received later than November 30, and I would very much appreciate a much earlier reply. The questions on which information and opinions are desired are the following:

1. To what extent is unemployment in our large cities due

---

* Mr. Jacob H. Schiff's memorandum, given in Introductory Note, page 3.
† Several of the correspondents declined compensation.

merely to mal-adjustment, *i. e.*, to the failure of men out of work to find in their own neighborhood existing opportunities for employment?

Distinguish different kinds of work, clerical, skilled, unskilled, etc., organized or unorganized. Would the fact that the Bureau charges employers a fee be a hindrance or an advantage, etc.?

2. To what extent is there mal-adjustment as between communities, *i. e.*, how far could the surplus of labor in a large city like New York find employment in other communities?

The reference here is not to a change of occupations as from industrial to agricultural, but merely to change of locality. Is the apparent over-supply of labor in cities a local, or a part of a national situation? Is it a feature of "congested populations"?

3. What are the natural limits of mobility of labor as to changes from one occupation to another, and what bearing has this on the possible usefulness of an Employment Bureau?

It is obvious, for example, that a tailor cannot readily ordinarily become a dairyman. But within what limits might an over-supply of labor in one occupation be relieved by finding other reasonably similar occupations? In other words, discuss occupational mobility, as distinct from geographical mobility.

You will gather from the above that the fundamental question is as to the real need for and the probable utility of an Employment Bureau. The above questions are intended as suggestions, and are not exhaustive. Anything which you wish to say on the general subject will be appreciated.

Sincerely yours,
EDWARD T. DEVINE.

APPENDIX II
Replies to Letter of Inquiry (Appendix I)

REPLY FROM MR. WILLIAM H. BALDWIN,
OF WASHINGTON, D. C.

I approve heartily of the proposal to place the Bureau under a manager of great executive ability. Anything done in a perfunctory way by salaried officials, certain of their pay at the end of the month whether any good is done or not, is not likely to be of much practical value. Nothing, in my opinion, can take the place of the stimulus which the responsibility for success or failure puts upon men who must account to stockholders or others from whom they receive their position. I believe such a bureau as you propose would in this respect be far more efficient than any government agency, such as is proposed in Pennsylvania, is likely to be.

The fee is quite proper, but the undertaking would have to be worked up like any other enterprise and by its conduct show that the fee is not the principal purpose of its establishment. Employers would patronize it as they do the advertising columns of newspapers if experience proved that it was worth while for them to do so.

1. As to the local mal-adjustment in cities, I do not know. So much depends upon a man's make-up as to his getting employment or keeping it after it is obtained; and I imagine that the quality of work done by those who have grown up in New York City, and by many of the emigrants, is not of a high order. Unquestionably an efficient agency, which keeps up a knowledge of the wants of employers of various lines in different quarters of the city, would

be of great assistance in enabling men to find quickly some employment which they were fitted for.

2. The wider question of mal-adjustment as between communities presents some of the same difficulties, but undoubtedly much good could be done in supplying workmen for other communities which need them. It is not probable that some of the men from New York could stand up in the wheat fields of Kansas where men are so much needed at times, but I believe that there is a good deal of work throughout the country for which these men would be fitted if they could be properly placed.

The congestion seems to be a part of the national situation, a result of the tendency to crowd together, but is apparently worse in New York than elsewhere and an intelligent effort to get large numbers of people past this dead-point, and enable them to exercise this crowding tendency in other communities, would be of great benefit.

3. The limit of mobility of labor as between occupations depends largely upon the man. One of ordinary intelligence who is anxious to work has considerable range. To illustrate: In the plant of the Ohio Steel Company, with which I was connected, the men earning more wages than common laborers had their positions, and a man capable of running a steam engine, for instance, could not be given a place off-hand. It was our custom to let any man who applied for work go into the labor gang, from which men were assigned to different tasks as necessities arose. These men were watched and if any one displayed a commendable industry or capacity in any direction, he was given the first chance at any desirable work. In this way there was a constant promotion of those who were fit for anything better; and we were just as anxious to get men for these better positions as they were to get them. Of course there were many men whose habits were bad, or who were indolent or incapable of doing anything more than common labor; but the opportunity was there, and my experience is that a man of ordinary capacity, but with the will to do, could adapt himself to quite a

range of diverse tasks which might present themselves in such a large plant.

The men presented by such a bureau as you propose to employers for work to which they were not accustomed might not at first earn the highest wages, but if they could get something to do, and be learning, there could be a progress towards better work and permanent employment which would be well worth while. Any occupation sorts out the capable men. Those who are first dropped or who first drop out, and are compelled to seek something else, are the incapable.

Finally, such a bureau in charge of a man of ability, similar to that required to run a railroad, for instance, would develop the possibilities of the situation and not only find work for large numbers of those desiring work, but would take away the excuse which many now seem to have for not working, and I believe that in this last respect, as a sifting agency eliminating one large element in the problem of dealing with the unemployed, it would be well worth while.

The newspapers last week reported a shortage of workmen in Sharon, Pa. From what I know of this work I believe that a man of ordinary capacity, if sent out from New York, could soon learn to do the work in one of the positions in question, even though he had known nothing about it previously.

NOVEMBER 24, 1908.

LETTER FROM MR. FRANK L. BALDWIN,
ATTORNEY-AT-LAW IN YOUNGSTOWN, OHIO,
SUPPLEMENTING THE PRECEDING LETTER FROM MR. WILLIAM H. BALDWIN

I have just had a short talk with one or two of our employers of labor, and they seem to think that it (the Bureau) would probably work well in the larger cities, but seem to doubt its usefulness in places like Youngstown and vicinity. Good positions in towns of this size are pretty well filled, and the men go along up from the ranks below as fast as places become vacant. What is needed in the industries in this vicinity is the unskilled laborer with brawn and muscle and good health. Men of this class here are largely foreigners, principally Italians and Austrians, such as the Slovaks, Hungarians, and men from other neighboring districts in Europe. This class of men begin as laborers here, and as they show improvement are advanced to better positions. Our larger industries have departments that keep in touch with that class of labor, and when men are needed have no difficulty in getting as many as they want by going to their padrones or leaders.

Men are badly needed at the present time in the coke regions and also in the industries of the South. Whether the unemployed of New York City could be utilized is questionable. For the coke regions sufficient men could probably be obtained without much difficulty from a city like Pittsburgh and its vicinity.

Unemployment in our large cities is due principally to maladjustment. Men who are out of work find it difficult to find employment in their own neighborhood, and also find it extremely difficult to look for work elsewhere, by reason of lack of means and necessary information. An Employment Bureau such as is contemplated would be a great benefit to such men.

The unemployed of New York City are more numerous in the winter months when work on the large enterprises is suspended. Whether such unemployed could be moved out of New York City to work elsewhere is a serious problem. Most of such men probably have families dependent upon them, making it extremely difficult to transfer them. Clerical and skilled labor usually fill such positions locally, and there would be places only for the unskilled laborer or workingman.

NOVEMBER 30, 1908.

REPLY FROM PROF. ERNEST L. BOGART,
OF PRINCETON UNIVERSITY

Some years ago I had occasion to look up the matter quite thoroughly in connection with an article on Free Public Employment Agencies in the United States for the *Quarterly Journal of Economics* (Vol. XIX, pp. 341-377). From that and subsequent studies I am convinced that the problem of mal-adjustment of labor is not at all adequately met by existing agencies, and that there is real need of an institution that shall attempt to meet the problem on broader lines than has yet been attempted—perhaps national. New York City is certainly the strategic center from which such an effort should be made.

I. Is there a lack of adjustment within New York City between workers and existing opportunities for work?

Yes, there is, although this differs greatly in the different branches of labor. It is probably greatest in domestic service, owing partly to the temporary and shifting character of this employment. But in this field the need is probably fairly well met by existing commercial agencies. If the proposed Bureau were established, it would be necessary to guard carefully against being swamped by this kind of labor, as has occurred in the various State bureaus. Skilled labor, especially where organized, has generally depended upon its own agencies, often very specialized, to bring about an adjustment in the labor market. It would be very difficult to meet the peculiar needs of employers or workers in this field, and I personally should doubt the wisdom of trying to do so. There is of course a large amount of unemployment among skilled workers, but so far as this is caused by the seasonal character of their work, the generally accepted economic view is that they receive a sufficiently higher wage during the period of employment to compensate them for the period of unemployment. A great deal of the unemployment among this group is undoubtedly due to absolute lack of work to be done. Thus the Twentieth Annual Report of the Bureau of Labor Statistics of New York State reported the amount of idleness among the members of labor organizations in the State for the year 1900 as due to the following causes:

Idleness due to—

    Lack of work........................75.5 per cent
    Bad weather, etc..................... .5
    Strike or lockout.....................13.0
    Sickness, etc......................... 4.7
    Other................................6.3

How to deal with this is a very difficult problem, but it would certainly seem undersirable to try to secure any considerable occupational shift to other occupations or any geographical shift to other places. The difficulty is probably a temporary one, at least on any such abnormal scale as presented in the above table.

The proposed Bureau would probably deal principally with the unskilled and unorganized laborers. Here the need of a bureau seems, too, most evident, and in dealing with these classes the free public employment bureaus have achieved their greatest successes.

The technical and skilled trades have their trade organizations or special agencies; but this group, numerically far surpassing the others, is taken care of in rather haphazard fashion. The first problem to be met in dealing with this group, however, is the strict separation of the "won't-works" and the unemployable class from the unemployed. It would be the duty of the Bureau to try to solve only the problem of mal-adjustment, and to hand over to other organizations the care of the unemployable. Charles Booth calculated for London that over 8 per cent of the population belong to the unemployable group. Nor, as I have said before, does it seem to be feasible for the Bureau to deal with such unemployment as arises from seasonal fluctuations due to the character of the work, bad weather, etc. But, on the other hand, industrial mal-adjustment due to industrial depression, changes in fashion, the introduction of new machinery, etc., must be met by the Bureau and an attempt made to introduce the unemployed laborers to some other occupation. Possibly the greatest problem in connection with this class, and the one which would keep the Bureau busiest, would be the treatment of the casual laborers. Forced by the very nature of their occupations to find a new job at periodic intervals, they would have constant recourse to the Bureau. It would be necessary, therefore, to keep in touch with large employers of labor and to secure their co-operation with the Bureau.

The question as to whether the Bureau should charge a fee or not is an administrative one, which I should unhesitatingly answer in the affirmative. It should be placed as far as possible upon a business basis. It must avoid trying to "run out" other existing commercial agencies. But an even stronger reason for charging a fee is in the effect it has upon both employers and employees: where no fee is charged, it is apt not to be patronized; or, if employment is found for an applicant, little obligation is felt because the service was a free one, and at the slightest provocation a rupture occurs. If it seemed undesirable to charge the unemployed applicant for a position an initial fee, it could be deducted subsequently from his wages. But it would certainly seem desirable to make a charge to employers, quite aside from any voluntary contributions they may make to its support.

II. Is there a mal-adjustment of labor between communities?

I should answer yes to this question less unhesitatingly than to the former one. At bottom, it seems to me, the problem which would confront the suggested Bureau in New York City is the problem of congested population. There is today much less opportunity in the far West to attract workers, now that the free land has practically all been taken up. Many persons, too, are attracted to the cities, quite irrespective of the existence of any actual demand for their services. New York City has also, of course, peculiar problems of her own, as a result of the influx of foreigners, of whom so many remain there. But that normally there is room and work for all the workers in this country admits, it seems to me, of no doubt. So far, therefore, as it is a question of mal-adjustment, especially if it be geographical, the proposed Bureau should certainly cover as large a territory as possible. The success of the German system is largely due to its national scope. It should at least comprise a whole State, in which there should be several branches, or affiliated institutions, working together. The most successful institution of the sort in the United States, so far as I know, is the Seattle Free Employment Bureau, which has secured the co-operation of the large employers of labor throughout the State, and sends men, especially unskilled workers, to the most distant parts of the State.

There seems to be a standing demand for labor in the agricultural parts of New York State. A List of Farms Occupied and Unoccupied in New York State, published by the Bureau of Information and Statistics (Bulletin No. 1, Department of Agriculture), states that "probably fifty thousand agricultural laborers can find employment on the farms of New York at good wages. Families particularly are wanted to occupy rented houses and work farms on shares." Perhaps some of the three hundred thousand aliens who settled in the cities of New York State during the year 1904-5 could be persuaded to leave them for the farms if the matter were fairly presented to them. My own experience as a charity worker in New York City was that many of those asking for assistance had come from rural districts or from farms in the Old World. It would therefore seem reasonable to suppose that they might be willing to accept similar work here. There is, of course, the difficulty of ignorance of the language to be met; possibly this could be met by colonization on a fairly large scale of farm laborers of the same nationality in the same district.

III. The relation of the mobility of labor to the proposed Employment Bureau.

The main usefulness of the Bureau, it seems to me, must

consist in promoting geographical mobility of labor. It is a curious historical fact that with the increased ease of geographical movement of labor, its occupational mobility has declined. As it becomes easier to move bodies of men from one place to another. there is less inducement to wage-earners to shift their occupations, Among the native-born Americans, consequently, there is comparatively little occupational mobility. Perhaps because they have made such a radical geographical change, there is also a greater tendency to occupational changes among the foreign-born. But as two-thirds of the immigrants are probably to be classed among the unskilled, the occupational change is not very great. The Bureau would deal very largely with this class, and would doubtless find it feasible to promote occupational changes in many cases, where it would mean a gain. In general, however, such movements, especially for skilled labor, mean a social loss rather than a gain, as it connects a sacrifice of specialized skill. There is, however, a strong temptation to exchange the uncertain prospect of good wages in a specialized trade for the immediate high returns that can usually be obtained by an able-bodied, muscular, unskilled worker. The conclusion that this leads to is that what is needed in the last analysis is industrial training that will promote general intelligence and thereby render possible a certain amount of occupational mobility without at the same time entailing loss of special training.

My own conclusion would be that there is ample scope and need for the proposed Bureau in New York City, and that it would fill a need that is at present met in no other way.

NOVEMBER 28, 1908.

REPLY FROM MR. HERBERT S. BROWN,
OF NEW YORK CITY

I. Every energetic workman, so far as my experience extends,—and this reservation applies to all that is said below,—knows other workmen in his trade, and through them and through personal visits to the various employers, he keeps in fairly close touch with possible demands for his services. Members of trade unions may frequent the headquarters of the union, in the chance of getting one of the jobs that come to the union direct and are passed out there on some uncertain plan not fully understood by me. Strangers in the city, of course, have fewer such means of getting located.

Similarly, every employer has lists, often very large, of applicants for work and of men who have previously worked for him. By reference to these lists and by inquiry among his own men it is possible for him to get about all the help he needs, in the skilled and semi-skilled occupations, even in busy times. In the case of unskilled labor, it is more difficult to put men where they are wanted at the moment they are wanted. In seasonal occupations, as among the garment workers, it is not always easy to get extra help for the few weeks it is needed,—not because of maladjustment, but because of full employment of all skilled in the trade.

Crude and inefficient as the above-indicated methods of buying and selling labor are, yet by their means some kind of a market for his services is always open to the active workman, except in "hard times" when nobody is buying labor. At such times no amount of individual canvassing or underbidding would materially increase the available supply of work,—the turn in the tide of which, in my judgment, depends primarily upon entirely different factors. I do not think that an employment bureau, working within trade lines, would be any more successful in remedying unemployment in "hard times" than such men as I have indicated working singly.

II. I have little direct knowledge of possible mal-adjustment, in the same trade, between different communities. It is my impression that in the East we have less mobility in the working population than obtains in the West. The influence of the trade unions is, I believe, against such geographical mobility. Newcomers, even with the proper credentials, are not over-welcome in any city. Witness San Francisco.

"Over-supply" of labor, so far as it exists in normal times, is due, in my opinion, to inertia (rather than immobility) on the part of the workman, together with a partly unconscious, partly studied policy of very many large employers—the Metropolitan Street Railway Company, for instance—of keeping more men on their pay-rolls than they can possibly employ for full time. As I take this to be an economic rather than an ethical inquiry, I will not express my views on the responsibility of employers for the part-time men. Distinctly, the latter *is* a feature of "congested" populations.

III. The natural limits to occupational mobility are, I believe, vastly less confining than those narrow bounds set down by custom, by habit, by employers, and by trade unions. The long apprenticeships demanded in some trades are sheer humbug, designed to keep down the total of workmen available in the craft. That the apprentice appears slow to learn means almost always that he is not given the chance to learn—assuming, of course, reasonable energy and natural fitness for the work.

Back of each skilled trade and occupation lies primarily nothing more mysterious than a certain deftness of hand, accuracy of eye, co-ordination of muscles, sense of rhythm, commercial instinct, or whatever else it may be, essential to the profitable prosecution of that occupation. Many a one of such human qualities will open the way to success in more than one trade,—the more general of them to a large number of trades. For example, the man who has the "mechanical instinct," and has had sufficient training in any one of the score or more of mechanical trades to have acquired accurate and quick co-ordination of brain and muscle, can and frequently does pass freely from one trade to another, with no greater handicap than the few weeks' or months' delay requisite to learn the special processes of the new trade and to bring his speed up to that of the man whose longer experience has made the work practically automatic. And the lower the grade of skill required, the easier to make transitions. It is unreasonable to expect, and secure, of the men who carry on the difficult work of the world the astonishing mobility which history relates of Julius Caesar, or Goethe, or the ex-plumber Croker, with many another immortal not yet dead enough to mention by name, and then deny to the deft fingers that roll cigarettes in hopeless competition with automatic machinery the chance at a dozen other occupations unknown to them but known to us where the deft finger is a valuable asset.

I believe that it is possible to weave through the maze of endlessly divided and subdivided craft and occupation a comparatively simple classification based on the underlying essential, human qualification, rather than on a technical knowledge of trade peculiarity. I believe it would be possible to pass men properly qualified under such a classification from one occupation to others closely allied with comparative ease. And I believe that the encouragement of such inter-occupational mobility would be of very great benefit to the community. It is part of my creed in life that every man has a place, perhaps a dozen places, into which, when at last found, he will fit with definite profit to himself and every one else concerned. I believe that "congested" population means congested wealth, and that with proper mobility facilitated, the tangle will resolve itself, so that ultimately we may be able to say—the more people the more prosperity.

The proposition to establish an employment bureau that shall amount to something is in substance a proposition to upset the time-honored barter of services indicated in Section I above and substitute for it, in New York at least, a method which shall be modern and efficient in somewhat the same sense as are all our great commodity markets of wheat, cotton, and money—subject to undesirable speculation and fluctuation, to be sure, but on the whole acting as marvelous balance wheels of industry. Again I will say that it is unreasonable to be able to put wheat, or gold, or telephone switchboards by less than the turn of a hand into any part of the world where they are *instanter* needed, and yet think we cannot devise means for shifting our most valuable commodity, human service, from where it is not wanted to where it is wanted, without waiting till sheer starvation forces that commodity blindly to shift for itself.

The first requisite in facing this problem is to tuck any missionary notions we may have about us away in our pockets where they will be thoroughly out of sight, and handy for reference in private. Our transactions in themselves must be business-like to the last degree. Men buy labor only when they can see a profit to be made by so doing. The employer who takes on men merely because they need work is so rare a species that he can be left out of our count.

The second requisite is that, as salesmen, we must know our goods. At this point every employment agency I ever heard of, except perhaps one or two very high-class teachers' agencies and possibly some abroad, breaks down. A hasty interview, the scanning of a few references (notoriously meaningless), and the applicant is sent out to win or lose the job as good luck and his own native wit may determine. Result: not many employers apply a second time to such bureaus.

It should be possible to establish an employment bureau which would know its merchandise—its applicants—so thoroughly that the man possessed of the bureau's certificate of fitness for work in a certain grade would have therein the highest recommendation available in this city. By proper care such a certificate could be made the *sine qua non* of entrance to many of the larger industrial concerns. By proper publicity young men could be stimulated to fit themselves to obtain certificates for higher grades and better opportunities than those they previously held.

Suppose, for example, a young man working in a street-railway office, computing conductors' returns fifty hours a week at six to ten dollars a week, with a family to support and a possibility of increase after years of service to perhaps fifteen dollars. If one of the classifications of the proposed Bureau should be, say, "accounting clerk," qualifying for positions of a certain grade in insurance, bankers', brokers', contractors', and many other kinds of offices, and if this young man, otherwise likely to stay put till sheer necessity drove him out, hearing of the Bureau, pulled himself together, qualified for and secured with good credit its certificate for this grade, he might now pass, on his own initiative or on the Bureau's recommendation, to a better position in, say, a contractor's office. Thence by successive advances in qualification, he could take up other and higher grades of work, until he found the place where his services were of maximum value to himself and the community. The people in the railway office on their part would now have room for a clerk of lower grade, or, if they were actually underpaying their men, the mobility induced by the Bureau's activities would soon make this evident, and justify them in increasing wages to the market standard.

The suggestion is, broadly, to establish for industrial service in New York a classification and standards of fitness just as are already being worked out for the civil service. Guaranteeing work to applicants is not contemplated. The function of the Bureau would be simply to point out the road to those who want to better themselves, and to indorse fitness in those who qualify under its standards.

Necessarily this means examinations and tests, which will be expensive, particularly at the inception of the enterprise. This expense, and other reasonable expenses of the Bureau, should rest, as in most commercial transactions, on the seller rather than on the purchaser. I think the employer should be free from financial obligation in the matter. Every inducement should be afforded him to encourage co-operation with the Bureau. Let his contribution, if any, be in furnishing skilled overseers to advise with the Bureau in preparing tests of fitness. The prospective employee will gladly pay for the services of the Bureau (note how the padrone prospers), and if successful in getting work he will be able to pay. Generous latitude should be allowed as to the time of payment, and responsibility should be put on him rather than on the employer to see that the obligation is met when due. I believe there would be a surprisingly small number of defaults. With reasonable charges and a large clientele, such, for instance, as has been built up by the Provident Loan Society, the enterprise could be made commercially practicable, in the same sense as is that society or the City and Suburban Homes Company. The missionary part will be in the inception; in later years the Bureau, if rightly conducted, would be likely to become as commercial and unsentimental a factor in the city's life as are its savings banks.

A classification emphasizing the distinguishing human quality as a cut through the maze of occupational detail would, if found and proved worthy, carry with it the relatively prompt solution of the vexed and intensely practical problem of what constitutes the right schooling for boys and girls about to enter the industrial ranks. Years must intervene between practice and proof in attempts to work out the latter *an sich:* the touchstone of immediate success or failure awaits any application of theory to the industrial army itself.

The name chosen would be important Brevity, dignity, and a hint of official authority are desirable. "Employment Bureau" suggests too much the "out of a job" atmosphere. The institution must be constructive, not palliative. "Bureau" any way is an unfortunate word in its leaning toward bureaucracy. Something like "The Service Registry," or "The Industrial Service

Registry" might convey a more favorable impression, correlative in the public mind with the "Civil Service Commission."

Verily, it is interesting ground your inquiry has entered. A ground where you can *do* things.

DECEMBER 11, 1908.

REPLY FROM MR. H. L. CARGILL,
OF NEW YORK CITY

Referring to that part of the question relating to a bureau charge, while I might modify my opinion through further knowledge of your plans, my impression is that such charge to employers would be a help rather than a hindrance. You will probably find some reluctance on their part at first through fear that your movement is an effort to promote the incompetent and load them with inefficient labor. As I understand your purpose, however, you propose a real service to employers as well as to employees, and when that service is given or the employers are convinced of it, most of them would prefer to pay for it. In such case they would feel that you are under obligations to select your candidates more carefully; and they would be freer to complain at a poor supply. It will be more businesslike all around.

In reply to question No. 3,—Occupational Mobility. In unskilled labor, of course, the range is pretty large and the zone of employment wide. Such labor, for example, can be shifted from the dock to the warehouse, can be transferred to gang work, and could make itself useful in most forms of agriculture, etc. Passing to the semi-skilled trades, the zone is narrower, though still wide enough to give considerable employment, and the individual mobility, though restricted, is enough to admit of considerable accommodation. In the purely skilled trade the limits are sharply drawn. The modern specialized workman is apt to make poor shift of it when he turns his hand to anything outside of his specialty. The clerical employee is perhaps the most handicapped of all.

There is one modifying consideration, however, that is worth keeping in mind in this connection. The American *per se* has more mobility, more "jack-of-all-trades" about him, than the man of any other race; and so far as the Bureau deals with the American pure and simple it would find him comparatively easy to place. From the nature of the case, however, the bulk of your unemployed would be of foreign stock. Among skilled aliens, occupational mobility is much less developed, in many instances entirely wanting.

In regard to the need of this Bureau: Speaking without such special examination as is implied in your first two questions, but from a general knowledge of the subject, it seems plain that there is a place for such a broad, sane, co-ordinated movement as you suggest; and it ought to fill a large field of usefulness. The utility of your Bureau, however, will depend upon its organization and administration, upon how efficiently and wisely your plan is carried out. In this connection I should especially emphasize the need of making haste slowly. From the unique character of the venture, unusual problems that cannot be anticipated will present themselves, and they will have to be worked out through experience. It would therefore seem ill-considered to establish outlying agencies until such questions had been carefully settled through the results of the New York office.

There are two specific, vital things to be done on the start: First, you must secure the confidence of employers. Second, you must enlist the co-operation of the labor unions, without conceding to them undue voice in your movement. There is a chance for headwork right here.

It is not by any means impossible that you may have also to overcome considerable apathy or suspicion on the part of the unemployed themselves. All this means much time and work aside from the usual detail and work of an organization.

Another important fact must be kept in mind. Employers, in common with most business men, are shy of enterprises which are partly business and partly philanthropic, and objection may be made to your Bureau on this ground. From the start, therefore, it is vitally important that the business aspects of your movement, its efficient administration, and its real service should be so kept in the foreground that any philanthropic purpose which attaches to it should not be overmuch in evidence.

In reply to your question as to whether this venture can be made a paying enterprise, I should say again that it all hinges upon administration. As a business there ought to be a good deal in it, but it will require unusual skill and care to prevent failure. In any event, immediate profits could hardly be obtained. The first year would necessarily be one of organization and experiment, but with these well done and conducted it would not seem unreasonable to expect the second year to show some return on capital.

DECEMBER 21, 1908.

REPLY FROM PROF. JOHN B. CLARK,
OF COLUMBIA UNIVERSITY

In my view loss of employment by large bodies of men personally fit for it is invariably due to mal-adjustment, since there is never a time when there is not within the limits of the society to which the men belong a need of their labor and a chance, with proper adjustment, to dispose of its product. The rearrangements needed may be too extensive to be made within the neighborhood in which the men reside, and herein lies the largest practical difficulty. The change needed is occupational and, when made in a large scale, involves a local change as well.

In the main, in the period following the recent crisis, the change needed has been from occupations catering to the mere luxurious wants to those producing necessaries of life and comforts of the lower grade. The trouble would now be relieved by a migration from manufacturing and commercial centers to the country. Agriculture and mining would absorb a large amount of new labor and relieve the congestion elsewhere. The change, if made by persons specially fitted for these rural occupations, would open the way for persons not so fitted to find employment within their own communities. The mere increase of the output of agriculture and mining would create a demand for more products of urban labor.

Minor changes, such as those from community to community, would afford a valuable though less comprehensive relief. A large system of intelligence bureaus would make known in congested centers important fields for labor, though they would be capable of receiving fewer persons than the absolutely rural occupations. Probably in connection with changes automatically making, they would relieve most of the serious distress of New York City.

It is a happy circumstance that labor, thanks to modern methods, has become increasingly "mobile." Formerly much of it was tied to its occupations by the fact that most trades required long apprenticeships. The maker of shoes could not make cloth or set type or make tools. He cannot do this now without some instruction, but at present most mechanical trades consist of specialties that can be easily learned. Many of them involve only the tending of certain machines, and it is not hard to learn to run different machines. Old men may not readily change their trades, but young men can do so, and do it easily where the change is not too great. Occupational mobility is sufficient, in these days, to transfer a vast number of persons quickly from one trade to another. The larger difficulty is the local one—changing work means moving, which is costly and is hazardous when no assurance of employment is afforded before the move is made.

In my view, no philanthropy could be better than one which

should seek far and wide for plans where workers are needed and make the facts known where they are present and unemployed.

The plan of charging a slight fee is the right one in the long run. Whether it should be adopted at the outset, while the trouble from lack of employment is most acute, is doubtful. Anything to ensure quick employment in an emergency might be the rule. In time—and in a short time—the fees should be charged, in order that the system might be self-supporting.

November 23, 1908.

REPLY FROM PROF. JOHN R. COMMONS,
of the University of Wisconsin

It is possible that if one were to make a thorough field investigation and to give some time to the matter he might discover features of your proposition that would be worth taking up, but the attention that I am able to give to it leads me to question very much whether the plan as you outline it will secure results which seem to be hoped for.

In the first place, it appears to me that an experiment of this kind which would attempt to distribute the surplus of labor of New York into other cities or industrial communities (I perceive that you do not contemplate agricultural distribution) would lead to such great friction that its success would be doubtful. So far as I am able to learn, the depression in industry and resulting unemployment is general throughout the country. I should not be surprised if it were worse in some cities, say Pittsburgh, than it is in New York. If, therefore, New York labor were sent to employers in other cities, objection would immediately be made on the part of the local wage-earners and especially trade unions. If, on the other hand, the New York emigrant secured employment, there seems to be no guarantee possible that the employer would keep him, provided he is dissatisfied with his work. In such a case the laborer would be thrown on the local charity and would need to be carried back to New York at the expense of your proposed Bureau. In such a juncture the municipal authorities and the charity organization would be after you. It is possible, however, that if you had very capable agents in the several cities to which you send surplus labor, and these agents were thoroughly able to master the local employment situation and to get beneath the representations both of employers seeking cheap labor and of trade unionists hostile to imported labor, you might avoid the difficulties suggested. The expenses, however, would be so great in securing this kind of competent help, that I do not think it is practicable.

Omitting then, the proposal to distribute the surplus labor of New York in other cities, there remains the question of what should be done by an employment bureau designed to make work for the unemployed in New York or nearby.

If it is true that existing employment bureaus are unreliable, that they take advantage of the unemployed, it might be worth while to establish a model bureau both as an example to others and as a means of driving out the unreliable ones. This is the only ground on which it appears to me it would be worth while to establish such a bureau as you propose. If you are planning to go further than this and to provide work for the unemployed, it cannot be done except by enlisting the State or city or private capital in starting up public works or labor colonies or something of that kind. I assume that the existing bureaus are adequate to make the transfers and the interchanges needed for those employers who actually are looking for workmen. But, seeing that private employment cannot be increased until the general industrial conditions start up, there remains only this alternative of making work independent of existing establishments. In other words, it appears to me that the best thing that could be done under the circumstances would be to go ahead on something like the Swiss and German relief stations, labor colonies, etc., and to plan out in co-operation with the State and municipal authorities a large project by which, whenever private industry lets down through panic or depression, these supplementary means of employment could be started up.

As to the occupational mobility of labor, it does not appear to me practicable so far as private employment is concerned. A dairy farmer certainly would not want to take on a tailor for his work. The proper way to get at the extent of mobility in occupation would be to bring together the agents of the Charity Organization Society and get their experience in the matter. I should think, however, that with the supplementary methods of employment which I have suggested, it would be found possible to make work that would be suitable for all kinds of the unemployed.

I have, perhaps, stated my views with more assurance and abruptness than are warranted; and, as I said in the beginning, a thorough investigation, especially if there is promise of adequate expenditure and competent managers and agents, might develop features that would modify what I have said. The great balance of evidence, however, seems to me just now to support the position above taken.

NOVEMBER 24, 1908.

REPLY FROM PROF. H. J. DAVENPORT,
OF THE UNIVERSITY OF MISSOURI

I believe it well at the outset to distinguish between normal times and periods of panic, or of post-panic depression. Any analysis of these last is possible only after the settlement of some very fundamental issues in economic theory. For my own part, I am convinced that the difficulty is not so much one of disturbed production reacting upon consumption, as of disturbed consumption reacting upon production. The period preceding the depression is one in which society has achieved a technicological development affording the possibility of a high standard of consumption; society now turns in temper and disposition temporarily toward a policy of postponed consumption and of saving. Emphasis, that is, is temporarily transferred from goods for consumption to the accumulation of purchasing power. In some measure, the supply of goods does not now furnish a demand for other goods, but merely a demand for the medium of exchange or for rights of deferred consumption expressed in this medium. Each man is trying to produce and sell more than he buys or consumes. This —socially speaking—is an *impasse*. Enlarged industrial equipment is not called for in time of restricted markets for goods; instrumental goods are in fact already in surplusage. Therefore only soon such saving can take place for individual purposes as connotes an increased consumption with others, and an enlarged indebtedness against them.

And this means that the essential fact of industrial depression is commonly a temporarily lowered standard of living in a society technicologically equipped for a higher standard.

In times of this sort, it is not possible that the total labor force of society be employed. The only question is whether some of the laborers shall be fully employed, and others totally lack work, or each shall work at reduced time. A shorter labor day is by far the preferable alternative.

It follows, also, that this time of restricted individual demands for goods is precisely the time in which public work should be especially undertaken. What is accomplished by laborers who would otherwise be unemployed, is, socially speaking, a pure saving,—a costless accomplishment. Public debts should be incurred in times of low interest and of lax employment, and should be paid in times of prosperity, rather than be incurred on terms of diverting labor from other employments and at a high wage cost and on a high interest level, with the result that the payment, when it does take place, takes place through taxes collected at the maximum of burden and hardship.

I am not sure how far an employment bureau can make itself effective here, otherwise than as in some degree a force merely of amelioration or of readjustment. Something, however, is doubtless possible in this direction.

What would happen if the principle were to come to be generally applied over the entire field of industry, is, I suspect, past the theoretical reach of the economist, and must rather be referred to the legislator, the agitator, or the revolutionist. So far as the difficulties of non-employment are due to the fact that, in times of stress and liquidation, prices tend to fall more rapidly than wages, an employment bureau should be able to do something in finding for the employer laborers who are willing to work upon a wage level making their employment an *entrepreneur* possibility. I see no reason why the employer should not pay for this, particularly if the employment bureau accepts some responsibility in investigating and reporting upon the quality of the labor.

Turning, however, to normal conditions: something like a problem parallel to the foregoing is presented so far as concerns the work of the monopoly principle, as applied (1) by employers, (2) by employees.

No combination can raise the price of its product on any other terms than of diminishing its output. This involves a reduction of the labor employed. The wider spread the application of the monopoly in production, the larger must be the restriction of the labor market. Under present conditions the restriction of output by the monopolized industries must result in the congestion in those fields still backward in the application of the monopoly principle.

A precisely parallel analysis applies to the activity of labor unions, so far as their methods involve an increase of wage costs and of commodity prices. Higher wages can be enforced by the unions, and can be granted by employers only upon the basis of a higher market price upon a restricted output. The penalties are paid in part by the consuming public under the guise of higher prices for goods, and in part by displaced laborers lacking employment.

But even were the problem of non-employment free of complication by industrial depression or by monopoly organization, it would still be serious enough, though serious in aspects more readily submitting to amelioration through the methods of employment bureaus.

Imagine yourself in a great city, even in prosperous times, seeking employment. Ask yourself to whom you would apply. It helps little that the demand is there if you cannot find it. The very employer seeking further help will probably not accept you; he does not know you. Who are you? What are your credentials? Why are you not already at work? He can wait—you cannot. He seeks a contented, steadfast, trustworthy servant. You may be all this, but he does not know it. For his purposes, therefore, you are not all this. He needs more than an efficient worker, more also than a trustworthy worker; he needs one whom he knows to be both efficient and trustworthy. All these adjustments of supply to demand take time. An employee losing his place and finding another within thirty days may count himself fortunate beyond the average. The intermediate period is to be charged up to friction, lost motion, in the interplay of demand and supply. This loss quantity is never a small one. Consider the transformations constantly occurring in modern industry,—new inventions, new processes, new factories, changing demands of time and season, new fashions, new centers of trade, bankruptcies, retirements, restrictions of output, new schedules of tariff, speculations, booms, strikes, and lockouts,—a very kaleidoscope of change, —and one begins to appreciate the causes which lie back of disturbances in employment. Give each change its time for completion, for the fitting of each industrial block to its new niche, and the phenomena of non-employment are seen to be inevitable. The best-disciplined regiments require time for reforming after ranks are broken. The streets are thronged with people, by the mere going to and fro from one place of business to another; for several hours of the day the ways are filled with passers to and from their meals.

There is, then, a normal and, in a certain sense, healthful volume of non-employment.

Even were seekers of employment informed of the various opportunities for employment, and did questions of fitness and proof of fitness present no difficulties, there would still be a great measure of immobility in labor, resulting in non-employment. Men dislike changes of home even if they are able to make them, and are often unable to make them even if disposed. When, for example, the lace factories of Nottingham close for lack of demand, it is small help to the operative that in Glasgow or in Dublin there is employment in ship-building or iron-working. Assume, also, the knowledge of the opportunity and the disposition to embrace it. But the workman cannot move his cottage. It is, indeed, common enough that he is unable to undertake the expense of moving his family and personal belongings. And always the risk of misfortune or failure is menaced by new surroundings, strange people, and new methods.

Nor have we yet done with the important influences recruiting the army of the unemployed. The leading characteristic of the modern industrial system is the division of labor. As has already been remarked, this principle applies not only to individuals, but in large degree to communities, states, and nations. In sociology as well as in biology, specialization of function involves interdependence. In complicated machinery, when one wheel fails to turn, all stand still. In our present society production depends upon exchange. The agriculturist employs the mechanic and vice versa,—the steppes of Russia, the workshops of Germany. So if the American Northwest ceases to produce, and in default of production ceases to buy, the industrial centers experience a partial paralysis. A crop failure in several states, chiefly agricultural, works some measure of non-employment in those manufacturing centers with which the barter of commerce commonly takes place. At the best, the manufacturer must reach out to new and difficult markets of low profit-paying quality. Shut out by trade restrictions from the world's currents and price levels, the process is necessarily slow and painful. For the agricultural states the case is evidently still worse.

In short, there comes about a condition of want, of acute necessity, which yet affords no demand for present labor, but rather for immediate purposes a diminished demand. Ultimately, we must remember, product furnishes demand for product. The Northwest will not demand hats or shoes until it can produce wheat or meat. The manufacturing states must do their exchanging with such agricultural producers as have produced. Low prices, therefore, tend to follow for the products of the factory. Possibly enough, also, slow or hard collections in the districts of crop failure may permanently embarrass some centers of production. At all events, the condition is one of abnormally low social product accompanied for a time, not by correspondingly large outlay of productive energies, but by a reduced outlay. The world acutely needs more grain and meat. What of it? It must wait until another year. This larger requirement will mean increased activity when next year comes; it means stagnation now. Agricultural production is mostly periodic. Were the question of hats or shoes, a disproportion of product to wants would bring about a stimulus to production. Not so with the industries of agriculture. When these fail in product, it is an empty mouthing of generalities to assert the adequacy of employment as the necessary corollary of hunger. Months must pass before agriculture will renew its opportunities of employment. Other industries are over-manned at present, in view of the abnormally restricted market. Even did they offer possible employment, they are so far away as to be practically inaccessible. That agriculture is prospering on the other side the equator helps the agriculturist on this side not at all, and the manufacturer not much.

Recurring conditions of non-employment are thus inevitable in society as at present organized. But the difficulty is not fairly to be ascribed to the manner of organization. It results from the uncertainties of climate and the periodic nature of agricultural production. These failures of product could not be avoided under any circumstances. Systems can differ only in their manner of distributing the disaster.

But I take it as evident that in these later aspects of the case there is a large field of service open to the employment bureau, not merely in pointing the employer to a certified quality of labor, but in directing the laborer to that industry or to that locality having need for his services,—and possibly in some cases by extending the laborer financial aid in moving to that locality where the call for his labor exists.

NOVEMBER 24, 1908.

REPLY FROM PROF. HENRY W. FARNAM,
OF YALE UNIVERSITY

My general impression is that while many of the public employment agencies are useful, especially in providing for seasonal laborers, they have not done very much towards handling the mass of unemployment which comes with a financial crisis, or adjusting the supply to the needs of different occupations; for instance, drawing the surplus labor of the cities into the country districts where labor is often at a premium. My own view is that a mere employment bureau cannot do very much for these cases, but that an effort should be made to go much deeper and to pursue the aim of giving each man two trades. This sounds quite impossible, but the idea is not in my judgment impossible. In itself, the main thing is to educate the public sentiment and especially labor organizations up to the idea of the double-barrelled man. The extent to which immigrants change their occupations and the number of individual cases, doubtless known to us all, where a man can do more than one thing, all prove that there is nothing inherently impossible in it.

NOVEMBER 21, 1908.

REPLY FROM PROF. FRANK A. FETTER,
OF CORNELL UNIVERSITY

In the lack of reliable statistics on the topics you have suggested, our dependence must be on the impressions of observers. Naturally those in contact with the problems of the unemployed in our larger cities, and especially in New York, are most competent to form judgments in this matter. But some facts bearing on the question may be evident to one with a non-metropolitan outlook which may be either overlooked entirely or seen in a different light by city workers.

1. MAL-ADJUSTMENT OF EMPLOYMENT IN CITIES. Certain general considerations lead me, in the absence of exact figures, to the belief that unemployment is, to a considerable degree, due to mal-adjustment. This is in part a common observation. It is apparently inevitable to some degree because of the more complicated nature of industry in large cities. There is less chance for the city wage-earner to turn to a side occupation than there is for a rural worker. The higher working pace in the cities more quickly throws out a man suffering from sickness, accident, or old age, a fact that is reflected by the figures showing the larger proportion of old men engaged in agriculture. City industry has more of the lottery element, giving larger prizes to the successful

at the price of more failures for the average man. The German census of the unemployed in 1895, the only statistics on this subject that I know of for an entire country, gives the following result.* To one thousand inhabitants there were unemployed in

	June.	December.
Cities over 100,000	11.2	16.9
Communes 10,000 to 100,000	4.5	10.7
Communes under 10,000	1.7	9.6

That a similar difference would be found in America as between communities of different density of population can hardly be doubted as is in part shown by figures to be given below. These facts may be interpreted as indicating a permanent excess of labor in cities as compared with agricultural districts, but it seems reasonable to infer that in part they indicate mal-adjustment of the working force in the cities.

As to the fee I hesitate to express an *a priori* judgment, but I question whether, on the whole, a reasonable fee would be a disadvantage. With or without a fee, however, it must be recognized that a considerable portion of the unemployed will fail to make use of an agency. A German investigation in Stuttgart gave the remarkable result that only 19.9 per cent of the unemployed attempted to get employment through the Labor Bureau which was (probably, though of this I am not certain) public and free.†

2. MAL-ADJUSTMENT BETWEEN COMMUNITIES. The few facts at hand indicate that there is a large measure of such mal-adjustment in the sense that a considerable number may be unemployed in the cities when a paying occupation, either their own main occupation or one which they could successfully follow, could be found for them not far away. As suggested above, unemploy-

---

* (See Georg Schanz, *Neue Beitrage zur Frage der Arbeitlosen-Versicherung*, 1897.)

† (See Schanz, Op. cit., p. 191.)

ment is a greater problem where industry has become largely specialized. The connection would seem to be between specialization and unemployment rather than between congestion of population and unemployment, but as a matter of fact, the specialization goes in most cases along with larger aggregations of population, or "congestion," as your question suggests. But this is not always the case, for a smaller population given almost entirely to one industry, as in a mining town, or in a manufacturing city dependent on one industry, feels the effect of hard times in an extreme degree. Agricultural communities and smaller cities supported in large part by agricultural trade nearly always appear to advantage in seasons of industrial distress. The replies from the different states to the questionnaire of the National Conference of Charities in 1908 showed that the southern and western states in a number of cases were hardly aware of the existence of industrial depression and had no problem of unemployment. In a general way it appeared that the distress was most marked in proportion to the dominance of manufacturing and large cities. On the occasion of the state conference recently, citizens of Elmira (in private talks) boasted of the prosperity of the community and the freedom from unemployment and said it was the policy to attract to Elmira a large variety of industries so that the effects of a panic would be little felt. The city of Ithaca has had no problem of unemployment in any special sense in the past year. Several members of labor organizations have told me that work has been abundant in the building trades the entire year, there has been a relative scarcity of skilled labor and of unskilled, and only some small reduction in the factories which caused no local distress has taken place. The columns of *Charities and The Commons* have reported that even domestic servants have been in superfluity in New York City during the present year, but it is certain that many of them could find employment in Ithaca and similar cities at the present time at wages quite as high as ever have been paid here, which are probably higher than in New York City.

3. Natural Limits to Mobility of Labor. Mobility of labor as found among the unemployed would seem in some cases to indicate inferior intelligence and skill and in other cases superior intelligence and skill in those adapting themselves to the need by shifting their occupation. A few words of explanation of this paradox will be ventured.

Broadly speaking, the unemployed are the relatively inefficient in any occupation, a statement that is almost a truism. It must happen, therefore, in many cases, that those unemployed are most likely to be forced to change their occupations either in the perennial hope of the inefficient of bettering their condition, or from necessity, dropping down the industrial scale when forced out of an occupation for which they have proved unfitted. An investigation in Dresden showed that of 1,632 unemployed men in June, 526 had been engaged just before in some other than their main occupation, and of 3,503 unemployed in December, 1,176 had been last engaged in other than their main occupation. This kind of mobility is not ideal, and yet is hardly all bad if it means in part the change from a calling for which one is not fitted to one which can be better done. The main explanation, however, is probably to be found in the shifting purpose and planless lives of the cases investigated.

Mobility in other cases is the indication of superior intelligence and skill. It takes greater natural ability to adapt one's self to a sudden emergency such as loss of employment, and this adaptability undoubtedly can be strengthened by industrial training. The change from agricultural to manufacturing and from rural to city conditions has been so rapid that our education, as is now generally recognized, has not kept pace with it. The present degree of immobility is not to be deemed inevitable, and the possibility of its decrease with machine workers is surely great. Instead of a rule-of-thumb knowledge of a single machine, there needs to be more general training in mechanical principles and the cultivation of adaptability in the great mass of the working population.

Mobility is affected by seasonal changes and there is large chance for adjustment between agricultural and manufacturing occupations. We living in the country hear the constant call for farm help from early spring to the end of summer. It is true that the conditions of work on the farm are such as are not familiar to the city worker, and doubtless some changes must be made in this regard before the desired mobility as between city and country can be obtained. The busy season in manufacturing is in the months September, October and November,* when not only the busy canning season, but special orders for the holidays are crowding. The average number employed per month during these three months exceeded the average number for the entire year by 155,000.† It has been the social ideal of many reformers to provide an alternation of employment and especially to enable workers in city factories to spend a part of the time in the country. Therefore, anything that would reduce unemployment by increasing mobility in this regard would be a double blessing.

One of the greatest difficulties in such an adjustment is the subjective one, the inertia of the city worker and his feeling of helplessness in taking an unaccustomed occupation. Specialization gets men out of the habit of adapting themselves to new conditions of employment. I believe that we need to recognize that this difficulty is more psychological than merely physical or because of lack of manual training. In smaller cities, only a little less than is the case on farms, the worker does many things in the course of the week. Trade union rules perhaps help to confirm this habit of immobility in large cities. For the past year or more a good deal of my gardening and lawn work has been done by a stone mason, who works regularly at his trade at full union wages when the build-

---

*See Census Bulletin 57, p. 11.

†Idem. p. 23, the total given under "greatest number" is, I judge, a statistical fallacy.

ing season is on. In the West I have known many factory workers with their entire families to go out to work in the country, for example, in Oregon at hop-picking. I dwell on these things indicating tasks outside of the usual functions of employment agencies to raise the question whether those functions should not be thought of more broadly, especially in their educational aspects.

The work of such a bureau might well be directed in other unconventional lines; for example, the possibility of using public work, as road building, etc., as a balance wheel is well worth studying, for we have not done as much in America as has been done in other countries in this matter. The proposed Employment Bureau will, I hope, be conducted with a larger social aim than any of the efforts in the past. The application of sound principles of industrial education, the developing of better relations between the different industries, the study of the individual workers and their capacities, the classifying of them in accordance with their various degrees of adaptability, are all problems calling for consideration. The reasonable hope of benefit from such an undertaking is great when we consider that the change of a few workers will help to preserve the equilibrium in industry both as between the different occupations at a given moment in a single community, and as between the different communities making up our national economy. The delicately adjusted employment machinery should act like a gyroscope by shifting the free labor supply promptly to the point where it is most needed.

NOVEMBER 28, 1908.

REPLY FROM PROF. (EMERITUS) WM. W. FOLWELL,
OF THE UNIVERSITY OF MINNESOTA

In regard to question 1, I will suggest that since it is safe to assume that in "large cities" many men are always out of work because they cannot or will not find jobs, it is not important that any precise ratio be established. The proportion should of course be largest in your great seaboard cities where immigrants are dumped, and smallest in our interior rapidly growing cities. In good times there is a shortage of all kinds of labor in some of the latter. I cannot think that employers would object to paying reasonable fees for efficient service. They would object to paying fees for men who would "skip out" soon after reaching destination.

As to Number 2, it seems to me that local mal-adjustment is to some extent national, and is due to the interplay of two great forces. One of these is attachment to home, which in spite of appearances is still powerful. A similar sentiment keeps immigrants in the places where they happen to settle soon after arrival. I remember the wrench it took to move me from the "Lake Country" of central New York to northern Ohio. The other force is the passion for adventure and movement felt by all of us at some time of life.

I do not see how anybody can tell beforehand "the extent" to which the surplus labor of New York City can be shipped to other cities. As new industries are opened in western cities the East is drawn on for skilled laborers. We have, for instance, in Minneapolis, considerable manufactures of shoes, hosiery, laborers' underwear, and overalls. I suppose the operatives were mostly imported from the East. I doubt if any considerable market will be found for unskilled labor shipped from the East. There is talk of the establishment here of an enormous packing plant by the Armours. In fact they have bought near a thousand acres of land about one mile from where I am writing. It may be that your Bureau could "ship" out two or three thousand men when the concern starts up.

As to Number 3, we have not statistics enough to warrant a guess. The distribution of labor to the several industries is, I think, beyond any calculus, and can only be solved by experiment, or perhaps I should say, experience.

When the country comes to be completely occupied, and immigration is reduced to an inconsiderable increment of population, and all the arts have been brought to perfection, we may begin to guess about a normal distribution of labor.

Without any statistics or estimated ratios, we have good ground to believe that such a bureau as you propose might do much good service. You will, in my judgment, do well to make an experiment, if you can find sufficient means.

I suspect that, if you undertake it, you will find very great difficulties of administration. You will be suspected of unloading paupers and dead-beats on the western cities. You will have to devise some means by which the men sent out shall actually stick to work for the employers who send for them. You will need reliable agents in many places. Competition of private employment agencies will embarrass. Advertising will be a great expense.

For one I should like to have the experiment made. It might furnish an excellent object lesson on which some day to form a national employment bureau. Perhaps a national "intelligence office" would best be tried at the first.

Query: Might it not be well for your proposed Bureau to begin as an "intelligence office"? I suspect that a force of field agents would be necessary to keep the office advised as to actual needs of localities. If you can get the money, try it by all means.

November 23, 1908.

REPLY FROM PROF. J. E. HAGERTY,
of Ohio State University

I am very much interested in your effort to organize an employment bureau. Of course, you know we have a public employment bureau in Ohio, with a local branch in Columbus. Up to date, the bureau has been worthless, and an expense to the state. The superintendent of the local branch has been, all along, a politician who has utterly failed to appreciate the duties of the office.

It seems to me the only way to establish an employment bureau, at least now, is to organize one under private control.

I will endeavor to take up your questions in order:

1. I believe that unemployment is due to mal-adjustment to a considerable extent, especially in that class of labor which would not be classified as unskilled. I presume organized labor has no difficulty in finding employment where employment is to be had. Clerical labor, or labor just above the unskilled sort, I think, meets with difficulty in finding employment. In many cases such a bureau would be of service to the unskilled. Of course, in times like the present, when unemployment is due to industrial conditions, is would be difficult for an employment bureau to be effective. At the outset, I believe charging the employers a fee would be a hindrance to the development of the bureau. On the other hand, I think that a small fee charged the employee in case he found employment, would be an advantage. He would appreciate the service rendered him, and I think that he could distinguish between the legitimate employment bureau which is under private control, and the one that is organized primarily to fleece the wage-earner.

2. There is a great deal of mal-adjustment as between communities. That mal-adjustment is especially obvious between communities like Columbus and rural districts. If frequently happens here that there is a strong demand for labor in the country, while men are seeking employment in the city. An employment bureau would be of service in getting this surplus population out on the farms. As between different communities, I think, too, that such an employment bureau would be of advantage. Industrial conditions may create a glut in the labor market at one point, and a dearth of labor at another point. A well-organized bureau which engages in an aggressive campaign in learning the conditions of the labor market, would, I believe, be of great value. I do not

think that the over-supply of labor in cities is a feature of "congested populations."

3. Of course, there are natural limits to the mobility of labor in change of occupation, but the unskilled labor and that slightly above it can change with ease from one occupation to another, and it is at these points that the labor problem is a difficult one. Here, I think you could get enough to shift from one occupation to another to relieve the pressure at one point and to supply the labor market at another.

I think there is a real need and that there are great possibilities in a thoroughly organized employment bureau. Such an employment bureau, of course, I need not say, would have close relations and a good understanding with employers of all classes, and a knowledge of labor, upon the other hand. No individual should be recommended for a position who is not qualified to hold it. The principle of "first come, first served," should not apply here.

NOVEMBER 25, 1908.

REPLY FROM MR. JAMES MULLENBACH,
Superintendent of the Municipal Lodging House of Chicago

Although I have had no time to prepare a careful statement, I am venturing to send you some information and a few opinions based on our observation and experience at the Municipal Lodging House. I shall take up each of your inquiries in order.

To what extent unemployment in our large cities is due merely to mal-adjustment.

The following groups seem to be especially affected by lack of information, or of false information as to where work is to be found.

1. Newcomers to the city from the country, naturally unacquainted with places of employment. They do not know where the jobs are.

2. Immigrants, also unacquainted with the city and the customs of the country and with the additional handicap of not knowing the language. This is not so true of those nations that have been sending immigrants to America for so long a time that they have been able to create their own agencies. For example, the Swedish National Association maintains one of the most efficient and reliable agencies in Chicago. Those nations whose people have only recently begun to come to this country, seem to be most open to exploitation, the Bulgarians, for example. An agency in Chicago charged a group of them as high as $5 for a job on the railroad.

3. Men who do not know how to approach an employer for a job. The art of getting a job sometimes surpasses the skill required to do it.

4. Those exploited by regular employment agencies. The number of labor agencies and the extent of their operations, their specialization, *i. e.* their division of labor, would indicate the need of a real Employment Exchange. In Chicago we have about 200 of these offices, and they negotiate employment from lowest casual and unskilled labor up to high salaried positions in our big business houses,—all this in competition with the newspapers. No complaint could be made, if honesty and efficiency generally prevailed, but I am sure that some of the unemployment in the city is due to their inefficiency and dishonesty of the agencies. Scarcely a night passes at our Lodging House that some victim of these agencies does not report. While I would not wish to place a percentage estimate upon this exploitation as a cause of unemployment, I am sure it is a very definite factor. It is my opinion that we shall not be able to deal with the general problem of employment until we get this matter of mal-adjustment taken care of in some intelligent way.

As to the various classes of help that you indicate,—clerical, skilled, unskilled, etc.,—so far as my observation goes the clerical seem to suffer less, that is, they seem to be able to know quicker where work is to be found, probably because of newspaper advertisements.

As for skilled men, the organized trades look after their own unemployed. In Chicago all of the leading trades are so well organized that most of the business agents of the unions act or their office acts, as the labor agent for the men. About one-third of our lodgers are skilled men, but union men in good standing have no trouble as a rule in getting work at once through their unions. As a matter of fact, they form only a small percentage of the number of skilled. The balance is made up chiefly of drifting craftsmen, whose unemployment is due mainly to the present depression, but in normal times to the increasing tendency toward rush and dull seasons in the trades. The unorganized workers find it much more difficult to find work on account of their lack of knowledge as to the jobs.

The unskilled fall chiefly into three groups, the factory workers, the casual laborers, railroad laborers, etc., and the local odd job men. As for the first group, I believe they are only partly dependent on the employment agency, and rely mainly on the "ad" and the legend "Help wanted" in the window. As for the casual laborers,—the railroad navvies, deck hands, ice-cutters, harvest-hands, loggers,—they are almost entirely dependent upon labor agents for the jobs. The same is true of all kinds of construction work, excavating, etc. This group is subject to all forms of exploitation by the agents,—overcharges and misdirection. It may be that this is peculiar to Chicago, as casual laborers, I have been told, are not so numerous in New York. Concerning the odd job men, only those employed in restaurants and hotels seem to depend very much on the agencies. A good share of the others get their "steer" for a job through the news "ad."

II. Mal-adjustment between communities.

So far as I have been able to observe, the demand for men outside of the city is confined mainly to casual labor, construction work and farm work, with here and there some factory demand.

I believe a bureau such as you are contemplating would do much to eliminate the exploitation of these groups by the regular agencies in Chicago. The difficulty has been to get the employers, railroads and others, to co-operate. I know this has been our experience and also the experience of the State Free Employment Bureaus. So far as the casual labor and the farm groups are concerned, permanent withdrawal from the city cannot be expected, so long as the present conditions of seasonal occupation continue.

Unemployed seek the city for several reasons;

1. There is always "something doing" in a city and, though there are more men for the jobs probably, the out-of-work prefers to take his chance.

2. One can always keep warm and alive in the city, with less risk of social isolation and ostracism than in a small town or the countryside. My observation at the Municipal Lodging House is that the chances for employment in the small town or country are not as good as in the city. If I were an out-of-work, I am sure I would rather take my chance in Chicago than in Rockford or Woodstock or some other well-to-do and eminently respectable Illinois town. A good employment agency might be able to negotiate a job for me at one of these places,—a job I could not find myself, and I probably would be willing to take it. While there is a good deal of feeling that a man can get a job in the country and the farmers are in need of men all the time, I think it will be found that they want the help chiefly during certain seasons, as for instance, at harvesting time.

On this point of mal-adjustment between communities, I would say that I do not believe that small communities will offer much opportunity for taking up the surplus labor of our large cities, and that an employment agency would be doing its best service in placing the casual and unskilled labor that is now placed and exploited by other agencies. On occasion opportunities for sending out men to permanent employment in the country or small town would arise, but they would not be so numerous as to greatly affect the city's unemployed. In other words I think the geographical mobility is confined to certain well defined forms of labor, seasonal and casual, and that our unemployed problem is not local but national; that the reason there is an over-supply of labor in the city is because the state of unemployment is more endurable in the city than in the country, having more hope for relief through getting a job or through charity, and suffering less hardship while waiting for either.

III. Natural limits of occupational mobility. We seem to find these limits much narrower than we had supposed. For example, we have found it difficult for a man trained as cabinet maker to become a carpenter, though the two trades seem nearly related. Good German farm hands are not acceptable on our Illinois farms because they do not know how to milk, even when the farms are not strictly dairy farms. In following the disintegration of trades as it has come to our observation, it is rare that the craftsmen as a body take up the machine that is exploiting them and use it for the foundation of a new trade. Just now the autos are putting the cab drivers "on the bum," to use the expression of one of them, but there are few cab drivers becoming chauffeurs. The same is true of the tanners and the glass workers. The limits of such a transfer from one calling to another seem to be determined on the part of the man by his youth and initiative, and on the part of the trade by the fact as to whether the disintegrating force at work on the trade or calling attacks it so suddenly and completely as practically to supplant the craftsman. Able-bodied tradesmen seem to drift into the unskilled and casual labor groups, while such weaker ones as printers take to such work as restaurant, hotel, circularizing and canvassing.

On this point my opinion is that while the Bureau you have in mind would doubtless help in placing misplaced or displaced men in better lines of work than they might be able to find themselves, the operation of the Bureau would be quite restricted by difficulties inherent in the situation.

To sum up, I believe an Employment Bureau would do much to cure the mal-adjustment locally. It would protect the innocent, the uninformed and the unwary from exploitation, would set a standard for other agencies, and render positive service to the community as a reliable and efficient clearing office for men and jobs. It would be able to negotiate for the transfer of unemployed from city to country where opportunity offered, and doubtless would turn up opportunities that are now overlooked or hidden, In the region of occupational mobility its service would be valuable, but somewhat restricted by the natural limits of the movement from one calling to another. Of course, no one is supposing that such mediation as a Bureau, even at its best, may be able to give, will "settle the question of the unemployed," as it is commonly put; but such an agency would eliminate some of the perplexing elements of the situation and give a better grip on it. Anything that will remove the subsidiary and get nearer to the bona fide causes of unemployment will help to "settle it."

As to fees and one or two other things concerning the operation, our experience at the Municipal Lodging House leads me to believe that it would be a good thing to charge the employer a fee. When employers get help without charge they are apt to consider the help as cheap, pay low wages, exact unreasonable service, alter original terms, and to be captious. Anything that would create the feeling among employers that the Bureau was a straight business proposition, gotten up for the relief of no one, but for the best service of any one who wanted good, well selected help, and willing to pay for it, would be a good thing. I believe the fee would help toward this. Too many employers assume that because a man is down and out he should be "willing to work for anything rather than accept charity." Hence it is wise to avoid the appearance of dealing only with the unemployed or the down-and-out men.

Nevertheless it will be necessary at the outset to get the active interest and co-operation of some employers in order to make a good start. The casual labor end of it can not be handled successfully unless the railroad and steamship managements co-operate.

Another group whose interest and co-operation will be valuable is organized labor. One of the matters that came up for decision soon after we began our employment bureau at the Municipal Lodging House was the policy regarding labor troubles. It seemed well not to send men to plants that were having trouble with their men. In case of strike we have always refused to furnish help. I may add that this is the policy of the State Free Employment offices of Illinois and of Ohio. Opportunities for mutual co-operation and assistance will arise from time to time between the bureau and the business agents of the unions.

NOVEMBER 27, 1908.

REPLY FROM PROF. E. A. ROSS,
OF THE UNIVERSITY OF WISCONSIN

In my judgment the labor situation in New York City is distinctly anomalous owing to the constant influx of ignorant and helpless immigrants who lodge there and depress the labor market because of their lack of knowledge of opportunities out in the country. In normal times there is more difficulty in equilibrating the supply and demand in the New York labor market than in other labor markets. In times of depression the unemployment there is more acute. I have long felt that artificial means ought to be provided for distributing the surplus labor in New York out through the country where the opportunities exist. The sending of local unemployed a considerable distance in quest of jobs requires, however, more conscientiousness and good faith than a private employment agency ordinarily exercises. As few of the seekers of employment are in a position to discriminate between the honest and the fraudulent agency, there is an opportunity for the latter to flourish and even to make difficult the survival of the honest agency. This summer there were shocking revelations of financial exploitation of helpless, newly arrived immigrants by certain Chicago employment agencies. The agencies charged them high fees for sending them great distances in search of jobs which were merely temporary or had long since been filled.

Besides its consciousness of a fiduciary relation to its clients an employment bureau of the kind contemplated would be able by a correspondence with the secretaries of local charity organizations and the offices of similar societies to build up an organization by means of which statements of employers in their vicinity as to the amount, duration, remuneration, and conditions of the employment they propose to furnish, could be promptly and reliably verified. In this respect the agency would have a great advantage over private agencies.

As yet state employment bureaus are subject to the dry rot of perfunctoriness. The time may come when the state can provide efficient machinery for getting the unemployed in congested centers like New York out to points where their labor is desired. But it is likely that this will not occur until some such bureau as is proposed shows the state how to do it.

Certain facts that have fallen under my observation lead me to believe that in ordinary times unemployment is far more a local phenomenon than is generally supposed. Last year our State Tax Commission concluded an investigation of mortgage loans in this state which demonstrated that the interest on such loans is almost out of relation to the course of the general money market, but depends upon the relation between the local supply of and the local demand for loanable capital. In the frontier counties of this state the rate of interest on such loans was with equally good security about double what it is in the counties that have accumulated more capital. This astonishing exhibit turned my thoughts in the direction of considering how far a local rate for labor or capital are special and how far they reflect general or national conditions. The result is a growing impression that local labor markets are not sections or provinces of a general labor market, but markets of a considerable individuality. There are parts of the country where the labor market is habitually a bull market. New York City, for the reason I gave above, is on the other hand a bear market. It is, therefore, rational to help the unemployed by taking advantage of the different complexion of labor markets.

NOVEMBER 24, 1908.

REPLY FROM PROF. HENRY R. SEAGER,
OF COLUMBIA UNIVERSITY

It gives me pleasure to reply to the questions contained in your letter of the 20th instant, although circumstances have prevented me from collecting any exact information to back up the opinions which I express. They are the fruit of some study of the labor problem during the six years that I have lived in New York, and some knowledge of the work of an employment bureau gathered through a connection with the Alliance Employment Bureau during the last two years.

1. Distinguishing between unemployment in periods of active trade and unemployment due to general business depression, and confining attention to the first, I should say that in New York City there is at all times a good deal of unemployment due to mal-adjustment between seekers after work and opportunities for employment within the city. The causes of this mal-adjustment are: (1) Irregular employment in many trades; (2) the rise and fall of particular employing firms, forcing a constant shifting of employees from employer to employer; (3) immigration and the unadjusted immigrant worker which results from it; (4) the absence of any satisfactory agency or agencies for properly classifying workmen in search of employment, so that employers can be relieved

in part of the task of trying-out new hands. Among working women and girls especially, there is a great amount of mal-adjustment owing to the frequency with which employees are engaged for work for which they are not fitted, only to be turned off after a short trial discouraged rather than benefited by the experience.

A complete classification of employments would show, I think, that this unemployment falls most heavily on the relatively unskilled and unorganized workers. Women suffer from it more than men; girls and boys more than women.

I don't believe that charging a small fee would deter employers from applying to a Bureau like that proposed *provided the Bureau gained a reputation for supplying the type of workers needed rather than workers many of whom would prove on trial to be unsatisfactory.* Employers complain a great deal of the service rendered by existing employment bureaus managed for private gain.

2. In a city like New York and a country like the United States mal-adjustment of the labor supply to the demand between different sections is, for obvious reasons, much more serious than in older, more conservative and more homogeneous communities. My impression is that the attractions of city life, the position of New York as the leading port of entry for immigrants to the country and the irregularity of many of the principal industries carried on in the city (*e. g.* the clothing trades, the building trades, etc.) give rise to a continuous over-supply of seekers after employment in New York City and that much more could be done than has yet been attempted to relieve the congestion of population there by finding work for the unemployed in other sections.

3. For purposes of discussion the following very rough classification of the workers who might be assisted by an employment bureau may be helpful: (I) Unskilled workers, (a) of the factory operative type, (b) those with the physical strength and mental characteristics of contented farm laborers; (II) Skilled mechanics, (a) directed, (b) self-directing; (III) Brain workers, (a) clerks, salesmen, bookkeepers, etc., (b) bosses, overseers, superintendents,

etc. Among these those most likely to be unemployed in large cities are I(a), II(a), and III(a). Within each of these classes I believe there is a large degree of mobility as industry is now organized. The work of factory operatives, for example, is similar for workers of the same grade, whether the product be bicycles or sewing machines, carriages or automobiles, boxes or baskets. Machine-tending calls for about the same qualities whether the articles turned out are of wood or steel or whatever the ultimate form that is to be given to them. Between these different groups of employments, however, (*e. g.* I, II, and III) and between employments of different grades in each group (*e. g.* I(a) and I(b) etc.) there is relatively little mobility partly because different capacities are called for and different training but also because the workers accustomed, for example, to farm labor dislike factory employments and vice versa.

An Employment Bureau would need to consider these distinctions in order to succeed in its task. Concretely, the contemplated Bureau would find in the smaller cities and towns of the country a more promising field for the unemployed in I(a) in New York City than on farms. At present one of the chief reasons New York manufacturers assign for locating in New York is the ample and varied labor market on which they can draw at will there. On the other hand, I am assured by manufacturers in small towns in the Middle West that one of the most serious problems with which they contend is that of obtaining as they require them competent workmen. An Employment Bureau that would enable such manufacturers to draw their hands from a larger area would confirm their preference for their present locations and attract other manufacturers away from cities to the smaller towns and villages. And what is true of I(a) is, I believe, true also of II(a) and III(a).

Without enlarging further on details along the lines of your definite questions, I am glad to have an opportunity to record it as my opinion that such an Employment Bureau as you describe could render an important service towards lessening the evils of unemployment. I believe there is a large amount of mal-adjustment both locally and nationally that a properly equipped and wisely directed Bureau could remedy. I am even more certain that such a Bureau could render an invaluable service by determining the causes of unemployment and discovering what other means are needed to bring about a less wasteful industrial organization. Among such means, I have no doubt that more adequate provision for trade or industrial education will be given an important place, and no one who has given any thought to the problem of the trade school can fail to recognize its dependence for its efficiency on exact information as to the kinds of workers called for in each community—the kind of information that an Employment Bureau alone can supply.

That an Employment Bureau like that proposed would have been of great assistance during the year of industrial depression through which we have just passed is so obvious that I will not enlarge on the point. Even now, when conditions seem to be improving almost day by day, such a Bureau could, I feel sure, render great service in facilitating the return to normal conditions, if it were only in existence.

As to the financial side of the undertaking I will not venture an opinion except to say that $100,000 seems to me, if anything, too small a sum to enter upon a task that is as gigantic as it is socially important.

November 29, 1908.

LETTER FROM MR. JAMES B. SEAGER,

General Manager of the Olds Gas Power Company, of Lansing, Michigan. Supplementing the Preceding Letter from Prof. Henry R. Seager

Your letter opens a very interesting subject and one in which we are keenly concerned. I most heartily endorse the proposition, and believe it would be one of the greatest steps in the right direction toward really benefiting the worker.

The difficulty is very great today of getting connections between work and the man who is out of a job. In our own case, when we want men, we are compelled to send personal representatives to different cities, advertise in local papers, and in fact, for the time being, set up a bureau such as you contemplate. It always works, *i. e.* in the end we get the men. Somewhere in this broad land we are always able to find men out of work, even though in our immediate vicinity there may be a strong demand for labor. This country is so big and wide that conditions are not uniform and, as stated, when one looks far enough, there is always a locality where good men cannot find work.

It is a curious fact also that the really best men seem to be the most helpless, if they lose a job, in the matter of getting another one. A man who has been employed for years and never had to hunt for work, seems utterly lost as to how to go about it, or where to look, if he has to hunt for a new position.

A friend of mine for years operated an employment agency in Chicago, handling only engineering talent, viz. he specialized on draughtsmen, tracers, superintendents and managers, charging the men good stiff commissions for positions secured, and the records showed that he placed men all the way from a few dollars a week to positions as high in value as $10,000 per annum, and his frequent observation to me was that he knew no man so helpless as an engineer out of a job, the better he was in his profession, the more helpless he was in hunting for a new position.

Were such a bureau in force as you outline, we would make use of it at certain times every year. We have been so hard put to it that we have sent men as far as New York City to collect mechanics and send them to Lansing, advancing their carfare to secure them.

November 27, 1908.

LETTER FROM MR. FREDERICK L. SMITH,
VICE PRESIDENT AND GENERAL MANAGER OF THE OLDS MOTOR
WORKS OF LANSING, MICHIGAN, SUPPLEMENT-
ING THE PRECEDING LETTER
FROM PROF. HENRY
R. SEAGER.

Answering your questions seriatim:*

(1) How do we proceed to get men when we need them?

The usual process is from our application files which are kept in the paymaster's office; to see first if the live applications will bring forth responses, stating the qualifications of the men —and since at a time of labor famine, so to speak, these applications are valueless because the men are all employed, we then use the offices of some employment agency, as, for instance, the one in Detroit which was established by the Manufacturers' Association there and from which fairly good results are had. In addition to this we always send our paymaster, who is familiar through long experience with the eccentricities of the laboring man looking for a job, to run an advertisement in the paper first in the large cities—Detroit, Cleveland, and Buffalo,—and select such applicants as come there on the ground. As an additional move still when these methods do not produce results, we send to the small towns,—Battle Creek, Kalamazoo and Grand Rapids, for example, and in addition to running an advertisement in these papers, make it a personal matter to ferret out good men who have employment but who would be willing to change for a slight additional compensation. The comment on the latter process, or indeed on the whole present process now of securing labor in time of a rush for labor during business expansion, or for highly specialized labor which is always in demand apparently, is very obvious. The function of a "na-

* This letter is addressed to Professor Seager, and the questions are not identical with those asked in the general letter of inquiry.

tional" employment agency absolutely unbiased and absolutely commanding the confidence of the working man himself first of all, would be that of a general distributing his forces over the field of action and preventing an often repeated spectacle of a temporary massing of the laboring army where there is only a field for the efforts of half of them, entailing an unnecessary expense for transportation, and entailing what every factory manager would explain to you as a feeling of unrest by the reason of unemployed floating labor in the small towns, which has not always a beneficial effect on the men in the shop,—although it would suggest itself immediately to you that the presence of unemployed labor in this town, say, would not be apt to quiet the uneasy feelings of men in the shop who might be fearful of losing their jobs.

(2) Would we "patronize" a well managed employment bureau with an office, for example, in Detroit?

We most certainly should not only patronize but co-operate with such an office to the full extent of our ability, since in our own case no matter what effort we make, our total force will fluctuate from five or even four hundred, low point, up to a thousand or eleven hundred men. It is, of course, unnecessary to suggest to you that at such times there is a corresponding increase in the demand for labor in this town as well as in other centers where we are having material manufactured for us, and since in many cases we create a labor famine against ourselves, it would be a very great advantage to have some sort of a clearing house to whom you could send in your data, the number of your men, your prospects for increasing or decreasing weeks or months ahead, and allow such an office to handle the entire work of reporting on conditions, the chief requisite of such a bureau, as I have suggested before, being in my mind its absolute impartiality. The moment anything else was allowed to creep in, the value to both the employer and the employee would be less than nil.

(3) Shifting of men. (a) Speaking from the standpoint of this business only, there is a certain amount of "drifters," probably

twenty or even twenty-five per cent, who, by reason of being unattached, "free lances" regarding domestic complications, etc., like to change not only from the small towns to the large ones but from place to place so that they can have the excitement and novelty of the change itself, also get the experience of different factories, different makes of cars, etc. This applies naturally to the younger employees, but it is noticeable in the entire automobile business at least. A visit through the factories will also show an astonishing percentage of *young* men, the traditional gray-haired mechanic being a rarity. At a rough guess I should say that in our own shop the average age would be this side of twenty-seven years of age; I have noticed the same thing in all the other factories which I have visited, and the free masonry among young mechanics from twenty to twenty-five leads them to recommend to each other a shift to localities where conditions are apt to chime in with their inclinations. Leaving aside, however, this floating element, it would appear to me that my own experience, dating back to 1899, would lead me to say that the tendency to settle down and stay with a good solid job is growing constantly, and the prejudice even on the part of the younger workers against smaller towns and cheaper living is also passing away.

(b) I take it you are inquiring as to "drifting" from one *class* of employment to another. In this regard I should say that in all mechanical lines specializing is becoming the order of the day to such a marked extent that a change of the class of employment is rather exceptional; in other words, from the machine shop point of view, the lathe hand, planer hand, drill press man, etc., pretty much follow the same tools in the same class of work wherever they go; and also the variation between, for instance, automobile work, small arms works, typewriter and cash register work, is not very marked to the eye, and yet as a rule the operatives coming from factories turning out these various lines of work, seek work of the same kind in the same kind of factories wherever possible. The class of work done by the two factories side by side here, one on gas engines and one on automobile engines, is of such a different nature that an exchange between the plants is rather an exceptional thing, and I should answer your question by saying that as far as I know anything of the general trend it was for employees to follow the lines of their last job.

Covering your last question as to what we think of such a scheme, and would it do any good: I can give you a shotgun answer to this effect, first: it most certainly would work provided the proper men took hold of it and it was in the first place carefully and very slowly worked out, so that the employer on the one hand would understand that his requests in time of urgent need would be treated on a parity with those of his brother employers; that the employee on his side would understand that the "National Employment Agency" on the start would not undertake to give an estimate of the man's value or an analysis of the claims that he made in his application, or statements that he made as to his ability to prove of value. In other words, my own humble opinion would be that the thing would fail of support instantly unless the employee knew that a National Bureau in handling his name at all would simply act as a clearing house possibly to the extent of taking his last references and getting letters from the employers as to his ability, etc., which in the last equation his new employer would ask from him in any event.

I do not profess, as you know, to any expert knowledge on the labor question *per se*. My own views on the many sided topic of capital and labor I observe have been forestalled by a few eminent thinkers, with none of whom I agree in full, and a disquisition on this subject I will reserve until you call for it, which is tantamount to saying that this communication will be probably final as regards any information you may ask from this source.

Regarding, however, the often recurring problem of the senseless concentration, or rather the non-distribution of labor, I certainly believe that a National Bureau of Employment, with the co-operation of the employers all over the country, would be the biggest "dividend payer,"—speaking from the standpoint of the prosperity of the country,—that has been launched for some years past. From your own knowledge you must have dozens of instances where unemployed labor is within a few hundred miles of unemployed capital seeking to get names on their pay rolls and offering solid inducements to solid men who are in ignorance of the fact. Have had the good fortune to know a very large number of our own men personally, and in going through the strike in 1901 I certainly had my eyes opened as to the astonishing mental capacity of the average machinist or worker in a trade like ours; and at the same time, an equally astonishing eye-opener as to the clumsiness and ineffectiveness of the methods of letting the fact be known to the right workers that work was looking for them. I could cite you hundreds of cases and could call your attention also to the fact that the daily paper is one of the most fruitful sources for the distribution of *misinformation* as to where labor is needed, and a National Employment Bureau, without much additional expense or red tape, could have a publicity department which the newspapers would be very glad to avail themselves of, so that real news items would be edited and dependable instead of stating, for example, that all the steel mills in Pittsburgh were starting up, that business at the Packard factory in Detroit and the Olds Motor Works in Lansing, was booming, more men being taken on, etc.,—these items having appeared all through December and January of 1907-8 and being read by the seeker for work, who in numerous cases begged, borrowed or stole money enough to come out here, only to find scores of our own men laid off temporarily and having, of course, first call on the positions as they were thrown open.

You will observe that I am heartily in favor of such a scheme as is being proposed, and I presume the fact that it appears to be taken up by the bankers, gives it a special significance. This country is in need of class harmony and a most intelligent cooperation between all the employing class and the people that handle the money on the one hand, since it must some time dawn on even the poor slave of an employer driving his own business at top notch, that at some period or other the prosperity of the whole country or even a general prosperity is apt to make or mar his business.

NOVEMBER 28, 1908.

REPLY FROM MR. SIDNEY WEBB,
OF LONDON

I

Unemployment in large cities can only in a restricted sense be said to be caused to any great extent by the mere failure of employers to find workmen, or of workmen to find employers. They do find each other now, even in the worst of times *though only after some delay*. If there were *no* unemployment, in the sense of there being exactly as many vacancies as there were men to fill them, there would still be a certain proportion of time lost in shifting situations. This even if no more than one day in each case, would appear in the statistics as a percentage of men unemployed. Experience of the best organized trades in England, at the very busiest of times, rather points to the fact that minimum of unemployment, if it can be so called, due to time lost in shifting from job to job, and analogous causes, may amount to something like 1 per cent of the whole of the working class population, indicating an average loss, from this cause alone, in the best of times, of 3 days per annum.

At the present time, in England, the chief means used to get situations, and to fill vacancies are the following:

(a) TRADE UNION ORGANIZATION.—This applies to about a million of the best organized wage-earners, mainly skilled artisans and mechanics. Each trade union branch in these trades tries to get situations for its unemployed members. Each member is bound to report vacancies, and to do his best to fill them from his branch. Sometimes a small fee by the union is paid for each situation so filled. Among trade unions, the old-fashioned journeymen Steam Engine Makers' Association (which has never joined the Amalgamated Society of Engineers) is specially distinguished for the trouble it takes to get its members into jobs. On the other hand, at least half the trade unions, including those of the unskilled laborers, and the less well-organized trades, do not and cannot, practically, do anything in this direction.

Foremen frequently use the trade union, when they retain their membership, as an agency for recruiting their staffs. Employers themselves do so less frequently; but in the case of the London Society of Compositors, in particular, it is quite usual for employers to send or telephone to the society's offices when they want men. This is also done in some small societies of skilled trades.

All this has an important bearing on the establishment of a Public Labor Exchange. Alike in Germany and in London the trade unions were at first opposed to such an institution. Gradually they realized that it need not be inimical to their interests, whilst, if they stood aloof, it might be used against them. They have accordingly become friendly, *on receiving some share in the management.* This is indispensable to secure their support. In London, many trade union branches already keep their "Vacant Books" at the Labor Exchange offices, and have thereby become subsidiary branches.

(b) NEWSPAPER ADVERTISEMENTS.—These, whether inserted by employers or employed, are the principal means of getting places as clerks, managers, porters and all sorts of nondescript occupations; together with some trades. Thus there are always advertisements of compositors wanted, or wanting places. There is obvious mal-adjustment here, as there will be, in a single column, dozens of advertisements of places vacant, followed by dozens of advertisements by persons wanting exactly that kind of places.

(c) "CALLING ROUND."—This is the customary method of getting work in the building trades and, in fact, among wage-earners generally (especially laborers). Those who are unemployed go round from shop to shop, or from job to job, asking whether any "hands" are wanted. The employer, or his foreman, is apt to rely on this happening. He waits till men come along, and then picks out such as please his fancy. This method may take the form, on the one hand, of the attendance of a crowd of men at the dock gates, or at a wharf, or at any large engineering work, from among whom the foreman picks as many as are needed. Or on the other hand, especially in the woman's trades, the employer puts up a notice in his window ("Blouse hands wanted") which always brings him applicants within an hour or two.

This "calling round" expands into the tramping from town to town of unemployed artisans, which was the first form of out-of-work benefit of the trade unions. It still survives among the bricklayers, compositors, stonemasons and coopers. The man draws sixpence or a shilling at each town from the local trade union secretary, but may not draw this more than once within a specified period. He must therefore tramp from town to town until he finds a vacancy. This, it will be noted, is essentially the system that breeds the Australian "sundowner," and the American "tramp."

(d) REGISTRY OFFICES.—Mention should be made of the private adventure Registry Offices ("bureaux de placement"), of which there are in London about five or six hundred. Under a recent act they are all obliged to register themselves under the London County Council, and to obey its regulations. They are used almost entirely for domestic servants,—for which they are practically the only medium of engagement,—but they exist also for hotel servants, waiters, etc., musicians and music hall artistes, and, curiously enough, also men and women teachers in high or secondary schools, or private families. They charge a fee to employers, and usually also one to those for whom they get engagements. They do not deal much with workmen, whether skilled or unskilled, women workers or clerks.

In spite of all these agencies there is, in England, a great lack of knowledge among workers, of opportunities for advancement, and even of situations vacant in their own occupations. The persistence of the aimless and vague "calling round" system, expanded into the tramping from town to town of the bricklayers, compositors, stonemasons, coopers, etc., shows how little organization there is. Every morning tens of thousands of men rise up not knowing where to go for work. They drift aimlessly about, and a certain proportion of them eventually run up against jobs, almost by chance, just as a cloud of flies in the sunshine will collide with each other from time to time. (See the recent life of W. Crook, M. P., "From Workhouse to Westminster," by George Haw, for instance of this haphazard hunt for work.) There is a considerable loss of time between job and job. Employers usually say they have no trouble in getting all the help they want. But it is clear that (a) they often put up with inferior labor rather than run the risk of having none, (b) that they let slip opportunities of profitably using labor, particularly in agriculture, because they can't get just what labor they want, at the moment they need it, and without having it on their hands after the emergency has passed. During the past two years there has been a constant demand for labor in South Wales, at a time when nearly every English town had unemployed laborers on its hands.

(e) LABOR EXCHANGE.—It is interesting to find that this has existed in England in one great industry for nearly half a century, and that resort to it is *compulsory* on both employers and employed. By the Merchant Shipping Acts it is obligatory that all engagements of seamen and other workers on shipboard should be signed before a government officer, the intention being to prevent the abuses of "crimping." There are 110 "Mercantile Marine Offices" maintained by the government at the several ports; each with waiting room for the sailors, etc., and messengers to fetch those not on hand. The captain desiring a crew goes and picks out the men he wants, and then signs contracts with them before the superintendent. Any engagement otherwise than before the superintendent is a penal offence.

In London, since 1905, there has been a system of Labor Exchanges run by the Central (Unemployed) Body, a statutory municipal authority, drawing its funds from the rates (local taxes). The score or so of exchanges of this body now fill over 25,000 situations annually, and are rapidly increasing in popularity. It may be expected that the president of the Board of Trade (Mr. Winston Churchill) will propose to Parliament next spring the development of these London Exchanges into a national system covering the whole country; either managed by municipalities under central control and with a government grant; or, more probably, as municipal areas do not coincide with industrial areas, and would not be very sympathetic with each other, managed by the National Government (Board of Trade), as a single united system, as the Mercantile Marine Offices already are.

These Labor Exchanges charge absolutely no fee to employers or employed. The Mercantile Marine Offices used to charge a shilling to the employer and a shilling to the seaman on each contract; but this was abolished in 1882 (probably in some bargain with the shipping interest). Employers get their labor too easily as things are (in the various ways described above) to make them willing to pay any fee. Moreover, the great difficulty (unless resort is made compulsory) is to induce them to make use of the Exchange. Any fee would be a hindrance. A system of labor exchanges at all generally used would, I am sure, not only greatly increase the worker's chances of improving his or her position, greatly lessen the time lost between job and job, greatly diminish the wearing anxiety of looking for work, and greatly facilitate the employer's getting all the labor he can profitably employ. It would not only increase the mobility of labor, but would actually increase the aggregate volume of demand, to the extent of the opportunities for profitable employment that the employer now lets slip because he can't get just what he wants when he wants it.

II

The experience of Great Britain and Ireland is that, whilst depression of trade may be universal, fluctuations in trade are very largely local. Even within the same trade, there is usually less surplus of labor in one town than another. This has been conspicuously true of boot and shoe manufacturing during the past few years. Whilst Leicester and Ipswich have had numerous workers unemployed, there have actually been unfilled vacancies, *in particular branches of the trade*, in Nottinghamshire villages. The causes of the geographical shifting of employment are various. For instance, the whole class of "navvies" and "ground workers" go from one engineering work to another. In one town there may be large water works to be built, requiring hundreds of men. These have to be drawn from other places, and when the work is completed, they depart to other places. At Woolwich, within the last two years, some 5,000 engineers and laborers have been discharged from the government arsenal. These have had to drift away to other towns, where many of them have found employment. Railway and steamship depots change from place to place, in the course of extensions and developments; and with them thousands of workers have to shift. At present this shifting is left to anarchy, and the result is chaos. The workers drift aimlessly about and, after more or less delay, and more or less individual suffering, the new situations are filled, when they might have been filled much more expeditiously and with much less suffering, by means of a national organization of Labor Exchanges.

But there is a further and continuous shifting of the demand for labor from place to place, even within the same year. Many industries, especially those connected with agriculture, have a demand for ten times as much labor at one season as at another, for harvesting, etc. There are industries, such as gas making, the theatrical profession, the Post Office, etc., which employ many more workers in the winter than in the summer. Other industries, such as building and house decorating, need far more labor in the spring and summer than in the autumn and winter.

Now, in the absence of any organized arrangements for transferring surplus workers from one industry at its slack season to another at its busy season, each industry *tends to have its own set of workers,* who are sufficient to meet the needs of the busy times, and who remain hanging about the industry in its slack season, half employed. Thus each of the industries that fluctuate seasonally, contributes a large quota of workers to the ranks of the unemployed, at the season when year after year the industry is slack. This seasonal fluctuation really applies to practically all trades. Careful investigation has shown that in all the industries having well organized trade unions having out of work benefit, there has been, during the past ten years, a well marked systole and diastole according to *the seasons of the year.* The interesting fact has come out that, among these two or three dozen industries in England and Wales, *there is no month of the year* in which one or other of these industries is not at its slackest; and similarly *there is no month of the year* in which one or other of these industries is not at its busiest. Although precise statistics cannot be obtained, there is reason to believe that the aggregate volume of employment among the trades taken together may quite possibly be fairly uniform throughout the year. Nevertheless, there are in any month of the year numerous workers out of employment, from one of these industries or another.

But the most important utility of the Labor Exchange has still to be mentioned. The investigations of the last few years in this country have proved beyond possibility of doubt that the most serious distress, and the greatest obstacle to the success of relief works or any other form of provision for the unemployed, is due not to unemployment at all—in the sense of the loss of definite situations of assumed permanency, and the inability to regain such—but to the existence of a vast mass of "underemployed" labor. In London, in all the seaports, and in all the large towns, there are hundreds of thousands of workers who never hold definite situations, or even work for as much as a week, but who live by a succession of short jobs, each for a few hours or a day or two, for different employers. The typical case is that of the dock or wharf laborer, who is engaged for a job of a few hours only. This would present no great difficulty if, like the bricklayer and the plumber, the dock laborer habitually got enough work in the week to yield him complete subsistence. Unfortunately, owing to complete lack of organization, there is no correspondence between the number of jobs and the number of men looking to them for a living. Each wharf in London, and each dock "stand" in Liverpool, attracts its own group of expectant laborers who wait there for work, and who are very reluctant to look elsewhere for it, lest by their temporary absence they lose their chance of that work. The consequence is that each wharf in London and each dock "stand" in Liverpool, tends to attract to itself enough men to satisfy its demand on its busiest day. In fact, it suits the employer to have such a number of men in waiting at his gate. Hence there accumulates at each wharf what may be called a "stagnant pool" of labor. And as the busiest day of each wharf does not coincide with the busiest day of other wharves, the result is, experience shows, that, alike in Liverpool and in London, the total number of laborers looking for these jobs amounts to about twice the number that are ever employed on the busiest day for the port as a whole. Thus, the whole tend to live a half-employed life, struggling among each other for the work, living partly on their wives' earnings, and existing always at a miserably low level. This class of casual laborers is a very large one in the large towns of the United Kingdom; and presumably the same class exists in New York. In times of good trade they get three or four days a week; in times of bad trade, only three or four days a month. This is not only bad in itself, but it stands in the way of providing relief works for other workmen. Whenever employment is offered, even at four shillings a day, this horde of casual laborers swarms in, and ruins the experiment.

Now, if all the employers sent for their casual laborers to a Labor Exchange, those who wanted men for Monday, and those who wanted them for Tuesday, and so on, would get them for the days that they want them, without involving the existence of a large army of half-employed labor. The analogy may be quoted of trained sick nurses. A nurse is sent for by a household when she is wanted, exactly for the period that she is wanted. But by suitable arrangements, the nurses go from case to case, with little interval, instead of there being twice as many nurses as there is need for.

It is strongly argued that the very greatest of all single reforms that could be effected in London, Liverpool, Glasgow and other large towns would be, by means of a Labor Exchange generally resorted to, the intermittent jobs by which so large a proportion of the laboring population lives could be "dovetailed," so as to secure practically continuous work and wages for such men as are employed at all. Largely on this ground, it is expected that a national system of Labor Exchanges will be instituted all over the kingdom by Mr. Winston Churchill, the president of the Board of Trade.

REPLY FROM MR. ADNA F. WEBER,
Chief Statistician of the New York Public Service Commission

(1) As to local mal-adjustment of demand and supply in the labor market, I should be disposed to say that the existing agencies and methods do, on the whole, meet the requirements of the situation; that is to say, in a period of normal activity there are relatively few workers without employment at a time when employers

are seeking help of the same grade or class. There is much room for improvement in the methods of the private employment offices, which may be obtained through more careful public regulation and possibly through the example of a well endowed Bureau; but that the latter could find local situations for the unemployed in any considerable numbers seems to me doubtful. Fees should be charged.

(2) As to mal-adjustment between communities, this seems to me of importance in but one industry, agriculture, so far as it is carried on by small proprietors. The railroads and large industrial corporations find no difficulty in transferring multitudes of laborers from one place to another and farmers on a large scale like those on western wheat farms can obtain harvesters in gangs. It is the isolated, individual farmer of the East who has no organization or machinery for obtaining labor, and his difficulties are being met by the creation of state bureaus of (agricultural) employment. In any case, the rule generally holds today that labor goes where it is most needed and wanted as expressed in high wages or other advantages.

(3) With reference to occupational mobility the situation is entirely different. While the geographical inability of labor in this country is highly developed—almost too much so for the interest of good citizenship—the capacity of the worker to take up a new occupation is not highly enough developed. Broader training in needed; but a high-class Employment Bureau might aid to a degree.

The Germans have perfected an excellent system of employment bureaus, but it is a system and it has grown out of German conditions. In this country, there is reason to look to private enterprise rather than the government for the development of such a system. A well-endowed Bureau, under the most capable management, ought to elevate the tone of the business and possibly introduce co-ordination now lacking. How successful it may be, will, I think, depend entirely on the manager.

REPLY FROM MR. ROBERT A. WOODS,
Of South End House, Boston

I cannot do more than give general results of experience in reply to your question.

1. I have known of many instances where the evidence of mal-adjustment in the matter of employment was convincing. These have occurred rather in the skilled and clerical grades so far as the situation in the city itself is concerned. There cannot be any doubt that employers and workmen both lose a great deal of time and meet with much demoralizing embarrassment in this matter, which an employment bureau could remedy if it went at its work with something of the scope and detailed accuracy of the weather and crop reports. In my opinion such a bureau, in order to be of the greatest public use, should throw its emphasis strongly upon assisting really capable men to get their appropriate opportunities rather than upon landing the incapable in a job.

2. There is mal-adjustment in the unskilled grade of factory workers as between the cities and towns of Massachusetts. I have known of some significant instances of employers from factories, in good times, trying to secure unemployed or ill-paid people in Boston and with indifferent success. In bad times there are always working people who, as a last resort, are willing to go out of town. Systematic organization might bridge this somewhat complicated gap.

3. The possibility of change from one occupation to another seems to grow less and less. Such change nearly always means a step down, except where there is less demand for skill but more for responsibility.

This whole subject has been pretty carefully studied by the Massachusetts Bureau of Labor, whose employment office is beginning to afford some more or less suggestive statistics.

November 28, 1908.

LETTER FROM MR. JAMES W. VAN CLEAVE,

OF ST. LOUIS

PRESIDENT OF THE NATIONAL ASSOCIATION OF MANUFACTURERS

Let me say that I am personally very much in favor of the establishment of free employment bureaus, and in this I believe that I not only express my own opinion but that of the large majority of the members of the National Association of Manufacturers. Untold harm is being done by bogus employment bureaus that oftentimes fleece the poor seeker of a job of the few pennies he has left. There are, of course, noble exceptions to this rule, but it is a fact that in many of our large cities unscrupulous owners and managers of employment agencies carry on drinking places in the same locality, and the amount of good that can be carried on under such conditions for our poor and needy is very questionable to say the least.

It is a fact that many of our states, recognizing the need for free employment bureaus, have established such bureaus in the larger cities; however, my own observation impresses me with the inefficiency of such state bureaus. I do not mean to throw the slightest reflections upon state officials in charge of such institutions as to honesty and integrity, but the special training required for this sort of work is missing.

Appreciating the need for free employment institutions, some employers' associations and citizens' organizations have established such bureaus of their own. The Citizens' Industrial Association of Saint Louis has maintained a free employment bureau for a number of years. No charges whatever are made either to the employer or workers. The bureau is sustained by the association's funds. Our bureau is in charge of an efficient specialist, and the service is so satisfactory that many of our manufacturers refuse to employ help direct, in all cases sending to our employment bureau for help wanted. The advantage is that some sort of an inquiry has been made by our bureau into the records of all those seeking employment. You may be interested in the system.

Any one making application for employment is sent immediately to a man desiring help, but the person making application must state where he has been working for the last year or two. Letters of inquiry are sent to former employers, but this does not prevent immediate employment of the applicant. As soon as replies are received they are forwarded to the employer in addition to keeping a record of them at the employment bureau. As our working people find that a good record helps them in securing other or better places they become stanch friends of our employment bureau, and little by little we expect to have this bureau a clearing house for labor, much as our regular clearing houses are for the financial institutions.

While at the present time there are at least two or three dozen employment bureaus of the type of ours in various cities in the United States, they cover but a very small proportion of what needs to be done. I said something on this question when discussing the formation of the National Council for Industrial Defense, a year or so ago, in the pages of the *Engineering Magazine* of July, 1907. I quote from this article the following:

> As shortages and surpluses of labor may exist simultaneously in different localities, we will create labor bureaus in all the country's important industrial centers, and through them the council can operate a labor clearing house by which all such abnormalities can be corrected and a balance established. Through these labor bureaus the council could look after the better distribution of immigrants in the regions in which the chances for their employment are greatest. It could also, through these bureaus, secure picked labor in Europe, so far as this can be accomplished under the immigration regulations and restrictions which go into operation on July 1, 1907, and direct it to the proper localities.

I look upon the establishment of free employment bureaus most favorably, first, from the standpoint of a man and a Christian, and secondly, as an employer, and you are at liberty to use my letter in any way in which it may benefit the good cause.

DECEMBER 21, 1908.

APPENDIX III

Plan for the Formation of an Employment Bureau whose Object shall be to Find Employment for Men Unfamiliar with the English Language

By Mr. Cyrus L. Sulzberger

In charge of a competent superintendent, there should be engaged eight employment agents as follows: one each for men's and boys' clothing; women's and children's clothing; furs, caps and leather goods; paper boxes; building trades; interior wood workers; metal workers; and two for miscellaneous trades.

After the applicants for employment are classified according to their trades, it will be the duty of these men to take them about to the various possible employers and find positions for them. In order to facilitate this, there will previously have been a letter addressed to a large number of the chief employers of labor in New York, setting forth the purposes of the Bureau, and signed by half a dozen representative men, who express their interest in the Bureau, their desire for its success, and requesting co-operation of the employers.

The employment agent, having previously delivered this letter and through it secured an introduction to the superintendent of the factory, will have the entree of those places willing to co-operate with us, and if opportunity offers, will be enabled to place the men in his charge.

It is believed that each employment agent will have daily

five persons to dispose of. Should the number prove larger, a larger number of employment agents will be required.

The plan here outlined is an extension and elaboration of the methods by which the Industrial Removal Office has succeeded in finding employment for a large number of men in all parts of the United States. It has never been tried in this way in New York, but there is no apparent reason why it should not work as well here, if intelligently conducted, as it has elsewhere.

The estimated expense of such a Bureau is:

Superintendent	$2,000
8 employment agents at $750 each	6,000
Stenographer and a boy	700
Carfares	1,500
Printing and stationery	500

making a total of about $11,000 per year. No item of rent is here included, for the reason that it is expected that the necessary premises will be secured free of charge at the Hebrew Sheltering House.

A great labor exchange which contemplates the bringing together with greater facility of laboring men and employers is as purely an economic instrument as improved machinery or methods of transportation. It facilitates production and is quite as much in the interest of the employer as of the employed. To bring together the man who is idle for lack of a job and the machine which is idle for lack of a man, is to perform an act of distinct economic value to the community, serving immediately both the man and the owner of the machine, and ultimately society at large, by reason of the productivity thus brought about.

The establishment, however, of an Employment Bureau for competent workmen who are laboring under a handicap by reason of unfamiliarity with the language of the country, is in point of economic value equal to a general employment bureau, and has in addition a distinct philanthropic worth. Other things being equal, it is, economically speaking, a matter of indifference whether A or B is the man at the machine, but if A is a foreigner, and by reason of his lack of English is unable to fend for himself in procuring the job, he will, in the event of his failing to get it, speedily become a dependent, whereas B being a native and free from the handicap with which A is afflicted, can more readily place himself in some other position and maintain his independence.

Employers ordinarily will not take the trouble of dealing with men to whom they cannot readily give orders, and it is therefore necessary to arouse their interest in that class of workmen, and experience has shown that such interest is most readily aroused by the co-operation of representative men in the community influential with large employers of labor.

The Industrial Removal Office has placed over twenty thousand men at work in various parts of the United States, and fully two-thirds of these did not speak English. The plan which has been successful in this large number of cases away from New York, could be applied here somewhat on the lines laid down in the above statement, and if it were deemed advisable to put it in effect, either as to New York or elsewhere, it could very well be made a part of the general Employment Bureau or labor exchange which is contemplated.

APPENDIX IV

Statements in Regard to Three Free Philanthropic Bureaus Conducted in New York City

---

REPORT ON THE COOPER UNION LABOR BUREAU

EXTRACT FROM THE REPORT OF THE NEW YORK ASSOCIATION FOR IMPROVING THE CONDITION OF THE POOR, VOLUME 10,—1899-1900,—PAGES 81-82.

The committee in charge of the Cooper Union Labor Bureau, after a careful review of the work of the Bureau and mature deliberation as to the advisability of continuing it, recommended to the board of managers of the Association for Improving the Condition of the Poor that the Bureau be discontinued at the close of the fiscal year, September 30, 1899. This recommendation was approved by the board, and the office in Cooper Union was closed on that date. Among the reasons which influenced the committee in reaching their decision were these:

1. Improvement of business conditions in the city, lessening the number of the unemployed. While there are still many men out of work, the number is much smaller than when this work was begun.

2. The announcement by some of the intelligence offices that employers can secure help from them without charge.

3. Free labor advertisements published in a daily paper of large circulation.

4. The establishment of a Free Labor Bureau by the state;

also by other philanthropic agencies. One of the objects which the committee has had in view from the first has been the fostering of enterprises that could take up the work and carry it on successfully.

5. The growing belief that the state is able to conduct a free employment office better than a philanthropic society can, because of its wider sphere of influence, its ability to ascertain the needs of different sections of the state, and also its power to secure legislation tending to decrease the evils of the average intelligence office. Important steps in this latter direction have already been taken, much-needed laws having been secured since the State Bureau was opened.

6. Lack of adequate support to compete with agencies which have an expensive office force, employ canvassers, and insert advertisements calling attention to their work and their available applicants. The committee has not felt that it had a right to ask for large sums of money given to the Association primarily to improve the condition of the poor. Students of the labor problem who favor a Bureau of this character say that it should cost from $20,000 to $25,000 a year in order to insure its success. The total expenses of our Bureau for the five years of its existence have not reached even the smaller sum mentioned.

FREE EMPLOYMENT BUREAU CONDUCTED BY THE UNITED HEBREW CHARITIES OF THE CITY OF NEW YORK

Statement by Dr. Lee K. Frankel

Immediately after the organization of the society in 1875, the board of directors authorized the establishment of an employment bureau. In the report which the committee on employment made in 1876, there appears the following: "The better class of mechanics usually avoid applying for work where charity is connected with it."

In 1879, the committee reported that "the results are no better than last year. This is due to want of interest by the public." The committee further stated: "Such labor as is offered by the Charities, is not in demand. Good mechanics can find employment without our assistance."

No further mention is made of an employment bureau until the 1884 report, in which it is stated that an employment bureau is more than ever needed. The previous report mentions a conference with the Charity Organization Society at which the establishment of a Central Labor Exchange was discussed, the annual cost of which (estimated at $5,000) was to be raised with the aid of all the charitable organizations in the city.

In 1885, the Employment Bureau was reorganized, and immediately became very active. In the following fiscal year 2,811 positions were found, representing 80 per cent. of the applications. As the work of the Bureau was largely among immigrant Jews, the effort was made to send as many as possible out of the city, to positions which had been secured for them. The need and desirability of such a step was evidenced after 1891, when the second large influx of Russian immigration began. The establishment of the Baron de Hirsch Fund at that time, gave the employment committee the means to materially enlarge its "out of town" activities. In fact two departments were opened, one for local positions, and the other for positions away from the city.

Between the years 1891 and 1903, the activities of the Employment Bureau were continued, and, while large numbers of positions were found for the applicants, it can not be said that, at any time during that period, was the work considered truly satisfactory. For this reason, re-arrangements of the Bureau were effected from time to time, in the hope of improving and increasing its efficiency. The same difficulties which were mentioned in the earliest reports of the Employment Bureau were encountered in the subsequent years. The competent, skilled mechanic found it possible, when work was obtainable, to secure employment either directly or through the medium of the trades union to which he would belong. For the handicapped, it was difficult to secure positions, owing to the unwillingness of the average employer to engage this class of help.

In addition, it was found that many employers refused to accept workmen who were sent to them by charitable institutions for obvious reasons. The claim was made in particular that applicants sent by the United Hebrew Charities, either by reason of incompetence, inability, or unwillingness, did not retain their positions for any great length of time, and gave trouble to the employer.

Since the organization of the Industrial Removal Office the work which formerly fell on the Employment Bureau of the United Hebrew Charities in finding positions outside of the city of New York, was no longer necessary.

The experience of all these years of the Employment Bureau is summarized in the report which the committee made to the board of directors, under date of December 9, 1903:

To the President and Board of Trustees of the United Hebrew Charities:

During the past year, the reports of the Employment Bureau did not show altogether satisfactory results. The committee has given the work considerable observation and believes that it is almost impossible to obtain satisfactory results in securing positions for the class of people who apply to us for the following reasons:

1. A large proportion of our applicants are men who have never learned a trade and are thoroughly incompetent. They are willing to work, but lack ability. It is only during unusually prosperous times, when there is a great demand for help, that it is possible to place such men.

2. We have a class of applicants who are incapacitated, either by sickness or age. No explanation is necessary in order to understand why it is extremely difficult to obtain positions for these men.

3. We have another class to deal with who have their own ideas as to the value of their services, and when offered a position at a lower figure than their own estimate of value, absolutely refuse to consider it.

4. We have a number of applicants who come to us only because we are a *free* Employment Bureau, and they feel that they may obtain positions through our

agency without any effort or expense to themselves, although able-bodied and *not subjects for charity.*

5. Another class take positions which are offered to them, hold them for a day or two, and then suddenly fail to appear, leaving with their employers a poor opinion of the Employment Bureau of the United Hebrew Charities.

6. The employers of labor throughout the city appear to have a strong prejudice against engaging men who are recommended by a charitable organization, one of their reasons being that sentiment enters into the question, and they feel that they cannot deal with subjects of charity in the independent manner in which they treat with other employees. A second reason being that they usually require men who are able-bodied and competent, and such men *should not find it necessary to* apply through our Bureau.

It has for some time been an open question in the minds of the committee whether the United Hebrew Charities should have a Free Employment Bureau as a branch of its work. A Free Employment Bureau, as we understand the term, is one that is open to the public, without expense to the applicant or employer. Why should an institution whose funds are donated by the public for charitable work only support a Free Employment Bureau which assists men who are not proper subjects of charity? We believe that our Employment Bureau, despite the fact that great efforts have been made to obtain good results, has injured rather than helped the reputation of our society. It is our opinion that the United Hebrew Charities is slowly but surely drifting in the direction of doing executive work only, instead of carrying on the various branches of work under its own personal supervision, and with that idea in mind we now make what we consider a conservative suggestion for the consideration of the board.

We believe that obtaining employment for other than relief applicants is not within the sphere of our society's work, and we therefore recommend:

That as soon as arrangements can be made with another institution, our Employment Bureau be discontinued as a Free Employment Agency, and that instead, our organization should make efforts to secure employment for *relief applicants* only.

By so doing, the expense of the department will probably be decreased fifty per cent. and the relief cases will receive far better attention than is now possible.

Application to an institution of charity brings with it a loss of dignity and self-respect to the applicant. This would be obviated by having all but relief cases taken in charge by an organization such as the Young Men's Hebrew Association or the Educational Alliance.

Respectfully submitted,
THE EMPLOYMENT COMMITTEE.

DECEMBER 9, 1903.

Acting upon the recommendation of the committee, the board of trustees of the United Hebrew Charities discontinued the Employment Bureau, and turned it over to the Independent Order of B'nai Brith, at the same time subsidizing the last-named society, so that it would be possible for it to carry on the Bureau. Eventually the United Hebrew Charities discontinued the subsidy, and, as the Independent Order of B'nai Brith was unable to raise the necessary funds to keep the Bureau open, it was found necessary to close it.

I may say, in passing, that, since the discontinuance of the Employment Bureau, the United Hebrew Charities has had the services of an employment agent, to secure work for the relief cases which come to its notice, particularly for men and women who are partially incapacitated, in other words, the so-called handicapped class. The work of this agent has been quite successful. In my judgment, the committee on employment pursued a wise course in recommending the severance of the Employment Bureau from the United Hebrew Charities.

It should always be the purpose of such a society to endeavor to secure work for those who are directly under its charge. The general proposition of finding work for all the unemployed hardly comes within the province of a charitable institution.

NEW YORK, DECEMBER 5, 1908.

FREE EMPLOYMENT BUREAU CONDUCTED IN NEW YORK CITY BY THE SOCIETY OF ST. VINCENT DE PAUL

STATEMENT BY MR. THOMAS M. MULRY

The censensus of opinion amongst those interested in this subject, bears out my own impression that it is a most difficult matter to operate successfully a free employment bureau. Our experience was by no means encouraging, as we found that the majority of the applicants were superannuated or unfit to fill the various positions which we endeavored to obtain for them. Employment was secured for a number of boys and girls who had just finished school, but undoubtedly they could have been placed without the assistance of an agency, as there is always a good demand for them.

In many instances we found that the employers who sought help through the medium of our Bureau expected to obtain men at a lower rate of wages than was prevalent at the time. Our Employment Bureau was, of course, principally to obtain work for the poor families which came under the care of the conferences. Frequently, when we had good positions on our list, we were obliged to have recourse to other organizations, as it was only occasionally that the applicants were qualified for these positions.

In such work as watchman the various firms, as a rule, had some pensioners who had grown old in the service, to fill the vacancy. In the different branches of the public service, such positions as laborer, foreman, etc., would generally be under the control of the political situation, for, despite the fact that there was always a large number of applicants who were physically and mentally capable of filling these places, it was very seldom that such vacancies came to our notice, simply because it required political influence to obtain these places.

To my mind, it will be very difficult to successfully operate an Employment Bureau on a philanthropic basis. In prosperous times there is no difficulty for a capable person to obtain employment and in times of business depression it is, as you know, a very difficult task for anyone to secure a position. But at all times, the class of applicants which comes under the notice of a charitable society is generally composed of those who have outlived their usefulness and whose poor health or incapacity make it almost impossible for them to qualify for any position. They will always be in the category of "cheap labor" because it is necessary to hold out some inducement in order to obtain positions for them.

NEW YORK, DECEMBER 8, 1908.

APPENDIX V

Experiences of Mr. Benjamin C. Marsh in Trying to Secure Work in New York City, on December 17 and 18, 1908

On Wednesday night, December 16, I went, at about half past twelve, to one of the cheap saloons on lower Chatham Street and talked with several men who were drinking there about opportunities to secure work. Three of them stated that they had been out of a job for several weeks, but one urged me to make application to the foreman of the gang laying tracks on the railway directly in front of the saloon.

At one o'clock I went to the bread line of the Bowery Mission, 37 Bowery, on the East Side, and found a place in the line on Bayard Street half way east on the block from the Bowery. The man ahead of me claimed that he was a broom maker and had never been out of employment before, but he had been ill and, although he had been to every broom-shop in New York City, he was unable to secure any employment. He cursed the men in the line some of whom he said had money saved up, several having $10 at least in pocket while they still sponged bread and coffee. Men who had been through the mission and secured their roll and coffee kept constantly coming back and lengthening the line.

It took about 20 minutes to get to the door where we were let in with another line forming in the Bowery north of the mission. When we got to the main floor there were 500 or 600 men drinking coffee, or hanging around until they were turned out. Most of them had left by a little before two. Several of them told me that they were iron-workers, carpenters, moulders, or had other trades, but had not been able to secure any work for a number of days. I followed them on the street until past three o'clock. Some of them curled up in halls, others went into the rear halls of several saloons which were open all night, where they could get in and stay for a five-cent drink. I found no difficulty in getting into several of these saloons. In one of them on the Bowery a schooner containing a pint and a half of beer is sold for a nickel. Several of the lodging houses were marked "Full," and Mills Hotels Numbers 1 and 2 were both full between 3 and 3.30 A. M., but I was referred to Mills Hotel Number 3, where I secured a room. Two or three of the men with whom I was talking said that they would be willing to go to the country if they could get a job where they would be sure of staying, and that they had applied to the Bureau of Information of the Immigration Service, but they could not be sent out into the country because they had no money to pay their fare.

The first thing Thursday morning, a little after nine, I went to R. H. Macy and Company's with a comrade I had picked up on the street, trying to secure a job as porter. The man had suggested that there was work in the department stores, but claimed that he had tried several of them for a number of days without any luck. He had been out of work for several weeks, for the first time, he claimed, although he was a painter by trade.

On Twenty-sixth Street, I asked a policeman where work could be secured and he held up his hands in horror, saying that if he knew where there was any work in town everybody would be after him. However, he suggested that I go to the manager of Madison Square Garden for employment, but I found that I was unable to secure any work there; the manager said that I might come around again about the middle of next month when there would be another show coming on.

In response to the following notice in the "Want" columns of the *World*, I went to William H. Reynold's:

> SALESMAN wanted; five first class salesmen of ability and tact; no canvassing, but hard workers wishing to make considerable money. Bennett, 9 East 26th Street, Room 226.

I was asked to canvass for lots belonging to the company in East New York. I was to have 7 per cent. commission on the value of any lots that were sold. The prices are from $300 to $1400. I promised to come back a day or so later if I wanted the job.

From there I went to the Bureau of Labor in the State Department of Agriculture and found the room full of men, but the clerk in the office refused to give any information or to take my application and told me to come back again the next morning. At the Information Bureau of the Immigration Department I found a crowd of men, Italians, Poles and some Germans, and the man at the outer counter stated that he had very little opportunity to get men out unless they could pay their fare, as the farmers were not advancing money. He said that men didn't like to work on the farm because the hours were so long and they were apt to get out of a job. He instanced cases of people who had been in to get men and they kept them for only a week or ten days and then turned them off as unsatisfactory, paying them only a small part of their wages. He admitted that they had received one application from a farmer for a man to work from 2.30 in the morning until 5 at night, and he didn't blame the men for not wanting to take such jobs. A man of 40 odd years, apparently a German, said that he had been on a farm where he had to work from 5 in the morning until 10 at night and had been getting only small wages, so that he would not think of such a job again for a minute. The attendant said that he had a job in Illinois but that the fare out there would be about $20, although possibly half-fare could be secured. They would pay $18 or $20 a month with board and washing, but it is the dullest time in the year.

A second visit to the Information Bureau of the Immigration

Service was equally unsuccessful, although Mr. Green, the manager, informed me that they had plenty of work for men in a sawmill in Alabama at wages from $1.25 to $1.50 a day. Board, lodging and washing are about $15 a month, so that one could clear quite a fair amount. He suggested my going to the Joint Application Bureau, to give a reference or two and see if they would not advance me the reduced rates which would amount to about $9, but I told him that I was not able to raise this amount. When I was coming out of the office I was called back to meet a Pole who wanted a boy to work on his farm to "break in." I asked him how much he wanted to pay and volunteered to work quite cheaply, but he said the money was no special object to him. Several of the men in the office came up during my conversation with Mr. Green and were evidently anxious to get hold of any job that was considered for me.

A second visit to the Bureau of Labor in the State Department of Agriculture, a little before noon, was almost as discouraging. The clerk told me there was no use in my trying to get work and they wouldn't take applications from any except married men. I asked whether paying $1 would help me in getting a job, but he informed me with some disgust that this was a state enterprise and that they couldn't take any money from an outsider.

The Dunham Cocoa Manufacuring Company claimed that they were working on half time. The Thatcher Company were planning to lay off their men from their iron works. The Berlin Analine Works had no jobs available. The A. S. Howard Polishing Company said that they had to struggle to keep the men busy who were working for them and that there was no chance to get in.

Three Employment Agencies along Greenwich Street all claimed that it was impossible to get any work at present. The Magyar Agency, at 53 Greenwich Street, claimed that they had employment for 25 laborers at $1.40 a day, transportation paid, but upon being questioned admitted that the work was all gone and they simply kept up the sign.

The Dilk Draying Company said that they couldn't get any work themselves. McRoberts and Company, contractors and stevedores, 42 Whitehall Street, were unable to give any jobs. Charles L. Hearst and Company, grocers specialties, at 16 Pearl Street, had been laying off men, since it was very dull. L. Schnellfeld's Employment Agency, at 6 Greenwich Street, claimed that they had work for everybody, Germans and all, but admitted that they had not given out any jobs for several days.

The Delaware, Lackawanna and Western and several other railroads on the North River piers, said that they had no employment, but might possibly be putting some men on about Monday or the first of the year. The Adams Express Company had no opening but advised me to come back again. Wells, Fargo and Company asked me to bring back two or three references and said they would probably put me to work within a week or so.

The employment office of J. Block, 135 Liberty Street, also had not sent out any man for a long time. The Laurenton Land Company had advertised, but their jobs were evidently the same as W. H. Reynolds, selling real estate.

The Moore Soap Company, 288 Greenwich Street, offered me a job selling soap, a $1.25 outfit containing seven cakes, for 75 cents. The agent was to get half of this and they would let him start with a very small stock. In addition the proprietor suggested that he could put me on a wagon in a city in another state, probably in Hartford, Conn., to earn $2.50 a day.

Thomas Harper and Sons, brass manufacturers, on the corner of Lafayette and Howard Streets, were laying off men and didn't expect work to pick up for some time. The American Brass and Copper Company, on the opposite corner, could do nothing for me, although I claimed to be an experienced brass maker, as they expected to lay off help within a short time. J. Gelb and Company, machinery, 5 Howard Street, claim that they haven't work enough to justify them in keeping the shop open.

The Schaefer Brewing Company, Fifty-first Street and Park

Avenue, claimed that they were shutting down one day a week in the bottling works and that some of the men were to be laid off in the brewery so that any task was hopeless there. They thought that most of the other breweries were in about the same condition.

R. Wolf, leather goods manufacturer, on the eleventh floor of the block bounded by Crosby, Prince, East Houston Streets and Broadway, were closing down to take stock until after the holidays, and doubted whether they would take back more than a small portion of their workers even when they opened again. Rosenthal's, eighth floor, manufacturers of men's and women's clothing, was visited, and the manager pointed to several men who were sitting around and said they were paying these fellows for sitting around and being idle and that they didn't intend to pay anyone else for doing that. There wouldn't be any more work for a good while.

In response to an advertisement for motormen and conductors I visited the Metropolitan Street Railway Company and was given an application in which I acknowledged the right of the company's officers to terminate my employment at any time without notice and also agreed that my wages should cease at the time of such discharge. I talked with several of the men looking for jobs and they said the chances were not good, and that a great many applications were made but that they didn't get the jobs. Here also references from the last places of employment were required. I did not hand in the application although the man in charge said there would be a chance of my getting work as they were taking on men occasionally. An application at the repair shop of the company on Fiftieth Street was equally futile, although I begged the man to give me a chance for a few days. A second visit on the day following to the maintenance and construction departments of this same company had the same result and I was told that they would not be taking on any men for some time and they might be obliged to lay a few off before long.

The New Idea Arc Light Company, 138 Leonard Street,

wanted me to go out selling arc lights on a unique basis, holding me responsible for the payment under rather strict conditions.

The Enterprise Coffee Company, 116 Wall Street, wanted canvassers and would furnish coffee at from 14 to 17 cents a pound, which could sell for from 20 to 35 cents, and tea which they would sell to me for 20 to 25 cents to be resold for from 30 to 60 cents. They would give a small sample package for five or ten cents, but they thought it was necessary to do this.

The Coston Signal Company, Moore Street, could not give any promise of employment, but remarked that work was very dull.

Brady and Gioe, general stevedores and contractors, 11 Moore Street, said there was nothing doing in the way of getting employment at present.

I registered at the Bowery Mission for a job, but they admitted that they had given employment to only a few men among the several hundreds from whom they had applications and that the chances of work were very poor. In the evening I called at the Bowery Branch of the Young Men's Christian Association, and they said that I could register in the day time, but they gave me very little hope of securing any employment. They advised me to go to the Twenty-third Street Branch, although they said that they too were not giving many jobs. A man whom I met on the street and asked for work, mentioned the Bowery Branch of the Young Men's Christian Association and said he had heard from several of his companions that they took two-thirds of the first week's salary. I didn't have any opportunity to confirm or disprove this statement.

I made an application to the Subway Construction Company on Park Row and found that over 20 men had been making application, but without any immediate success for most of them. Some of the men claimed that they had had their application in for several weeks and that they had good references, but it didn't amount to anything.

The manager of a coach company asked me whether I could paint and upon learning that I could said that there might possibly be a job, but later withdrew and said that they should probably lay off 100 men within a few days. The Manhattan Storage Company claimed that times were very dull and that there was no chance of their having any work.

An application at the new building being erected on the site of the old Fifth Avenue Hotel was futile and I was referred to the Hedden Construction Company where the manager advised me not to be discouraged, but that they were going to lay off most of the force on that building shortly, and probably lay off a good many men in other parts of the city. Coming down from the elevator in the Metropolitan Building I overheard a man, who gave his name as Nicholson, state that construction in the Bronx had fallen off 70 per cent. I asked him if he could help me get a job and he admitted that prospects were pretty bad particularly when I told him that I was not a union member.

Several employment agencies on Greenwich Street visited later in the afternoon did not give any better results and in not a single case did I get any definite encouragement from any one of the employment agencies to which I applied. Following the suggestion of my saloon friend I went to the foreman of the gang putting in tracks on Chatham Street, but it was wet and he informed me that they wouldn't do any work during the day so that it was no use for me to wait for the job.

A second visit to the saloons on Thursday night enabled me to see a number of the men whom I had seen the day before and I talked with some of them. Two or three of them told me that they had been looking for jobs all day and weren't able to get a thing. A man I talked with this second day admitted that he would go to work on a farm if he got a chance. One man, a brakeman on the Central Railroad of New Jersey, advised me to apply there as they were taking men for braking, but he had no very definite statement.

Experiences in Brooklyn were fully as unpropitious as in Manhattan. Robert Gair had a sign out "No help wanted" and earnest entreaties on my part did not succeed in getting any more favorable reply to my request for work. The Union Lead and Oil Company, the automobile works and a nearby machine shop, although I applied at all three places as an expert machinist, had no hopes for me.

D. T. Soper and Company, who were starting a new printing office, said that in two weeks they might possibly have a job, but there was no chance at present. Erbe, Crombie and Lamothe, bindery, had no chance. The Phoenix Paper Box Company had signs out "No help wanted" and confirmed the statement upon application. The American Can Company claimed that they were laying men off, but that they might possibly have a job within a month. Two small novelty works in the immediate vicinity said that there would not be any employment for additional men for several weeks.

Mason, Au and Magenheimer, confectioners, had out a sign "No help wanted" and they said that they could hardly get work for their regular employees. The Curran Machine Company and W. B. Conrad and Company, manufacturers of clothing in the same building, had no work, but the latter thought they might possibly be able to give me a job the first of the year.

E. W. Bliss and Company were not giving employment to any men in any of their departments, either in Adams Street, Plymouth Street or First Avenue, and claimed that they would not be able to put anyone at work for some time.

Arbuckle's in the early morning advised me to come back at six at night when I would probably have a chance. I was there a little before that hour and found a crowd of 47 men, Poles, Swedes and nationalities indistinguishable in the dark, many of them not able to speak English. We blockaded the doorway when the men were coming out and at the close we were told that there was no job. Several of the men told me that they had been there every night for a week, but that very few of the men had been successful in getting work.

An application at the Adams Express Company resulted merely in the suggestion that I come back with a letter of recommendation on Monday when I might possibly have some chance if the letter were good enough.

The list of the 54 places at which application was made in the two days is as follows:

Employment Agencies	8
Railroad Docks	5
Specialties	4
Express Companies	3
Contractors	3
Foundries	3
Machine Shops	2
Printing Establishments	2
Real Estate	2
Clothing Manufacturers	2
Cigar Manufacturers	2
Automobile Works	1
Leather Goods Manufacturers	1
Showmen	1
Department Stores	1
Cocoa Manufacturing Company	1
Confectioners	1
Analine Works	1
Soap Manufacturer	1
Polish Manufacturer	1
Draying Companies	1
Breweries	1
Coffee and Sugar Manufacturers	1
Binderies	1
Paper Box Companies	1
Metropolitan Street Railway, Subway Construction Company, Bureau of Labor State Department of Agriculture, Information Bureau Department of Commerce and Labor,	4
	54

CONCLUSIONS.—As far as conclusions are possible from the list of factories, places of business and employment agencies which I visited, and the conversations with the men, they were as follows: First, it was an extremely bad time of the year, just before Christmas, for a man who could not give any references to make any attempt to secure employment. Even making allowances for this situation, however, the position is rather desperate and the giving of free meals, the bread line, etc., not only have a demoralizing influence upon the men, but befuddle the real issue. There are scores, if not hundreds, of the men who are drifting from one place to another, getting food from missions and simply "making out." A good many of them would not take employment if they could get it, but in conversation with over 40 men I found eight or nine who I believe, from their own statements, had been making continuous and earnest efforts to secure work.

The employers may have hesitated to give me work when they knew that I did not belong in the city as I stated to several of them. In any event the depression in lack of employment is serious and is aggravated by the inability of the men to get away from the city and their fear of being exploited if they go on farms.

APPENDIX VI

Study of Newspaper Advertisements as a Medium for Securing Work and Help

WANT ADVERTISEMENTS AND THE LABOR MARKET
By H. G. Paine

"WANT ADS" AND THE LABOR MARKET.—At the request of the general secretary of the Charity Organization Society, the writer conducted an investigation of the "want ads" ("Situations Wanted—Males" and "Help Wanted—Males") in two New York daily newspapers, at twelve selected periods from April, 1902, to November, 1908, for the purpose of learning how far they reflect the general trade conditions prevalent at those times, and, more particularly, the relations between demand and supply in the labor market as affected by those conditions.

PERIODS.—The periods selected were the months of April, August and December of 1902 and 1908, the month of October, 1907, just before the recent disturbance in the financial market, and the months of December, 1907, February, May, July and November, 1908, following the so-called "panic." The first six periods may be taken as representing normal conditions in the labor market during the spring, summer and winter in years of general prosperity. The second six periods were chosen to study the effects of hard times on the labor market and to illustrate the present condition of that market.

NEWSPAPERS.—The New York *World* and New York *Herald* were chosen, those newspapers printing the largest number of "want ads," and also effectively supplementing and complementing each other, by attracting different classes of "want" advertisers. The issues of the second Sunday in each of the selected months were taken for examination. The original intention was to include the New York *American* in the investigation; but an inspection of two or three numbers showed that, in spite of the large circulation of that newspaper, it was not regarded as a good medium by "want" advertisers. Very few such advertisements were printed, and many of those seemed to be of a doubtful and even spurious character. Scarcely any of them gave addresses other than some letter-box in the American office, and they were frequently so vaguely worded as to be little likely to attract inquiries.

CLASSIFICATION OF LABOR.—For purposes of comparison and analysis, the labor field was divided into six general classes: clerical, skilled, unskilled, agricultural, domestic and professional.

Clerical labor comprises bookkeepers, cashiers, clerks, collectors, correspondents, salesmen, secretaries, stenographers and typewriters, managers and superintendents of stores and offices, and agents and representatives of reputable business houses. Drug clerks are included under this head, as being primarily salesmen.

Skilled labor comprises all mechanics and others engaged in trades where a recognized degree of manual dexterity is required; chauffeurs, chefs (as distinguished from cooks in private families and boarding-houses), designers, draughtsmen, foremen and superintendents in factories.

Unskilled labor comprises all those not otherwise specifically classified, "useful men," those "willing to do anything" (not clerical), bartenders (large numbers of them), caretakers, drivers (as distinguished from coachmen), furnacemen, janitors (of buildings not requiring licensed engineers), laborers, waiters (in restaurants, mostly of the cheaper sort), watchmen, and so forth.

Agricultural labor comprises farm-hands, farmers, and gardeners (almost exclusively the last named).

Domestic labor comprises butlers, coachmen (as distinguished from drivers), cooks (as distinguished from chefs), footmen, grooms, housemen, second men, waiters (in private and boarding-houses).

Professional labor comprises actors, artists (as distinguished from designers), dentists, editors, lawyers, ministers, musicians and physicians.

CLASSIFICATION OF EMPLOYERS.—A classification of employers was begun, but was abandoned as greatly increasing the labor of investigation without adequate results. An analysis of the employers advertising in a single number of the *World* showed that while some merchants wanted mechanics, and some manufacturers and contractors wanted clerks, the balance was virtually maintained, as shown by the following figures:

```
Merchants advertising..........................  128
Clerks and salesmen wanted....................  127
Manufacturers, contractors and builders advertising.  343
Skilled laborers wanted........................  347
```

METHOD OF INVESTIGATION.—Score sheets, one for "Situations Wanted" and one for "Help Wanted," were prepared for each copy of each newspaper to be examined and were furnished to the examiner. In addition to the six classifications already mentioned a separate heading on each sheet was made for "Boys" and on the "Help Wanted" sheets an extra heading, "Fakes," was made for noting down any advertisements that, on close examination, did not appear to represent a genuine job awaiting the applicant.

The examiner read each advertisement, calling out the name of the class within which it fell to an assistant who kept tally on the score sheet. In the case of the "Help Wanted" advertisements, he noted also if the advertisement called for more than one worker, and if the help was wanted outside of the five boroughs. The assistant placed a dot over the tally in the first instance and crossed it in the second. A tally with a cross and a dot, accordingly, signified that an out-of-town employer wanted more than one worker.

The writer visited the Astor Library, where the examination was carried on, twice a day, and gathered up the score sheets, making his own additions, and tabulating the figures on other sheets, one for each date and for both papers. The figures for the two papers were then added together and set down in a third column. These totals represent very accurately the relations between demand and supply in the labor market at the specified periods as reflected in the "want ads" of those dates, and indeed very nearly represent the entire number of "want ads", the sum total of "want ads" appearing in all the other newspapers being a small fraction of those in the *World* and the *Herald* combined.

CHARTS.—For further convenience of reference, the figures thus gathered were transferred to three charts: one for the *World* (Chart No. 1), one for the *Herald* (Chart No. 2), and one for both papers combined (Chart No. 3). These charts are so arranged that by reading downward it is possible to compare the numbers of "Situations Wanted" and "Help Wanted" advertisements in each class on any given date, and by reading across, to compare the figures for any date with the corresponding figures on all other dates. In Chart No. 3 the percentages were worked out and set down in horizontal columns to show at a glance what relation the number of "Situations Wanted" advertisements of a given class bear to the total number of "Situations Wanted" advertisements of all six classes on that date, and similarly for the "Help Wanted" advertisements. In the case of the "Help Wanted" advertisements the percentages were similarly worked out and set down in perpendicular columns to show the relation between the legitimate and the total apparent demand for each date.

WANT ADVERTISEMENTS, NEW YORK "WORLD" (ALL SUNDAYS)

(CHART NO. 1)

	Class of Labor	1902 April 13	1902 Aug. 10	1902 Dec. 14	1905 April 9	1905 Aug. 13	1905 Dec. 10	1907 Oct. 13	1907 Dec. 8	1908 Feb. 9	1908 May 10	1908 July 12	1908 Nov. 8	Summary 12 Sundays
Clerical	Situations Wanted (1)	74	61	45	41	77	114	52	58	93	72	51	173	911
	Help Wanted (2)	*68*	*75*	*71*	*47*	*108*	*130*	*132*	*66*	*80*	*58*	*46*	*127*	*1026*
	More than One Wanted (3)	4	5	10	12	11	2	21	11	13	6	4	9	108
	OUT OF TOWN WANTED (4)	3	2	2	2	1	2	2	2	4	3	1	2	26
	Out of Town, more than One (5)		1		1		1		1	2				6
Skilled	Situations Wanted	260	147	181	104	247	298	176	207	252	284	205	392	2753
	Help Wanted	*350*	*218*	*193*	*130*	*303*	*365*	*340*	*133*	*157*	*195*	*126*	*347*	*2062*
	More than One Wanted	87	68	59	54	81	93	106	30	24	35	17	99	753
	OUT OF TOWN WANTED	36	14	9	17	21	7	12	3	2	16	17	18	164
	Out of Town, more than One	7	5	6	12	3	3	3	1	1	2	5	7	50
Unskilled	Situations Wanted	193	160	153	57	193	300	90	123	96	176	190	229	1960
	Help Wanted	*103*	*96*	*70*	*35*	*181*	*225*	*100*	*25*	*30*	*83*	*51*	*79*	*1096*
	More than One Wanted	20	18	25	8	37	40	17	8	7	18	1	10	209
	OUT OF TOWN WANTED	7	4	3	6	2	3	4			1			31
	Out of Town, more than One	2	1	2	3		1							8
Agricultural	Situations Wanted	6	5	2	4	3	4	2	1	8	14	7	11	67
	Help Wanted	*17*	*5*	*4*	*4*	*1*	*1*	*2*		*3*	*5*	*4*	*6*	*52*
	More than One Wanted		1								1			2
	OUT OF TOWN WANTED	17	5	4	4	1	1	2		3	5	4	6	52
	Out of Town, more than One		1								1			2
Domestic	Situations Wanted	25	10	6	9	10	17	76	103	131	26	9	19	441
	Help Wanted	*6*		*7*	*1*	*1*	*4*	*41*	*46*	*45*	*11*	*2*	*2*	*166*
	More than One Wanted							4		1	4			9
	OUT OF TOWN WANTED									1				1
	Out of Town, more than One													

134

														Total
Professional	Situations Wanted	39	32	32	10	39	68	38	66	52	50	44	21	500
	Help Wanted	*25*	*24*	*16*	*15*	*12*	*41*	*26*	*27*	*23*	*24*	*25*	*11*	*269*
	More than One Wanted	..	..	..	1	1	4	..	..	..	..	3	..	12
	OUT OF TOWN WANTED	2	1	3	1	..	1	1	..	2	2	3	..	17
	Out of Town, more than One	..	1	1	..	..	1	..	..	..	..	1	..	4
Total Classified	Situations Wanted	597	415	419	234	569	801	434	558	632	622	506	845	6632
	Help Wanted	*569*	*418*	*370*	*241*	*696*	*775*	*647*	*297*	*356*	*376*	*254*	*572*	*5571*
	More than One Wanted	111	93	97	75	129	130	148	49	45	64	25	118	1093
	OUT OF TOWN WANTED	65	26	21	30	26	14	21	5	17	27	13	26	291
	Out of Town, more than One	9	9	9	16	3	5	3	2	3	3	1	7	70
Fakes, etc.	*Help Wanted*	*127*	*92*	*85*	*111*	*191*	*235*	*72*	*71*	*263*	*341*	*257*	*381*	*2226*
Total Men	Situations Wanted	597	415	419	234	569	801	434	558	632	622	506	845	6632
	Help Wanted	*696*	*510*	*455*	*352*	*887*	*1010*	*719*	*368*	*619*	*717*	*511*	*953*	*7797*
Boys	Situations Wanted	34	35	24	13	46	41	15	23	49	47	37	51	415
	Help Wanted	*124*	*73*	*95*	*40*	*140*	*280*	*133*	*59*	*57*	*48*	*32*	*63*	*1150*
Total Males	Situations Wanted	631	450	443	247	615	842	449	581	681	669	543	896	7047
	Help Wanted	*820*	*583*	*550*	*308*	*1027*	*1290*	*852*	*427*	*676*	*765*	*543*	*1016*	*8947*
Total Advertisements		1451	1033	993	645	1642	2132	1301	1008	1357	1434	1086	1912	15,994

WANT ADVERTISEMENTS, NEW YORK "HERALD" (ALL SUNDAYS)
(CHART No. 2)

	CLASS OF LABOR	1902 April 13	1902 Aug. 10	1902 Dec. 14	1905 April 9	1905 Aug. 13	1905 Dec. 10	1907 Oct. 13	1907 Dec. 8	1908 Feb. 9	1908 May 10	1908 July 12	1908 Nov. 8	SUMMARY
Clerical	Situations Wanted (1)	299	251	324	372	288	395	492	484	508	427	328	572	4740
	Help Wanted (2)	166	227	220	304	287	322	204	133	166	121	122	181	2552
	More than One Wanted (3)	8	17	11	22	15	22	24	11	5	11	2	11	149
	OUT OF TOWN WANTED (4)	5	5	4	8	7	4	2	..	5	3	1	3	47
	More than One out of Town (5)	..	..	1	3	..	..	..	..	..	..	..	3	7
Skilled	Situations Wanted	89	86	86	167	114	107	244	178	141	261	167	206	1846
	Help Wanted	91	74	61	125	105	112	90	30	45	35	43	68	807
	More than One Wanted	16	12	3	11	18	19	20	5	4	3	4	7	122
	OUT OF TOWN WANTED	10	3	4	2	2	6	7	1	3	..	1	6	45
	More than One out of Town	6	1	1	..	1	1	3	..	1	..	..	..	14
Unskilled	Situations Wanted	145	141	141	185	114	151	240	178	163	202	137	253	2050
	Help Wanted	33	44	55	61	46	75	66	38	20	15	8	16	477
	More than One Wanted	4	5	15	4	6	18	14	10	3	2	2	2	85
	OUT OF TOWN WANTED	1	2	2	1	2	2	2	..	2	..	..	..	14
	More than One out of Town	..	1	1	..	1	..	..	..	..	..	..	..	3
Agricultural	Situations Wanted	54	17	7	61	41	15	32	25	56	67	43	47	465
	Help Wanted	11	4	2	21	12	6	12	6	8	6	5	6	90
	More than One Wanted	..	1	..	..	..	..	..	..	..	..	..	..	1
	OUT OF TOWN WANTED	11	4	2	21	12	6	12	6	8	6	5	6	99
	More than One out of Town	..	1	..	..	..	..	..	..	..	..	..	..	1
Domestic	Situations Wanted	228	97	110	319	86	179	355	215	242	411	204	299	2745
	Help Wanted	11	7	8	10	8	4	13	2	4	8	5	11	91
	More than One Wanted	..	1	1	..	..	..	1	..	1	..	..	..	..
	OUT OF TOWN WANTED	2	..	..	..	..	..	..	..	..	..	..	..	6
	More than One out of Town	..	..	..	..	..	..	..	..	..	..	..	..	..

		1	2	3	4	5	6	7	8	9	10	11	12	Total
Professional	Situations Wanted	26	31	38	56	33	29	52	43	24	50	26	50	458
	Help Wanted	16	20	14	24	22	19	27	17	13	17	12	21	222
	More than One Wanted	..	1	2	1	..	1	..	3	..	2	1	..	11
	OUT OF TOWN WANTED	2	2	2	2	..	2	4	1	..	..	..	..	15
	More than One out of Town	..	1	2	..	..	1	..	..	..	..	..	..	4
Total Classified	Situations Wanted	841	623	706	1160	676	876	1415	1123	1134	1418	905	1427	12,304
	Help Wanted	328	376	360	545	480	538	511	235	256	202	195	303	4338
	More than One Wanted	28	36	31	38	39	60	58	29	12	8	9	20	368
	OUT OF TOWN WANTED	31	17	15	34	23	20	28	8	19	9	7	15	226
	More than One out of Town	6	4	5	3	2	2	3	..	1	..	..	3	29
Fakes, etc.	Help Wanted	231	237	279	359	313	343	403	309	367	373	324	366	3904
Total Men	Situations Wanted	841	623	706	1160	676	876	1415	1123	1134	1418	905	1427	12,304
	Help Wanted	559	613	648	904	793	881	914	544	623	575	519	669	8242
Boys	Situations Wanted	21	28	21	51	26	19	36	14	33	28	36	44	357
	Help Wanted	89	63	117	156	101	147	171	50	32	27	29	43	1025
Total Males	Situations Wanted	862	651	727	1211	702	895	1451	1137	1167	1446	941	1471	12,661
	Help Wanted	648	676	765	1060	894	1028	1085	594	655	602	548	712	9267
Total Advertisements		1510	1327	1492	2271	1596	1923	2536	1731	1822	2048	1489	2183	21,928

For convenience in differentiation, different faces of type were employed in making the entries under different heads. For the figures for "Situations Wanted" advertisements No. 1 (plain Roman) type was used, and No. 2 (italics) type for those for "Help Wanted." No. 3 (dark face) type was selected to indicate the number of "Help Wanted" advertisements calling for more than one worker, and No. 4 (dark face capitals) type to indicate those coming from outside of Greater New York. No. 5 (title) type was used for out-of-town advertisements calling for more than one man. These advertisements formed so small a fraction of the total number (exactly 1 per cent.) that they were disregarded in Chart No. 3. On Chart No. 3 the percentages of the total "more than one" and "out of town" advertisements to the total number of legitimate "Help Wanted" advertisements were set down, enclosed in brackets, in the last column.

ANALYSIS.—In studying the results obtained it will be found best to begin at the end and to work backward. Thus, taking Chart No. 3 and referring to the figures in the right-hand lower corner, it will be seen that on the Sundays selected 37,992 "want ads—Males" were printed, in the *World* and the *Herald* combined, an average of 3,166 for each Sunday. The figures directly above show that of this total 19,708 were "Situations Wanted" and 18,214 were "Help Wanted," which would indicate an excess of only 1,494 of the former over the latter.

BOYS.—This inference, however, is seen to be misleading as soon as the figures next above are noted. Nearly 3,000 of the total "want ads" refer to boys, and the figures 772 and 2,175, show that there were 1,403 more boys wanted than there were boys seeking situations. It is impossible from the wording of the advertisements to classify boy "want ads," and no attempt to do so has been made. The demand for and supply of boys may bear some relation to the condition of the labor market, but a little consideration will show that this relation is not likely to be reflected in the "want ads" of the newspapers. Experience, at least,

WANT ADVERTISEMENTS, NEW YORK "HERALD" AND "WORLD." (ALL SUNDAYS)

(CHART No. 3)

Class of Labor		April 13, 1902 Number	April 13, 1902 Per Cent.	August 10, 1902 Number	August 10, 1902 Per Cent.	December 14, 1902 Number	December 14, 1902 Per Cent.	April 9, 1905 Number	April 9, 1905 Per Cent.	August 13, 1905 Number	August 13, 1905 Per Cent.	December 10, 1905 Number	December 10, 1905 Per Cent.
Clerical	Situations Wanted (1)	373	..	312	..	369	..	413	..	365	..	509	..
	Help Wanted (2)	*234*	*16.5*	*302*	*24.0*	*300*	*22.8*	*351*	*24.1*	*395*	*20.6*	*461*	*20.0*
	More than One Wanted (3)	**12**	..	**22**	..	**21**	..	**34**	..	**26**	..	**24**	..
	OUT OF TOWN WANTED (4)	**8**	..	**7**	..	**6**	..	**10**	..	**8**	..	**6**	..
	Percentages (5)	25.9 **26.**	..	30.1 **38.**	..	32.8 **40.6**	..	29.6 **44.7**	..	29.3 **33.6**	..	30.4 **35.2**	..
Skilled	Situations Wanted	340	..	233	..	267	..	271	..	361	..	405	..
	Help Wanted	*441*	*30.0*	*202*	*23.2*	*254*	*19.3*	*264*	*18.1*	*408*	*25.0*	*477*	*20.5*
	More than One Wanted	**103**	..	**80**	..	**62**	..	**65**	..	**99**	..	**112**	..
	OUT OF TOWN WANTED	**46**	..	**17**	..	**13**	..	**19**	..	**23**	..	**13**	..
	Percentages	24.3 **49.2**	..	22.4 **36.8**	..	23.7 **34.4**	..	19.4 **33.6**	..	20.0 **42.3**	..	24.2 **36.3**	..
Unskilled	Situations Wanted	338	..	301	..	294	..	242	..	307	..	451	..
	Help Wanted	*136*	*9.0*	*140*	*11.1*	*134*	*10.1*	*96*	*6.6*	*227*	*11.8*	*300*	*13.*
	More than One Wanted	**24**	..	**23**	..	**40**	..	**12**	..	**43**	..	**58**	..
	OUT OF TOWN WANTED	**8**	..	**6**	..	**5**	..	**7**	..	**4**	..	**5**	..
	Percentages	23.5 **15.2**	..	20. **17.6**	..	26.1 **18.2**	..	17.4 **12.2**	..	24.7 **19.3**	..	26.8 **22.8**	..
Agricultural	Situations Wanted	60	..	22	..	9	..	65	..	44	..	19	..
	Help Wanted	*28*	*1.9*	*9*	*.7*	*6*	*.6*	*25*	*1.7*	*13*	*.7*	*7*	*.3*
	More than One Wanted	..	..	**2**	..	..	..	..	..	..	..	..	..
	OUT OF TOWN WANTED	**28**	..	**9**	..	**6**	..	**25**	..	**13**	..	**7**	..
	Percentages	4.1 **3.2**	..	2.1 **1.1**	..	.8 **.8**	..	4.7 **3.2**	..	3.5 **1.1**	..	1.1 **.5**	..
Domestic	Situations Wanted	253	..	107	..	116	..	328	..	96	..	196	..
	Help Wanted	*17*	*1.2*	*7*	*.6*	*15*	*1.1*	*11*	*.7*	*9*	*.5*	*8*	*.4*
	More than One Wanted	..	..	..	..	..	..	..	..	..	..	..	..
	OUT OF TOWN WANTED	**2**	..	..	..	**1**	..	..	..	..	..	..	..
	Percentages	17.7 **1.9**	..	10.3 **.9**	..	10.3 **2.**	..	23.5 **1.4**	..	7.7 **.8**	..	11.7 **.6**	..
Professional	Situations Wanted	65	..	63	..	70	..	75	..	72	..	97	..
	Help Wanted	*41*	*2.8*	*44*	*3.5*	*30*	*2.3*	*30*	*2.7*	*34*	*1.8*	*60*	*2.5*
	More than One Wanted	..	..	**2**	..	**5**	..	**2**	..	..	..	**5**	..
	OUT OF TOWN WANTED	**4**	..	**3**	..	**5**	..	**3**	..	**1**	..	**3**	..
	Percentages	4.5 **4.5**	..	6.1 **5.6**	..	6.2 **4.**	..	5.4 **4.9**	..	5.8 **2.9**	..	5.8 **4.6**	..
Total Classified	Situations Wanted	1438	..	1038	..	1195	..	1304	..	1245	..	1677	..
	Help Wanted	*807*	*61.4*	*704*	*63.1*	*730*	*56.2*	*786*	*53.0*	*1176*	*61.3*	*1313*	*56.7*
	More than One Wanted	**139**	..	**120**	..	**128**	..	**113**	..	**168**	..	**199**	..
	OUT OF TOWN WANTED	**96**	..	**43**	..	**36**	..	**64**	..	**49**	..	**34**	..
	Percentages	100. **100.**	..	100. **100.**	..	100. **100.**	..	100. **100.**	..	100. **100.**	..	100. **100.**	..
Fakes, etc.	*Help Wanted*	*358*	*24.5*	*329*	*26.1*	*364*	*27.8*	*470*	*32.2*	*504*	*26.2*	*378*	*24.9*
Total for Men	Situations Wanted	1438	..	1038	..	1125	..	1304	..	1245	..	1677	..
	Help Wanted	*1255*	..	*1123*	..	*1103*	..	*1256*	..	*1680*	..	*1891*	..
	Percentages	..	..	..	..	..	..	..	..	..	..	..	..
Boys	Situations Wanted	55	..	63	..	45	..	64	..	72	..	60	..
	Help Wanted	*213*	*14.1*	*136*	*10.8*	*212*	*16.0*	*202*	*13.9*	*241*	*12.5*	*427*	*18.4*
	Percentages	..	..	..	..	..	..	..	..	..	..	..	..
Total for Males	Situations Wanted	1493	..	1101	..	1170	..	1458	..	1317	..	1737	..
	Help Wanted	*1468*	*100.0*	*1259*	*100.0*	*1315*	*100.0*	*1458*	*100.0*	*1921*	*100.0*	*2318*	*100.0*
	Percentages	..	..	..	..	..	..	..	..	..	..	..	..
Total Advertisements		2961		2360		2485		2916		3238		4055	

Class of Labor		October 13, 1907 Number	October 13, 1907 Per Cent.	December 8, 1907 Number	December 8, 1907 Per Cent.	February 9, 1908 Number	February 9, 1908 Per Cent.	May 10, 1908 Number	May 10, 1908 Per Cent.	July 12, 1908 Number	July 12, 1908 Per Cent.	November 8, 1908 Number	November 8, 1908 Per Cent.	Summary Number	Summary Per Cent.
Clerical	Situations Wanted (1)	544	..	542	..	601	..	409	..	379	..	745	..	5651	..
	Help Wanted (2)	*426*	*22.0*	*199*	*19.6*	*255*	*19.2*	*170*	*13.1*	*168*	*15.4*	*308*	*17.8*	*3578*	*19.6*
	More than One Wanted (3)	**45**	..	**22**	..	**18**	..	**7**	..	**6**	..	**20**	..	**257**	(2.6)
	OUT OF TOWN WANTED (4)	**4**	..	**2**	..	**9**	..	**6**	..	**2**	..	**5**	..	**73**	(0.7)
	Percentages (5)	29.4 **36.8**	..	32.2 **37.4**	..	34. **41.7**	..	24.5 **31.**	..	26.9 **37.4**	..	32.8 **35.2**	..	30. **38.**	..
Skilled	Situations Wanted	420	..	385	..	393	..	545	..	372	..	598	..	4590	..
	Help Wanted	*445*	*23.0*	*172*	*16.8*	*202*	*15.2*	*230*	*16.8*	*169*	*15.4*	*415*	*24.0*	*3859*	*21.1*
	More than One Wanted	**126**	..	**35**	..	**28**	..	**38**	..	**21**	..	**106**	..	**875**	(8.8)
	OUT OF TOWN WANTED	**19**	..	**4**	..	**9**	..	**16**	..	**6**	..	**24**	..	**209**	(2.1)
	Percentages	22.7 **38.4**	..	22.9 **32.3**	..	22.3 **33.**	..	26.7 **39.8**	..	26.3 **37.6**	..	26.3 **47.4**	..	24. **38.9**	..
Unskilled	Situations Wanted	330	..	301	..	259	..	378	..	327	..	482	..	4010	..
	Help Wanted	*166*	*8.5*	*63*	*6.2*	*59*	*4.4*	*98*	*7.1*	*59*	*5.5*	*95*	*5.5*	*1573*	*8.6*
	More than One Wanted	**31**	..	**18**	..	**10**	..	**20**	..	**3**	..	**12**	..	**294**	(3.0)
	OUT OF TOWN WANTED	**6**	..	..	..	**3**	..	**1**	..	..	..	..	..	**45**	(0.4)
	Percentages	17.9 **14.3**	..	17.9 **11.8**	..	14.7 **9.6**	..	18.5 **16.9**	..	23.2 **13.2**	..	21.2 **11.9**	..	21.1 **16.**	..
Agricultural	Situations Wanted	34	..	26	..	64	..	81	..	50	..	58	..	532	..
	Help Wanted	*14*	*.7*	*6*	*.6*	*11*	*.8*	*11*	*.8*	*9*	*.8*	*12*	*.8*	*151*	*.8*
	More than One Wanted	..	..	..	..	..	..	**1**	..	..	..	..	..	**3**	..
	OUT OF TOWN WANTED	**14**	..	**6**	..	**11**	..	**11**	..	**9**	..	**12**	..	**151**	(1.5)
	Percentages	1.8 **1.2**	..	1.6 **1.1**	..	3.6 **1.8**	..	4.0 **1.9**	..	3.5 **2.0**	..	3.5 **1.4**	..	2.8 **1.6**	..
Domestic	Situations Wanted	431	..	318	..	373	..	437	..	213	..	318	..	3186	..
	Help Wanted	*54*	*2.8*	*48*	*4.7*	*40*	*3.7*	*19*	*1.5*	*7*	*.6*	*13*	*.8*	*257*	*1.4*
	More than One Wanted	**4**	..	**3**	..	**1**	..	**4**	..	..	..	..	..	**29**	(0.3)
	OUT OF TOWN WANTED	**1**	..	..	..	**2**	..	..	..	..	..	..	..	**7**	..
	Percentages	23.3 **4.7**	..	18.9 **9.1**	..	21.1 **8.0**	..	21.4 **3.3**	..	15.1 **1.6**	..	15.1 **1.5**	..	16.9 **2.5**	..
Professional	Situations Wanted	90	..	109	..	76	..	100	..	70	..	71	..	958	..
	Help Wanted	*53*	*2.8*	*44*	*4.3*	*36*	*2.7*	*41*	*3.0*	*37*	*3.4*	*32*	*1.8*	*401*	*2.0*
	More than One Wanted	..	..	..	..	..	..	**2**	..	**4**	..	..	..	**23**	(0.2)
	OUT OF TOWN WANTED	**5**	..	**1**	..	**2**	..	**2**	..	**3**	..	..	..	**32**	(0.3)
	Percentages	4.9 **4.6**	..	6.5 **8.3**	..	4.3 **5.9**	..	4.9 **7.1**	..	5.0 **8.2**	..	5.0 **3.6**	..	5.0 **4.9**	..
Total Classified	Situations Wanted	1840	..	1681	..	1766	..	2040	..	1411	..	2272	..	18,936	..
	Help Wanted	*1158*	*59.8*	*532*	*52.2*	*612*	*46.0*	*578*	*42.3*	*440*	*41.1*	*875*	*50.7*	*0000*	*54.4*
	More than One Wanted	**206**	..	**78**	..	**57**	..	**72**	..	**34**	..	**138**	..	**1461**	(11.7)
	OUT OF TOWN WANTED	**49**	..	**13**	..	**36**	..	**36**	..	**20**	..	**41**	..	**517**	(5.0)
	Percentages	100. **100.**	..	100. **100.**	..	100. **100.**	..	100. **100.**	..	100. **100.**	..	100. **100.**	..	100. **100.**	..
Fakes, etc.	*Help Wanted*	*475*	*24.6*	*380*	*37.2*	*630*	*47.3*	*714*	*52.2*	*581*	*53.3*	*747*	*43.2*	*6130*	*33.7*
Total for Men	Situations Wanted	1840	..	1681	..	1766	..	2040	..	1411	..	2272	..	18,936	..
	Help Wanted	*1633*	..	*912*	..	*1242*	..	*1295*	..	*1030*	..	*1622*	..	*16,030*	..
	Percentages	..	..	..	..	..	..	..	..	..	..	..	..	..	..
Boys	Situations Wanted	51	..	37	..	82	..	75	..	73	..	95	..	772	..
	Help Wanted	*304*	*15.6*	*109*	*10.6*	*89*	*6.7*	*75*	*5.5*	*61*	*5.6*	*106*	*6.1*	*2175*	*11.9*
	Percentages	..	..	..	..	..	..	..	..	..	..	..	..	..	..
Total for Males	Situations Wanted	1900	..	1718	..	1848	..	2115	..	1484	..	2367	..	19,708	..
	Help Wanted	*1937*	*100.0*	*1021*	*100.0*	*1331*	*100.0*	*1367*	*100.0*	*1091*	*100.0*	*1728*	..	*18,214*	*100.0*
	Percentages	..	..	..	..	..	..	..	..	..	..	..	..	..	..
Total Advertisements		3837		2739		3179		3482		2575		4095		37,022	

NOTE.—Percentage figures in perpendicular columns refer to "Help Wanted" advertisements only, and indicate the percentage of each division to total number printed; including "Fakes" and "Boys."

Percentage figures in horizontal columns refer to legitimate advertisements by and for MEN only.

Bracketed figures in last column indicate percentage of "more than one" and "out of town" demands to total number of *legitimate* "Help Wanted" Advertisements.

demonstrates that the "want ads" do not reflect the real ratio between the demand and the supply of boys. Advertise for a boy to apply in person at your office or store, and you will very likely have more applicants than the total number of boys advertising for jobs, while other advertisers for boys are probably having similar experiences in various parts of the city.

The obvious conclusion is simply that boys as a class don't advertise. There are two principal reasons for this. One is that the average boy has no money to spend in advertising, and the other is that as a rule he has nothing to advertise excepting the fact that he is a boy. Probably few employers would take the time or trouble to answer advertisements by boys. It is easier for the employer to insert a "Help Wanted" advertisement, and by casting his eye over the crowd who apply, to pick out a few of the most likely looking for closer inspection; or, if the boy is wanted for office work, to have them apply in the first instance in writing, and then to invite those sending the best letters to call in person. The employer is looking for brightness, for capacity to assimilate instruction, not for experience, and he depends on his knowledge of human nature to guide him in the selection.

For the purposes of the present consideration, accordingly, the boy factor may and should be eliminated from the problem; and the figures next above show that when men alone are considered there are 18,936 "Situations Wanted" to 16,039 "Help Wanted" advertisements, a difference of nearly 2,900.

FAKES.—How misleading these figures are, however, will instantly be seen by looking at the line above, where it is shown that of the "Help Wanted" advertisements no fewer than 6,130, or 33.7 per cent., fall under the head of "fakes."

A great variety of advertisements come under this classification, which comprises every kind printed in the "Help Wanted" columns that does not represent a legitimate wage-earning opportunity. The great majority are advertisements calling for agents, canvassers, collectors, salesmen, solicitors and so forth (and for managers and superintendents in those cases where a close examination discloses that these terms are merely euphemisms for agent or canvasser), where the reward, if any, depends upon commissions and where the "employee" receives nothing until the commission is earned. Care was taken to differentiate these advertisements from those of responsible business houses who might desire to engage salesmen whose income would depend upon the amount of trade they would be able to control.

Other advertisements comprised under "fakes" are those of civil service schools and other offers of instruction, of employment agencies, and those evidently coming from employment agencies, as well as many more or less veiled efforts to dispose of various wares under the guise of "samples," "outfits," etc., including offers of "work to be done at home," where the dupe purchases raw material from the advertiser to decorate or otherwise to transform, but which is never accepted as "up to the necessary standard." All requests for "amateur actors to join dramatic company in process of formation" are classed as "fakes."

FLOURISH IN HARD TIMES.—Before proceeding to a consideration of the genuine "want ads," it may prove interesting to pursue the study of these "fakes" a little further. Run the eye to the left, following the line of "fake ads" printed on the twelve different dates selected. It will be seen that under fairly normal conditions of the labor market, they run from 24.5 to 34.2 per cent. of the total number of "Help Wanted" advertisements; but that, beginning with December, 1907 (when the excess genuine visible supply begins rapidly to increase), the percentage of fakes advances with leaps and bounds to 53.3 per cent. in July, 1908. There is a drop in November to 43.2 per cent., although in that month the actual number of fakes reaches its highest mark, 747. It would appear, accordingly that, roughly speaking, the percentage of "fake ads" varies inversely with the actual demand for labor. The harder the times, the more the fakes blossom out in the advertising columns. (Diag. 1, p. 143.)

AGENTS, SALESMEN AND CANVASSERS.—There are various reasons for this phenomenon. In the first place many of these advertisements are clearly traps to catch "suckers," and to draw from the pockets of the desperate and the inexperienced the few dollars they have remaining or can raise. Such are most of those requiring "security" or necessitating the purchase of "outfits," etc. In the second place, many concerns which regularly employ agents and canvassers, find their sales falling off in hard times, and seek to stem the tide by engaging more salesmen, or find themselves compelled to supply the places of former agents who have given up on account of the impossibility of making a living when people refuse to buy. In the third place insurance companies and other concerns employing canvassers and collectors endeavor at such periods to get in touch with men who are out of work and who would not ordinarily seek such employment, advertising for "managers," "superintendents," etc., from branch offices in different parts of the city.

Sometimes differently worded advertisements will lead to the same office. A concern with an office in the Brunswick Building used two forms of advertisement, each giving a different address, one the Fifth Avenue door, the other the Twenty-sixth Street door. This was discovered by a man who actually answered the two advertisements.

Again, men who have themselves been thrown out of employment, try to start in business for themselves with a minimum of capital, and adopt this way of selling their wares at a minimum of expense. The salesman gives his time and effort, and receives nothing if unsuccessful, although the fault may rest rather with the kind or quality of his wares than with the salesman himself.

A MEAN FORM OF GRAFT.—Advertisements for real estate salesmen are especially suspicious, and the experience of a friend of the writer's shows them to be mostly "fakes" and reveals a peculiarly mean form of "graft." A real estate speculator engages a man to sell lots on commission. A real estate deal usually requires considerable "working up" before it is consummated. The prospective purchaser must be visited two or three times, perhaps, before he will go to look at the suburb or "addition." His railway fares must be paid. He must be placated with lunch. This takes time, effort and money, all contributed by the salesman. Just about the time that the customer is ready to close, the speculator declares that it is clear from the time that has elapsed that the salesman is not up to his job, steps in and effects the sale himself, while the salesman gets nothing and is out his time and expenses. Even if the salesman, through inexperience, could not have made the sale himself, the speculator has been saved all the trouble and cost of the "working up" process. The customer has been told everything he is to be permitted to know about the property, excepting the interesting fact that he is going to buy it. To convey that information convincingly requires the intervention of the glib and plausible real estate "expert" himself.

GENUINE SUPPLY AND DEMAND.—Eliminating, then, "fakes" and "boys" from the "Help Wanted" advertisements, there remains a total apparent demand of 9,909 as against a supply of 18,936. (Diag. 2, p. 144, shows relation in each class.)

MORE THAN ONE WANTED.—These figures, however, fail to express the actual relation of demand and supply even as reflected in the "want ads"; for each "Situations Wanted" advertisement proclaims the desire of only a single worker for labor, while the figures in **dark face type** show that 1,461 employers wanted more than one worker. More than one means at least two, and may mean many more. Only occasionally is the exact number specified, as when one contractor calls for "twenty carpenters," and another asks for "ten sailors to paint ships," or when a tailor asks for "two bushelmen." Usually the advertiser contents himself with the use of the plural, stating that "tinsmiths," "painters" or what not are wanted. It is clear then, that the total "Help Wanted" advertisements should be increased

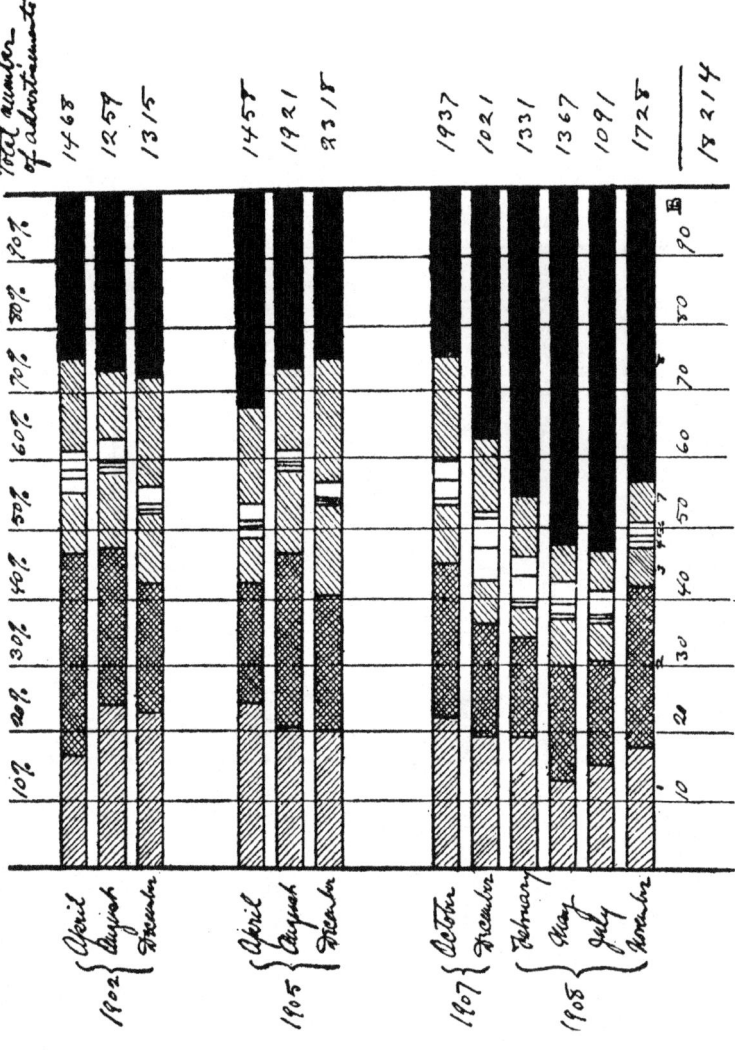

Diag. 1.—Percentage of each kind of "help wanted" among the advertisements studied. The order, reading from left to right, is Clerical, Skilled, Unskilled, Agricultural, Domestic, Professional, Boys, and "Fakes," "Fakes" being solid black.

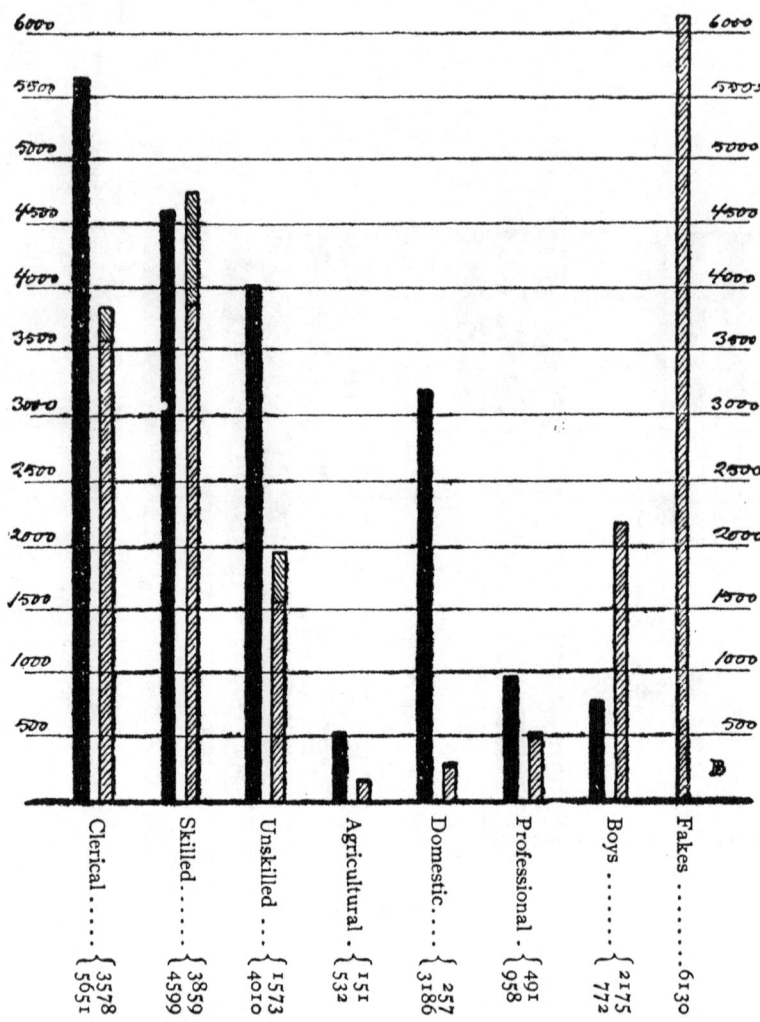

Diag. 2.—Relation of situations wanted and help wanted advertisements in each class of labor. Black columns, situations wanted; shaded columns, help wanted. At the top is added a section allowing one additional instance of help wanted for each advertisement calling for more than one.

to 11,370 by the addition of 1,461, as a minimum, and it would probably be within limits to add another 1,461, making 12,831.

HELP WANTED OUT OF TOWN.—So far as the labor market in the city is concerned, these figures would still further have to be revised by disregarding the 517 advertisements from out of town employers, although they undoubtedly offer opportunities to men living in New York who care to or who are able to move to another town. Although it does not appear on Chart No. 3, it is interesting to note that of these 517 advertisements from out of town 99, or 19.1 per cent., call for more than one worker, as against a per cent. of 11.7 of "more than one" advertisements to the total number of "Help Wanted."

APPARENT EXCESS SUPPLY.—In the period selected, however, there is still seen to be considerable excess of supply over demand, and a glance at the two first totals in each of the six classifications will show that this excess has been generally maintained.

PROFESSIONAL LABOR.—Taking the different classifications in order and still working upward, it is seen that professional "want ads" are of small importance numerically, forming only 5 per cent. of the "Situations Wanted" and 4.9 per cent. of the "Help Wanted" advertisements, while inspection proves them to be of small importance professionally. Most of the "artists," "dentists" and "musicians" sought for and seeking employment are of a grade below many of those appearing under the head of skilled labor. They are usually sought for singly, only 23 employers calling for more than one of a kind, while 32 were wanted out of town, indicating that New York is still regarded as the center of culture and the fine arts!

DOMESTIC LABOR.—The class of "Domestic Labor," next above, shows an amazing discrepancy between the number of those seeking employment and these seeking help,—3,166 to 257. On the face of it, no such ratio of difference can exist between the actual supply and demand. If it did, men servants would seek other employment. The natural explanation is that as a rule employers of male domestic labor do not advertise, but prefer to interview servants at responsible agencies and intelligence offices, or to answer advertisements, asking a few selected men to call at hours when they will not encounter one another and be able to exchange notes. Experience also indicates that this great number of servants constantly seeking situations is due in part to the ease with which servants can get engagements when out of work, which makes them ready to leave places on little provocation, or if things do not exactly suit them. The servant problem has always been a difficult one, but the excess of supply has never seemed to be a factor in it. The problem has usually stood by itself, as apart from the general labor problem, and it would perhaps have been better to treat it separately in this investigation. The elimination of "Domestic Labor" from the division of classified labor in Chart No. 3 would make the total figures for "Situations Wanted" 14,750, and for "Help Wanted" 9,652, and counting each of those calling for more than one to mean at least two, 14,750 to 11,341.

JAPANESE AS SERVANTS.—While still considering the question of "Domestic Labor" it is worth while to note how largely the Japanese figure in both supply and demand columns, as valets and houseworkers. And it may be worth noting, also, that experience has shown that the Japanese are notoriously inconstant in their allegiance to white employers, changing places frequently, although usually ready to supply a substitute. The substitute, however, is often unsatisfactory, with the result that the next day a Japanese boy is advertising for a place and an employer is looking for a boy.

AGRICULTURAL LABOR.—Agricultural labor figures so slightly in the "want ad" columns of the New York newspapers as scarcely to warrant a separate classification. Gardeners form the bulk of those noted, and it has been assumed that all were wanted for places out of town, although it is possible that a few may have been employed within the city limits. When an advertiser gives his address as the *Herald* office or somewhere in Worth Street, it is impossible to determine whether he lives in New Jersey or Staten Island.

UNSKILLED LABOR.—"Unskilled Labor," next after "Domestic Labor," shows the greatest discrepancy between supply and demand. Even allowing for those cases where more than one were wanted, the apparent supply was more than double the apparent demand.

SKILLED LABOR.—"Skilled Labor," however, shows a close balance between supply and demand. The difference, only 740, is more than made up by the 875 cases where employers wanted more than one worker, affording the only instance in classified labor where the total demand exceeds the total supply. "Skilled Labor" also shows the greatest percentage (exclusive of "Agricultural Labor") of "out-of-town" demands. Note that skilled labor amounts to 38.9 per cent. of the total demand for labor and only to 24.2 per cent. of the total supply. It would appear that the skilled laborer has a better chance to procure employment than any other kind of worker. It was observed in the course of this investigation that "housesmiths" did not figure at all in the "want ads," and that the building trades in general made little use of the "want" columns. There were some carpenters and painters wanted for jobs and in shops, and for out of town demands, and occasional masons and plasterers, but the labor for big building operations appears to be secured independently of the newspapers. The noticeable increase of chauffeurs, advertising and advertised for, during the last two years prompted a rough comparison with "coachmen," with the result that there was noticed an apparent increase in the supply of the latter, indicating some relation between the two employments, and that the character of one kind of service was in process of elevation from the grade of "domestic" to skilled labor.

CLERICAL LABOR.—"Clerical Labor" bulks numerically most largely of all the six classes in the "want ads," but only slightly more than Skilled Labor, as will be seen by adding together the figures for demand and supply in both cases, which is not done on the chart. The totals are 9,229 for "clerical" and 8,458 for "skilled," but adding 257 and 875 respectively for "more than one" demands, the results are changed to 9,486 and 9,333. Supply largely exceeds demand, however, in the case of "Clerical Labor," as is shown by the actual figures as well as by the percentage. Compared with "Skilled Labor," it is interesting to observe the difference between the "more than one" demands and also that between the "out-of-town" demands,—73 to 209. It is evidently easier for an out-of-town employer to find the clerk that he wants in his own neighborhood than it is to find the skilled labor that he needs. Any one who can read, write and cipher is a potential clerk, but skilled laborers, when the local demand is exhausted, are naturally sought in the great centers of industrial activity.

The greater number of "more than one" demands in the case of skilled labor is possibly due to the fact that productive labor responds more immediately to trade fluctuations. If a manufacturer receives a sudden demand for more goods than he can normally produce with his usual force of operatives within a specified time, he must increase his force until the emergency has passed. The order may have come through a mercantile establishment which will find the handling of the additional business no special tax upon its normal force of clerks.

The average tenure of service may be longer in the case of clerks than of mechanics as a result of this slower response to trade fluctuations, and this might account for the greater excess of supply in one case than the other, without necessarily implying an inferior condition in the labor market,—the average clerk having to wait longer for his job than the average mechanic, but holding it longer when he has obtained it. This is merely suggested as a subject for possible further consideration or investigation.

A considerable proportion of those advertising for clerical situations are foreigners, and the chief examiner in this investigation, himself of foreign birth, volunteers the comment that "many of these men, while without any particular trade or profession, are of more than ordinary culture and attainments." The examiner is a man of long residence and newspaper experience in New York. It may be noted that banks, banking houses, trust companies and other financial concerns do not figure in the "Help Wanted" columns. They have, as a rule, more applications on their waiting lists than would supply them all with a full force of employees.

COMPARISON BY PERIODS.—A comparison of the totals of classified "Situations Wanted" and "Help Wanted" advertisements printed on each of the selected dates will afford an interesting study. If in 1902 and 1905, the misleading item of "Domestic Labor" will be disregarded, and an allowance of one additional be made for each "Help Wanted" advertisement calling for "more than one" workers, the results will show much less difference between supply and demand than appears from a superficial examination. As these figures were not worked out in the chart, they are given here (see Diag. 3, p. 151):

	1902			1903		
	April	August	December	April	August	December
Situations Wanted	1185	931	1009	1066	1149	1481
Help Wanted	1019	916	852	888	1335	1504
Excess Supply	166	15	157	178	..	..
Excess Demand	..	..	..	..	186	23

It will be seen that in August and December, 1905, demand actually exceeded supply and that there was a negligible difference in August, 1902. The figures for 1907 and 1908, however, tell a different story:

	1907		1908			
	October	December	February	May	July	November
Situations Wanted	1418	1363	1393	1603	1198	1954
Help Wanted	1310	562	620	631	476	1000
Excess Supply	108	801	773	972	722	954

In October, just before the "panic," the balance was very nearly maintained; but in December the demand had fallen off tremendously, and it is odd to note that the supply had actually fallen off also. This may indicate that employers were keeping on old employees, so far as possible, but without taking on the extra hands that the holiday trade usually calls for. The figures for 1908 seem to indicate that the conditions so far as the labor market is concerned, have not improved, the figures for November 8 showing a greater volume of demand, indeed, but a corresponding increase of supply.

COMPARISON BY PRINCIPAL CLASSES.—Taking up the three principal classes of labor,—clerical, skilled and unskilled,—and comparing them with respect to demand and supply at the selected periods, and allowing for the advertisements calling for more than one, it is seen that in every month up to December, 1907, the apparent demand for skilled labor was in excess of the supply: 236 in excess in August, 1905, 184 in excess in December, 1905, 151 in excess in October, 1907. (Diag. 4, p. 152.)

At the same seven periods the supply of clerical labor was somewhat more than the demand, excepting in August, 1902, and in August, 1905, when the balance was the other way. The greatest excess of supply was in April, 1902, when it was 127. It was only 48 in December, 1902, only 28 in April, 1905, only 24 in December, 1905, and 73 in October, 1907. (Diag. 5, p. 153.)

On none of these dates did the demand for unskilled labor approach anywhere near the supply. The most favorable months were August and December, 1905. (Diag. 6, p. 154.)

Beginning with December, 1907, each of the three principal classes shows a persistent excess of supply, the demand being consistently strongest in the case of skilled labor (rising to 521 "Help Wanted" as against 598 "Situations Wanted" in November, 1908) and weakest in the case of unskilled labor, falling to 62 as against 372 in July, 1908, and to 107 as against 482 in Novem-

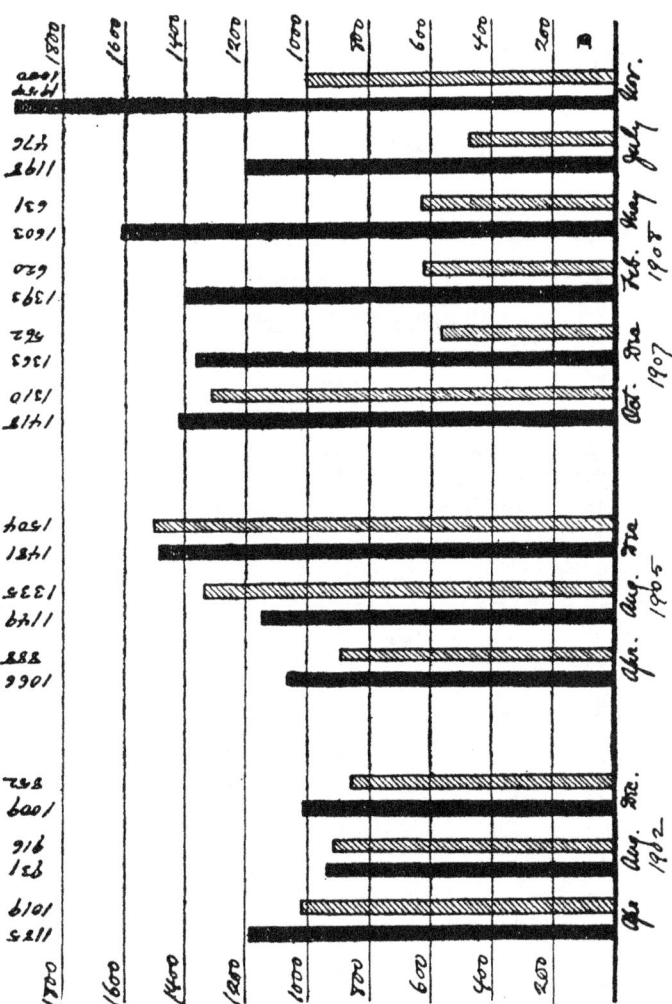

Diag. 3.—Advertisements for and by "males" in the N. Y. Sunday *World* and *Herald*, on 2d Sunday of each month, excluding fakes, boys, and domestic labor, and allowing two for each "more than one" wanted. The black column represents situations wanted (total 15,750); the shaded column help wanted (total 11,113).

152 AN EMPLOYMENT BUREAU FOR NEW YORK

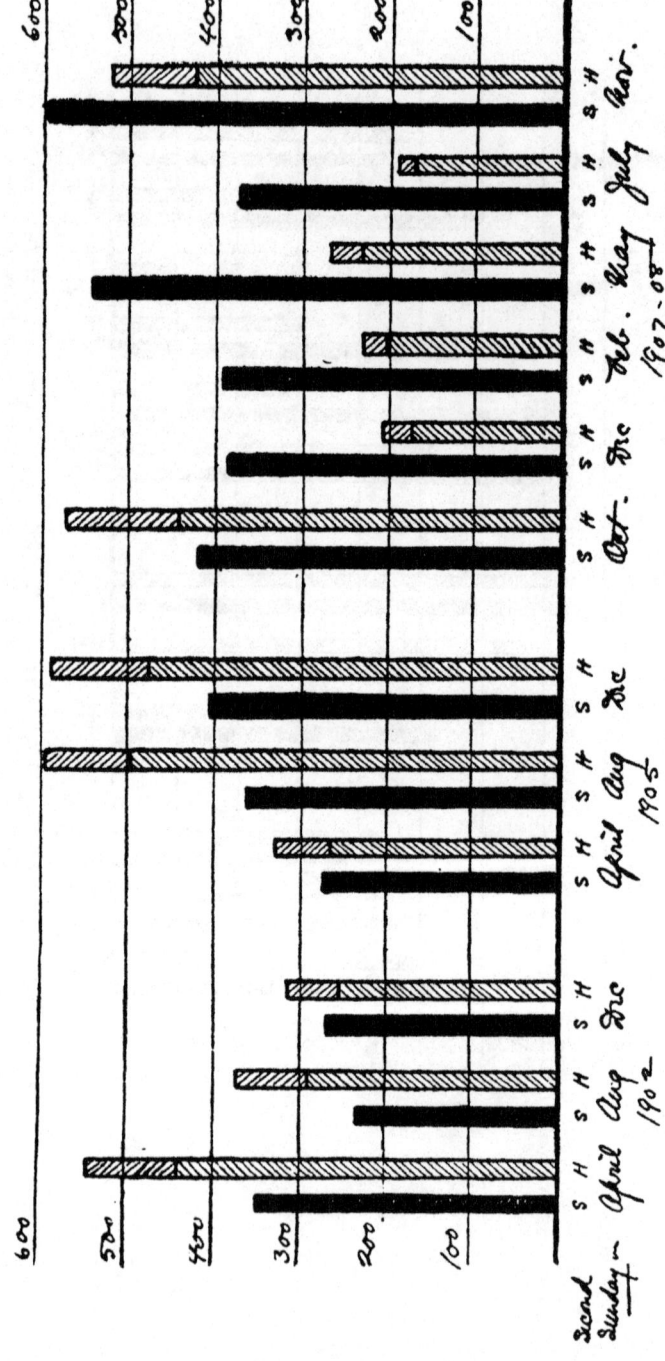

Diag. 4.—Skilled labor. Relation between situations wanted and help wanted at different periods.

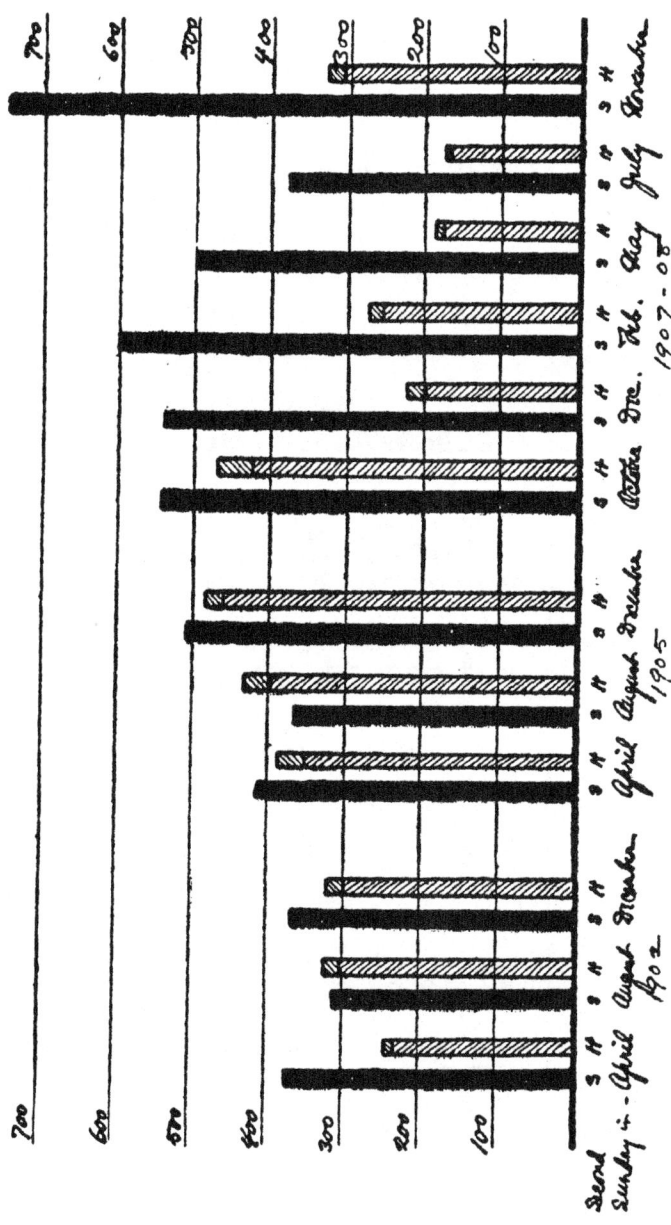

Diag. 5.—Clerical labor. Relation between situations wanted and help wanted at different periods.

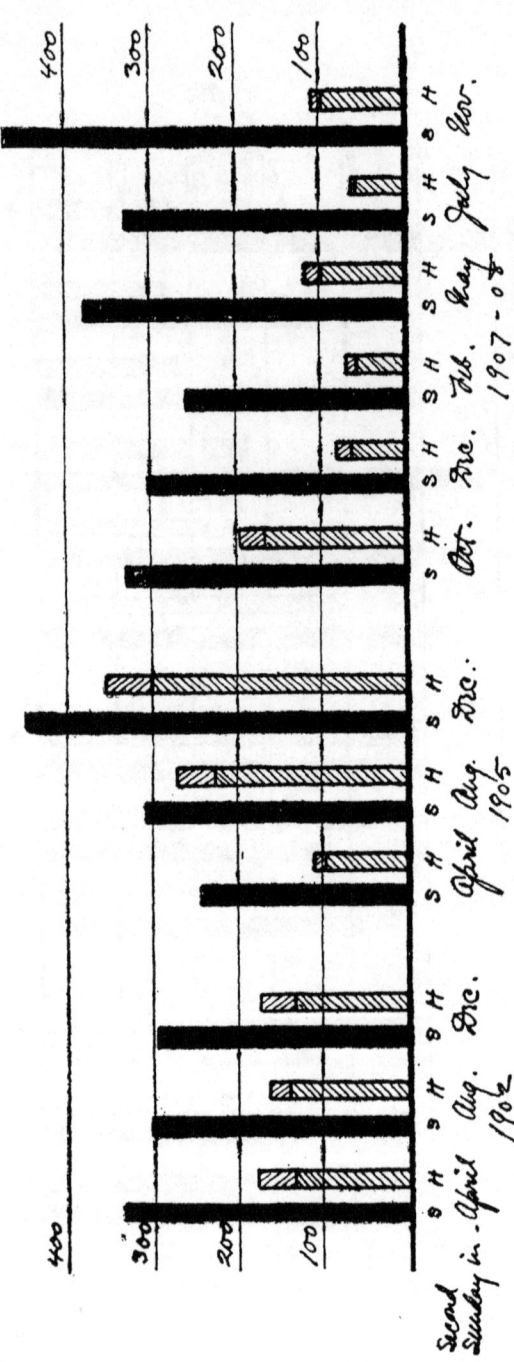

Diag. 6.—Unskilled labor. Relation between situations wanted and help wanted at different periods.

ber, 1908. At no time since October, 1908, has the demand for clerical labor equalled 50 per cent. of the supply.

OBSERVATIONS.—It is apparent, accordingly, that to some considerable extent, at least, the "want ads" reflect the condition of the labor market, when certain obviously misleading factors have been eliminated. How far other factors not herein taken into account may affect the apparent result one way or another it is not possible from the data at hand to determine. In spite of the large number of "want ads" published every week, they must comprise a very small proportion of the actual labor exchange. The actual relations of supply and demand may be quite different from those of the want columns. It would seem as if the "Help Wanted" advertisements would be likely to stand in a closer relation to the actual demand than the "Situations Wanted" advertisements; for no employer with an unsatisfied demand for labor would spare the trouble or cost of an advertisement, while with many men out work, the "want ad" is only made use of as a last resort.

Several men who have advertised for situations were interviewed, but not enough to form the foundation of a judgment as to the effectiveness of this means of getting employment. A great deal must depend upon the class of labor offered, the manner in which the advertisement is worded and the period at which it is printed. Some said that the only answers they had received to "Situations Wanted" advertisements were from employment agencies and from concerns wanting agents and canvassers. Others have received notifications to call which did not result in employment. A few had been successful in obtaining work by this means. As in the case of men who depend upon answering the "Help Wanted" advertisements, success must inevitably depend largely upon the persistence, the personality and the capability of the applicant.

"WORLD" AND "HERALD" COMPARED.—Turning from Chart No. 3 to Nos. 1 and 2, it is interesting to note the different impressions as to the relative volume of supply and demand in the different classes of labor conveyed by these two charts.

In spite of the falling off in demand since October, 1907, the *World* shows a slight excess of demand in its grand total, 6,664 to 6,632; while the *Herald's* corresponding figures are 4,706 to 12,304. Thus, it is seen that the *Herald* is preferred as a medium by those with labor to sell, while more employers patronize the *World*. Clerks and servants figure most largely among the patrons of the *Herald's* "want ad" columns, while skilled labor and its employers take up nearly half of the *World's* "want ad" space. Unskilled labor advertises almost equally in both newspapers, but finds more than twice as many jobs waiting for it in the *World*.

The arrangement and classification of "want ads" is much better managed in the *World* than in the *Herald*. In the former, it is easy to find what you are looking for, if it is there. In the latter, it is necessary to read carefully every advertisement to be sure you have not missed what you may be searching for. Other comparisons and reflections thereon might be made; but it has been the aim only to point out the most significant differences between the two newspapers as labor clearing houses.

VOICELESS INCOMPETENTS.—One reflection demands expression before closing. It is on the pitiful inability of many of those seeking work to say so in a way likely to bring it. There will be dozens of them together, especially under the heads of "clerical" and "unskilled labor," that are worded almost identically, and so as to repel rather than to attract inquiry on the part of possible employers. Willingness "to do anything," which so many advertisements proclaim, inevitably creates the impression of ability to do nothing worth mentioning. Perhaps some such inferential incompetents obtain work through advertising their putative incapacity; but it would seem as if in most instances they were simply giving their money to the newspapers without possibility of return.

EXTRACT FROM LETTER FROM MR. ARTHUR I. STREET,

Of Chicago, Editor of Street's "Pandex of the News."

I enclose herewith statement compiled from the Chicago *Tribune* and the Chicago *News*. The *News* carries no "Situations Wanted," but specializes on "Help Wanted." The *Tribune* is the only other considerable "want ad" medium in the city.

You will observe that I have taken somewhat different periods from those upon which Mr. Paine has been working in New York, but I made the change after going very carefully into the statistics of the different papers here. It appears, curiously enough, that 1906 was the biggest year in Chicago in classified advertising, also, in general, the maximum of want advertisements appears in April and the minimum in August. The judgment of the managers of the different papers was that you would get your best estimate of conditions by using these two months only, except in the case of November, 1907, when the effect of the panic was first felt.

I am cautioned against laying too much stress upon the indications of "Situations Wanted" advertisements. A large percentage of these is false, the columns being "stuffed;" also a considerable variation in the aggregate is made according to the variations in price asked by the papers. When a newspaper wishes to make a special run on want advertisements it cuts the price per line.

While, of course, "Help Wanted" columns reflect more the demand for labor than advertisements for situations, they are a better guide to the extent to which want advertisements fill the function of a labor medium.

The manager of the Chicago *News* calls my attention to the fact that in the ten months ending October 31, 1908, his paper lost 1,564 columns of classified advertising as compared with the totals of 1907, and of this amount 1,510 columns represented "want ads."

December 1, 1908.

WANT ADVERTISEMENTS IN THE CHICAGO "TRIBUNE"

Class of Labor.		1902. Second Sunday in		1906. Second Sunday in		1907 to 1908. Second Sunday in			Total (Seven Sundays).
		April.	August.	April.	August.	November.	April.	November.	
Clerical	Situations wanted	154	96	158	104	167	134	165	978
	Help wanted	368	298	442	494	251	347	351	2,551
	More than one	13	10	11	10	12	....	6	62
Skilled	Situations wanted	51	38	55	36	60	65	54	359
	Help wanted	147	118	220	132	95	77	86	875
Unskilled	Situations wanted	27	16	65	53	53	76	59	349
	Help wanted	18	3	33	25	9	8	13	109
Domestic	Situations wanted	13	8	29	18	37	33	44	182
	Help wanted	8	8	11	15	8	12	9	71
Boys	Situations wanted	4	4	2	....	2	....	3	15
	Help wanted	94	49	123	48	35	14	29	392
Miscellaneous	Situations wanted	56	62	71	53	90	48	65	445
	Help wanted	137	110	114	108	45	64	62	640
All classes	Situations wanted	305	224	380	264	409	356	390	2,328
	Help wanted	785	596	954	832	455	522	556	4,700
Total number of advertisements		1,090	820	1,334	1,096	864	878	946	7,028

WANT ADVERTISEMENTS IN THE CHICAGO "NEWS" "HELP WANTED" ONLY

Class of Labor.		1902. Second Tuesday in		1906. Second Tuesday in		1907 to 1908. Second Tuesday in			Total (Seven Tuesdays).
		April.	August.	April.	August.	November.	April.	November.	
Clerical	One	56	50	96	89	44	62	52	449
	More than one	3	....	2	7	3	3	2	20
Skilled		324	256	389	325	131	208	166	1,799
Unskilled: more than one		12	13	13	17	5	5	7	72
Boys		95	62	106	69	43	26	28	429
Miscellaneous		142	112	139	122	56	46	37	654
Total		632	493	745	629	282	350	292	3,423

APPENDIX VII

Reports Prepared in the Bureau of Social Research of the New York School of Philanthropy

Under the Direction of Dr. R. C. McCrea

TRADE UNIONS AS EMPLOYMENT AGENCIES,
By Mr. E. E. Pratt

The first fact of importance which stands out from a general visiting and questioning of the trades unions and labor organizations in regard to methods used in finding work for their members, is, that their systems, if indeed they can be called systems, are exceedingly haphazard. Although many of the unions announce that this is their reason for existing, closer inquiry reveals the fact that they probably keep an out-of-work list or book, from which men are sent to any job which happens to be reported to the office of the union. This is the most common practice and serves very well in a rough way. In some cases the men who happen to be at the union headquarters are sent out in answer to calls for help; in other cases the men are taken in order from the list, or according to their fitness for the position which is to be filled. In some unions all the information given out in regard to employment to be had is placed on a blackboard and as many men as wish may respond to the notice. However, the better organized a trade may be, the more effectively it controls a particular craft or line of industry, the more effective are its methods in trade-union activity, the better organized is its system of providing employment. In those lines of trade in which working agreements are in force with employers, the employment of union men is usually obligatory, and when any employer wants a man, he must send to the union headquarters. Non-union men have in these trades no chance to secure a job.

Probably the most effective organizations in the city are the Pattern-makers, the Newspaper Pressmen and the Building Trades. The Newspaper Pressmen are 100 per cent. organized and control the employment of their members exclusively; if work is short, the organization puts some of its men on half time, in order to give some work to all, and if any increase in the force is necessary, the organization fills the vacancies by promoting its apprentices. The Pattern-makers and Building Trades are about 90 per cent. organized and are very effective; the former sends its members from city to city, when in search of work, at the union's expense; the latter sends men to other locals in other cities, at the expense of the local asking for the help, and any such calls which prove to be "fakes" are paid for at exactly the same rate as if the men went to work during the time they lost in response to such calls. From these very effective systems, the methods of the unions deteriorate rapidly, almost in the same proportion as their grasp upon the trade declines, until among the garment workers (whose organization does not by any means control their craft), where over-supply commonly exists, and where parasitic labor hovers on the margin of the labor supply, the means taken to assist members in securing employment are few indeed. The officers of most of the locals admitted that they could usually do but little, and that the men sought work wherever and in whatever way they could, and therefore could furnish no information as to the numbers supplied with work through the unions.

Unskilled labor is but slightly organized, and therefore could furnish little data for this inquiry. It is, of course, very difficult to say exactly what occupations may be classed as unskilled labor; such jobs as street-paving, lamp-lighting, and the needle trades being called crafts or trades. However, among those occupations which are generally regarded as unskilled, the greatest need for accurate and reliable employment intermediaries is felt most keenly.

Any group of persons attempting to start an employment agency will need, I believe, in order to secure the support of the trades unions, to keep their hands strictly out of labor disputes, and never furnish or encourage men to work in shops where the full union standard is not openly or tacitly admitted to exist. The unions are, as a rule, not at all opposed to such a scheme as I could outline, *i. e.*, a central labor exchange, with branches perhaps in many cities. The well organized trades usually were of the opinion that no such agency was needed, at least in their own crafts, but were perfectly willing to coöperate in a friendly manner. Those trades which were less well organized were many of them fearful lest such an agency would furnish scab labor or, if not actually strike-breaking labor, men who would be willing to work under conditions inferior to those demanded by the union, which they maintain would weaken trade-union organizations. In the majority of cases, the business agents or the secretaries would not commit themselves upon the proposition, but were evidently willing to coöperate so long as such an agency did not interfere with trade-union activities. The unions of workers not so well organized (particularly the garment workers which in all its branches controls, according to the statements of its officers, about eighty-five thousand members in Greater New York, United Hebrew Trades 50,000, United Garment Workers 35,000; there are 237,648 persons employed in the clothing and allied trades in New York City, according to the report of the State Bureau of Factory Inspection, 1906) are willing to coöperate in any way with such an employment agency. Of course, the entire non-unionized field, largely the unskilled workers, does not come within the scope of these statements, and would probably be most largely benefitted by any scheme of philanthropic employment agencies.

In a very few cases, usually among the loosely organized trades, the unions sometimes found or gave employment to non-union members, sometimes with the pledge of joining the organization and sometimes without any such avowed intention; these were, however, sporadic cases, The better organized unions find employment only for their own members.

Again, in the matter of conditions under which men are allowed by union rules to work, those unions which control or nearly control their trades, allow men to work only under agreements with employers, or in recognized union shops; while in the less effectively organized unions the members are allowed to work wherever they please so long as they receive the union wages; in still other unions, such as the garment workers, wherever they are able to secure employment. There was a noticeable relaxing of union restrictions during the recent industrial depression.

In the international and national organizations there were usually some methods, more or less effectively organized, for disseminating information as to conditions of the trade in different sections of the country. This information may be sent out through the organization periodical, or it may only be circulated through the correspondence of the secretary. In some cases men are sent out of the city, in others they are brought into the city, and often both means are employed; traveling cards are provided by some unions, while others simply give a transfer to the particular union to which a member may be directing his course.

There are no exact data available as to the number of positions reported, the number of applicants, or the number of positions actually filled. This is due to a number of causes: (1) accurate records are not kept; (2) the men return frequently for work and several positions may be found for one man in the course of a year; (3) men sent out to accept the positions do not report; (4) out-of-work lists are kept, but the names are crossed off, whether the men receive positions through the agency of the union or by their own efforts; (5) lists of positions reported vacant are not kept.

The inclination to move about from city to city varies greatly in the different unions, some unions reporting that their men leave the city quite readily, while others report that their members very rarely leave New York City. The building industry exhibited in this respect the greatest mobility, while the garment workers and mechanical occupations are the least mobile. The printers seem to stand between the others.

It seems to be the opinion of the union leaders with whom I have talked, that the greatest need for an employment agency is between different cities, an agency which would be able to say exactly what the state of employment is in the various labor centers, and to place men where they are needed. Some of the secretaries and delegates received this suggestion with some degree of enthusiasm and were willing to give support to an agency doing such work. Most of the union officials seemed to realize their own inefficiency in this regard.

The organizations visited in this inquiry do not, by any means, include all the unions in the city of New York; it was necessarily limited to those which had offices, or headquarters, open during the day. The great numbers that had periodical meetings only, could not be visited. A list of the unions to be interviewed was made and classified according to localities, in order to economize time; they were then visited in order as the convenience of their location indicated; information was secured from the officials who were in the office; if there was no one there, none was secured from that particluar union. A second visit was made to a union only in case of a large and prominent organization whose opinion was especially desirable as representing a large body of organized labor, or a particular class of labor.

It seems, then, from the unions visited (some thirty, selected thus quite at random from all the trades, and representing, perhaps, a very large percentage of unionized labor in the city) that even for unionized trades and occupations an inter-city employment agency would be exceedingly useful; that in the less strongly organized labor groups within the city itself, a general employment agency would be able to place a large number of unemployed, and to adjust the labor supply to demands in the labor market to a considerable degree. Its functions would be, in some directions, restricted to gathering information as to where work was slack and where there was need for men. It would be quite necessary, I believe, to coöperate with the unions in some very intimate way, or their opposition might prove a serious handicap.

The chief facts shown by this inquiry may thus be summarized:

1. That while employment is taken care of reasonably well within the trade by the better organized and stronger unions, the weaker and less efficient do not meet the needs of the situation.

2. That in most of the unions, whether well or poorly organized, little is done toward the adjustment of labor supply as between different localities. In this field the agency would be most effective.

3. That the trade unions will be very favorable to a General Employment Exchange so long as it does not interfere with union activities.

NOTES OF INTERVIEWS WITH TRADE UNION OFFICIALS,

By Mr. E. E. Pratt

The following information was gathered in an inquiry relating to the efficiency of trade-union methods in finding employment for their members; in other words, the object was to find out how far the union organizations acted as employment agencies. The inquiry also aimed to find out what the attitude of the unions would be toward a General Employment Bureau. The attitude of the officers interviewed has not been put down, since such statements as they made were purely of personal opinion and not of trade union policy; and since all the other statements below are of actual facts, the attitude of the union can be better and more fairly summarized.

In not a single instance was opposition manifest; in all cases the proposition to establish a General Philanthropic Employment Bureau met with approval, although in some cases a qualified approval. The qualification usually had to do with a suspected danger to trade-union policies or activities, and in fact approval in every case was given with either the stated or the implied qualification that such an agency should act in harmony, at least, with organized labor and its program. In some of the unions which completely controlled their trades, or were very efficient in the administration of their employment features, such an agency was held to be unnecessary in their particular trades.

In the following summary, membership refers to Greater New York and its immediate vicinity. The membership in the international union is given in case of such a union being strongly organized. No assistance is given to non-members unless specified. Unless so stated, its members are not sent out of the city nor are any expenses paid.

I. BUILDING TRADES COUNCIL; membership 115,000. This organization is the Central Federation of the Building Trades in Greater New York. The trade is very completely organized. The council controls the building trades in all their branches and only a very few non-union contractors are to be found in the city. Whenever a contractor is in need of men he sends directly to the secretary at the central office, who refers the request to the particular trade which will be able to send the men to fill the position. A very strict system is maintained as to the applications for men to take positions, and for the employers to take men sent. For example, if an employer telephones for a man, one is sent to him and if, when that man has reached the particular address given, another man is found at work and the man sent from the central office is not needed, the latter receives a day's pay, whether he has worked or not. An efficient system of interchange of information between cities is maintained through a weekly paper of the building trades, and through the correspondence of the secretary. The transfer of workmen from city to city is accomplished in the following manner: If more men are wanted in the building trades in New York City than can be supplied within the city, a call is immediately sent to Philadelphia, as the nearest and most convenient city, and then if the surplus supply of men is not sufficient to meet the demand, calls are sent to Boston, Pittsburgh, Chicago, and even further. The association asking for men pays the traveling expenses. If, for example, a Pittsburgh union asks for 50 men from New York and only 40 receive work, the other ten receive their traveling expenses and are paid for their time at the expense of the organization which asked for them. This precludes any fake notice of employment. The building trades are very well organized and have one of the most efficient systems of finding employment and disseminating information which was found. The secretary feels that the building trades are sufficiently well covered in the matter of employment agencies.

II. AMALGAMATED SOCIETY OF PAINTERS AND PAPER HANGERS; 926 Third Avenue; 646 Eighth Avenue; membership 10,000, United States, 75,000. This union controls about 60 per cent. of the trade in New York City. The men are allowed to find work wherever they can, providing the union rate is enforced. This association maintains perhaps the largest meeting rooms and headquarters in the city. The secretary keeps an out-of-work list. Notices are sent out by the general secretary informing employers that the union is ready to furnish all help required. Employers send word when necessary and men are furnished. The system is evidently a very loose one and the secretary himself states that the men do most of the searching for work themselves. The notifications of help wanted are sometimes sent to the secretary of the Building Trades Council, who then notifies the union. About 10 per cent. of the men, during an ordinary year, get their employment through the union. Men are sent to other cities in answer to requests from employers, the latter paying the expenses. During the past year about 2,000 men have come to New York from other cities.

III. THE CARPENTERS' DISTRICT COUNCIL, 142 East Fifty-ninth Street; membership, 15,000 to 18,000, United States, 246,000. This organization controls about 90 per cent. of the trade in Greater New York. The union has affiliations in other cities and sends men out of the city or brings them in, according to the demand. If more work is needed in one city than can be supplied from the membership in that city, calls are sent to nearby cities. No traveling expenses are paid. The carpenters publish a weekly bulletin which reports the condition of business and employment in every city in the country. This gives the members accurate information as to where there is a probability of work so that they can go where the need is greatest. Members do this, however, on their own responsibility. The membership is somewhat restricted; the initiation fee is $20, a man must prove his ability as a carpenter before an examining board, and only citizens are accepted for membership. In Greater New York the union employs seventeen business agents who are thoroughly conversant with the condition of the trade employment throughout the city and vicinity, and furnish jobs whenever possible. The system of finding work in the carpenters' organization is rather loose. A blackboard is kept at the central office on which the addresses and names of employers wanting men are posted. The men come to the assembly rooms, which are large and where the members gather from day to day, and from which they go out in search for work. They do not report at the office and it is impossible to keep any record of those who find positions by this means, nor is any record kept of the positions reported. The business agents also report at the union meetings, held once a week, as to the vacancies in various parts of the city. During the last year (September 1907 to September 1908) about 3,000 men migrated from New York City.

IV. ELEVATOR CONSTRUCTION AND MILL OPERATORS, 154

East Fifty-fourth Street; membership, 900. The secretary keeps an out-of-work list, which is filled in regular order, unless one man is especially ill adapted for a position. This organization thoroughly controls its craft. The membership of the union is restricted and a thorough examination before a board of examiners is required before men are admitted to membership. Although a record is kept of the number finding employment through the union, this record is very unreliable because many men remain but a short time on a particular job; the men sent out by the office with the addresses of vacancies do not report whether or not they receive the positions. The union is an international organization, with affiliations in other cities. Members are supplied with traveling cards in order to enable them to find employment in various cities. Expenses are never paid. Members are allowed to work only under union agreements.

V. NEW YORK NEWSPAPER PRESSMEN, 74 Lafayette Street; membership 900, United States, 25,000. This union controls the entire trade and is probably one of the best organized in the city. An out-of-work list, properly speaking, is not kept, for whenever a man is unemployed he is put immediately at work, through a very efficient regulation of the members in their respective jobs, conducted by the union. If work becomes slack, the men who retain their positions work fewer days a week and the unemployed members are given the surplus which is caused by this curtailing of work on the part of the rest. If the number of men required increases, the supply is not enlarged from other cities but apprentices are immediately promoted to furnish the additional supply of workers. The Newspaper Pressmen have worked out a co-operative system of employment which effectively does away with unemployment.

VI. LITHOGRAPHERS' APPRENTICES AND PRESS FEEDERS, 41 Centre Street; membership, 500. An out-of-work list is kept and employers needing men immediately report vacancies to the secretary's office. Report of slack work is sent from city to city, but no regular bulletin giving the state of employment in the city is published. An initiation fee of $10 is charged and two years' apprenticeship is necessary for membership together with a special examination before a committee. The attitude of the union is favorable toward an employment agency.

VII. TYPOGRAPHICAL UNION, known as "Big Six," 74 Lafayette Street; membership in this particular union 7,000, total membership in New York 8,000, membership in United States 45,000. About 90 per cent. of the craft in New York City is organized. A list is kept of men out-of-work and the union acts as its own employment agency, furnishing work to its members, information of which is sent in by foremen and proprietors, all shops being under a working agreement. The international union furnishes information as to the state of employment in the different cities. About 100 traveling cards, which indicate the number of men usually out of work or traveling between cities, pass through the New York office every month. Information which these men gather in their travels from city to city, spreads among the members at the union meetings and forms the basis of their information as to the state of work in other cities. No traveling expenses are paid. The initiation fee is $5, otherwise membership is not restrictive. The men are allowed to work only in union shops. There are two classes of shops only, union and non-union. Union shops are those which work under an agreement with the union and under union conditions; the non-union, where members are not allowed to work, have no relations at all with the union.

VIII. NEW YORK STEREOTYPERS; membership, Locals 1 and 100, 865, membership in United States 3,500. About 90 per cent. of the trade in the city is controlled. A list of the unemployed members is kept and foremen and proprietors give information as to any vacancies. The foremen act as intermediaries between employers and the union, being members of the union and representatives of the employers. About 10 per cent. of the membership left the city during the recent industrial depression, while ordinarily many more may come to New York City than leave it. This is because a large proportion of this business is done in Greater New York. The initiation fee is $10, and an applicant must pass a satisfactory examination before an examining board. An international monthly journal is published which keeps the locals in different cities informed as to the conditions of employment. No expenses are paid when members leave the city.

IX. LITHOGRAPHERS' INTERNATIONAL UNION; membership 1,000. About 75 per cent. of the trade in the city is organized. Employers send directly to the secretary's office when in need of help. An out-of-work book is kept, and men are sent to the positions in order, as they appear on the book. The union occasionally pays expenses for men going out of town to secure work, but such aid is rather exceptional and usually takes the form of a loan from the union. Transfers are furnished by the secretary to any member leaving the city. There are no restrictions upon the membership other than that a man must be employed as a lithographer and have served an apprenticeship, be thoroughly familiar with the business and thoroughly competent to do the work. If there is any doubt about his ability, a test, before a committee appointed by the union, is required. The initiation fees are low, varying with the age of the man. No records are kept of the number of positions furnished to men during the year. Very few have left town in search of employment.

X. TYPE PRESS FEEDERS, 13 St. Mark's Place; membership 300. Notification of vacancies is sent to the union office and members who happen to be on hand are sent out in response. The method employed is very crude and no statistics of the number of vacancies reported or the number of men who found employment can be had. The initiation fee is $3.50, and the membership is limited to men over 18 who have had three years' experience in a printing establishment. The employment work here is very haphazard. Nothing is done outside the city nor are persons from outside the city given employment within.

XI. UNITED GARMENT WORKERS, International offices, Bible House, New York City, membership 35,000, United States 80,000. Each local has its separate arrangement for employment of the men and any calls which may be sent to the main office are referred to the individual locals, either in the different cities or in the particular lines of work. The garment workers, being an international union, are affiliated all over the country. They have succeeded in unionizing but a small proportion of the entire trade, but that portion is well organized and under very strict supervision by the international office. According to the secretary very few garment workers left New York during the recent depression: (1) because the trade is so largely concentrated in New York City, (2) because the Jews, who largely predominate, are not apt to move from place to place. The secretary believes that an Employment Bureau which would disseminate information as to the state of trade in many different cities, and would transport workmen from one city to another would be very valuable. Men often will not leave New York City because so many of them have been disappointed by false reports of work; if such an agency could insure against loss through a move to another city, it would be of inestimable help to the entire trade. Membership in the garment workers is not restricted; their initiation fee is, by constitution, limited to $5, and in a large majority of the locals it is less than that amount.

XII. THE CUTTERS' UNION, 41 Waverly Place; membership 3,000, United States 7,000; a local of the United Garment Workers. The union keeps a list of the men out-of-work and positions are found through the information of employers or members, who keep the secretary informed as to the state of employment in the different manufacturing establishments. Men are allowed to work wherever they can find employment, the only restriction being that they shall work in establishments where the salary is fair and which have minimum union conditions. The Cutters' Union endeavors to keep the quality of work done by its members up to such a standard that if an employer wishes the best help he must send to the union for it. The secretary is very favorable toward any movement which will attempt to provide men with employment so long as it is not directly in opposition to union policies and so long as it would coöperate with organized labor.

XIII. SHIRT MAKERS' UNION, 201 Broome Street; membership 800. One of the loosely organized garment working unions. Men are allowed to search for and obtain employment wherever they can. A list of places in which vacancies are reported is kept in the secretary's office; members who are out of work come to the secretary and are given the names of places where they are apt to find employment. Information as to where work may be found is furnished either by members or employers. Members are not sent out of the city to find employment. The initiation fee is $1; dues 40 cents a month, although at present they are fifteen cents a week, owing to the relief benefit being given. In 1907 this union had a membership of 1,600 which has fallen during the past year to 800,—500 men and 300 women; only half of this number are working in what may be called union shops.

XIV. TAILORS' UNION, 269 Broome Street; membership, 1,000; a local union of the United Garment Workers. An out-of-work list is kept by the secretary, and when the employers send in for men they are sent out in order. The union does not send men out of New York, nor are expenses of any kind paid. Just at present 25 per cent. of the membership is idle, but in spite of the depression in trade membership is increasing. The union attempts to find work for members and non-members. Employment may be found not only in union shops but also in open shops, and this union, like others in the garment trade, has very poor control of the labor market in its particular sphere.

XX. JACKET MAKERS, 437 Grand Street; membership 400, and affiliated with the United Garment Workers, controls about 40 per cent. of the trade. Men who are out of work leave their names with the secretary and are sent to employers who apply to the union. Employment is sometimes furnished for people outside the city and occasionally men go outside, which is not, however, a part of the union's scheme of finding employment for its members. The initiation fee is $5, weekly dues, fifteen cents.

XXI. UNITED HEBREW TRADES, 133 Eldridge Street; membership 50,000. This is a federated union of the various Hebrew trades, composed in all of about sixty subordinate organizations. Every local union in the organization acts as a bureau of employment. Any calls for help which may be sent to the central office are referred to the particular local which handles that trade or class of business. Secretaries of the local unions receive applications from members, and from employers. Men are never sent out of the city and the organization never brings men into the city as a union affair. The restrictions as to open or closed shops are loose, members being allowed to work wherever they can find a position. They would also, if occasion demanded, get positions for non-union men. This organization is the large central body for the Hebrew Trades, a sort of loosely organized federation, which handles the affairs of a large number of individual unions in a rather general way, giving advice and counsel to individual locals. The United Hebrew Trades does not by any means control the business, which is largely garment making, clothing manufacturing, and, therefore, is not very powerful; neither is the system of securing employment for members systematized or efficient.

XXII. KNEE-PANTS MAKERS, 133 Eldridge Street; membership 1,500. A local affiliated with the United Hebrew Trades. Men out of work apply to the secretary who keeps a list of the positions which are available and a list of members out of work, from which men are taken in order. Men are allowed to work wherever they can obtain employment, except "scab" shops or where strikes are in progress. The uinon is not strict as to wages or union conditions. This union is loosely organized, evidently with very little control over the trade. It not only supplies its members but also non-members with positions, in order to encourage the latter to become members. Sometimes men leave the city; it has never happened that any have come in and found positions through the help of the unions. Membership is in no way restricted; the initiation fee is $1.48 and the monthly dues forty cents.

XXIII. CHILDREN'S JACKETS (NON-BASTED) ORGANIZATION, 436 Grand Street; membership 1,200, affiliated with the United Hebrew Trades. Employers send to the secretary for men, and are put in touch with men who are out of work. The addresses of employers who wish men are kept on a blackboard in the meeting rooms. There is no affiliation outside New York City, nor are men sent from or brought into the city. Under ordinary circumstances the members of the union are allowed to work only in closed shops; in a season like the present they are allowed to work wherever they can get employment, which is at best very difficult. The initiation fee is five dollars, monthly dues thirty-five cents.

XXIV. THE INTERNATIONAL LADIES' GARMENT WORKERS, 25 Third Avenue; membership New York City 4,000, United States 8,000. Methods of finding employment for members out of work are as follows: (1) at union meetings the men tell one another of positions open which may be obtained; (2) the chairman, before calling the meeting to order, asks for information as to any positions which are open; (3) the business agents employed by the union incidentally receive information of vacancies and place men; (4) members come to the office for information which is obtainable from the secretary, employers having left notice of any vacancies in their shops. The secretary believes that employment agencies, so far as skilled employment is concerned, are frauds and fakes. There is no interchange of information between cities, and men are not sent from one city to another.

XXV. PATTERN MAKERS' ASSOCIATION, 192 Bowery; membership New York City and vicinity within a radius of 100 miles 1,000, United States 7,000. Men out of work sign the out-of-work book; the employers send to the secretary, and a man is sent by the central office immediately. The secretary allows no loafing around the office, and when a man has once signed the out-of-work book he need go to the office no longer, but when a position is found for him a telegram or a message, at the expense of the Association, is sent him. The union belongs to the National Brotherhood and is affiliated with other cities. Transportation expenses are paid for men going to take jobs in other cities and likewise for men coming into New York City. The union is composed of highly skilled men and it is their aim to control the very best men in the occupation. A few years ago this union was discredited by employers, but it has since changed its mode of action and today it succeeds in entirely controlling the pattern making trade by having a monopoly of the best men in it. If an employer wishes a good pattern maker he must send to the Pattern Makers' Association. The initiation fee is $16.50. From December 14, 1907, to July 18, 1908, the national association spent $3,300 in out-of-work benefits, at a rate of $5.50 a week per unemployed member. The weekly dues are at present $1.50, ordinarily fifty cents. This union has one of the best organized systems of any of those visited, controlling the entire trade, furnishing employment for its members, on thoroughly friendly terms with employers, and discouraging all strikes.

XXVI. THE SHEET METAL WORKERS, 25 Third Avenue; membership in New York City 2,500. This is a local of the International Metal Workers, head office Kansas City, Mo. This union has no regularly organized method of employment work, but when the secretary is notified of positions open, a notice with the address of the employer is put on the blackboard which is hung up in the union rooms; members come in and look at the blackboard, and go out to search for employment. No record is kept either of the number of vacancies reported or of the number of positions filled. This information is only for union men. Traveling cards are furnished which enable men to go from city to city and obtain what employment there is. The union employs four business agents who, in visiting the trade in different parts of Greater New York and vicinity, keep a list of the positions which are open and also the men who are out of work, and act as intermediaries in finding employment for those out of work.

XXVII. PORTABLE ENGINEERS, 154 East Fifty-fourth Street; membership 900. International affiliations. A system of reciprocal intelligence is maintained between different cities of the country and business agents are employed to look after the interests of the men and supply positions for the unemployed. Each business agent keeps a list of those men who are out of work and the employers either speak to the business agent or send word to the secretary when men are needed. This trade is very well organized and controls its craft in New York City. Traveling expenses are not paid from city to city. The members are allowed to take employment only under the union agreement.

XXVIII. THE INTERNATIONAL ASSOCIATION OF MACHINISTS, 23 Park Row; membership 8000, membership United States 100,000. The union controls about 90 per cent of the craft. The machinists keep an out-of-work book and the members bring information of positions vacant; the secretary sends men out in order as they appear on the list. Monthly reports are received from various locals throughout the country, but there is no regular system of publishing these reports. During the last year about 800 of the members in New York City left town. There is no reliable data as to the number of positions filled or the number of applications for men which have been made. The members are allowed to work both in open and closed shops. A committee examines applicants for membership. The initiation fee is $5. The policy of the union is not restrictive.

XXIX. FIREMEN'S UNION, 193 Bowery; membership, 3,000. This trade is not very well organized and controls only about half of the craft in New York City. An out-of-work list is kept. Engineers and superintendents send directly to the secretary, who sends men out, in order, as they appear on the list. Members leave the city occasionally; transportation expenses are occasionally advanced by the union as a loan. An initiation fee of $5 is charged, membership being in no other way restricted. The firemen are not inclined to travel from one city to another. During the year 1907 between 2,800 and 2,900 men got positions through this office. The secretary is very suspicious of any attempt on the part of an employment agency to secure work for its unemployed because he feels that it would be detrimental to the interests of the union in that men would be supplied with positions and allowed to work at terms and under conditions lower than those of the union and thus disintegrate the union. He would, however, be favorable if active cooperation with the union is anticipated.

XXX. THE ACTORS' PROTECTIVE ASSOCIATION, 8 Union Square; membership 1,100. This association is really an employment agency, licensed as such in the name of the business agent. The union not only finds employment for its members but also arranges bills or theatrical programs for various entertainments throughout the city. The membership extends to actors throughout the country. When persons are out of a job they apply to the office, which supplies them with work. This is the only theatrical or actors' union. During the past year about six hundred people have been furnished employment. No positions reported to them have gone unfilled. Positions are generally restricted to those who belong to the association, but the policy is a very liberal one and outsiders are taken in whenever application is made. The association belongs to the American Federation of Labor.

XXXI. THE PAVERS' UNION, 25 Third Avenue; membership, New York City and vicinity within a radius of 50 miles 3,000, United States 10,000. This union, which controls the trade to a very large extent, furnishes employment for all of its members; that is, whenever a contractor wishes an employee he sends to the secretary at the central office, who sends him any man who may be out of work. The union sends men out of New York City and finds work in the city for men from other places. The business agents take care of unemployment within a radius of fifty miles from City Hall. All long distance employment, *i. e.*, work that is reported from other cities, is done through the central office in New York City. The work is considered a skilled occupation and cannot be handled by unskilled individuals. There are fourteen locals in New York City, each taking care of its own unemployed so far as possible. There are four business agents in New York City. Initiation fees range from $25 to $50, according to the work done. This system of employment seems to be entirely adequate.

XXXII. THE ASPHALT-PAVERS' UNION, 154 East Fifty-fourth Street; membership about 400. All available work is controlled by the union, and all applications for jobs must be made directly to the secretary, who controls the working agreements which are in force with all contractors. Membership in the union is not restricted, but the applicant must satisfy the secretary or the business agent that he is qualified to do the work. About 50 per cent of the membership is Italian. About 10 per cent of the members left New York during the recent depression.

XXXIII. CIGAR MAKERS' UNION, 192 Bowery; local membership 1,500, in the cigar trade in the United States 44,000, in New York city 6,200 to 6,300. This is a local of the International Order of Cigar Makers. The union supplies employees not only to closed shops but also to open shops if union scales are paid. Reports of vacancies are sent to the secretary by employers or by members who may have been informed of jobs in their shop. Information as to the state of employment in the various cities is sent from local to local, but the system as a whole is inefficient and does not meet the needs of the situation.

XXXIV. THE LIBERTY DAWN, 145 East Fifty-third Street; membership 2,000, in United States 50,000. The union organization has been for the last seven years the only employment agency in this rather miscellaneous occupation, hackmen and drivers, who compose the union. It is well organized, and men are not brought to the city or sent to other localities if those out of work can be helped. In that way they control the occupations named to a large degree, but the benefits of the association are confined to union members. The initiation fee is $25. For six years prior to and including 1907, up to May or June, on an average of two hundred men a year have been provided with employment.

XXXV. BARTENDERS' UNION, 145 East Fifty-third Street; membership 2700, United States 185,000. The union controls about 50 per cent of this trade in the city and has working agreements with most of the establishments. Men are allowed to work wherever they can find employment, but preferably in establishments under agreement. An out-of-work list is kept at the secreatry's office and calls for men are sent directly to him and filled in order from the list. Membership in the union is restricted. The bartenders are not strongly organized and the employment feature is comparatively unimportant.

XXXVI. EAST SIDE WAITERS' UNION, 12 St. Mark's Place; membership New York city 500. An out-of-work list is kept by the secretary. The union furnishes the men with traveling cards, and as the union is affiliated throughout the country, men are often transferred from one city to another. The union does not pay transportation expenses. About fifty men have left town during the last year on account of the depression.

XXXVII. INTERNATIONAL BROTHERHOOD OF BOOKBINDERS, 132 Nassau Street; membership 2000 men, 1000 women; international membership 12,000. About 80 per cent. of the bookbinding craft in New York City is controlled by the union. Each local acts as an employment agency for its particular city or its particular line of employment. They keep a list of the members out of work and the first man on the list is sent in response to any reports brought in as to vacant positions which are given by members and employers. Through the international secretary information is sent from one local to another, giving the state of employment in different cities. Members have not left town during the past year to any extent owing to the fact that employment in other cities was as depressed as in New York. No records are kept of the number of persons securing employment through the union, while the secretary himself designates the system as "a haphazard affair." The bookbinders work under an agreement with the employers but they are not restricted to union shops. Membership is not restricted and any one employed as a bookbinder is eligible for membership. An initiation fee of $25 is charged.

XXXVIII. THE BREWERS' UNION, 193 Bowery; membership 4500, United States 44,000. About 98 per cent of the trade is organized. The Brewers' Union maintains a regular labor bureau for its members to which employers may send and demand help at any time. A very strict working agreement is enforced between the owners of establishments and the Brewers' Union, which enables the organization to completely control all help used in the breweries of Greater New York. This union is affiliated with the International Union and men leave the city when there is news of work elsewhere, but expenses are not paid. Members are allowed to work only in union shops. The initiation fee is $10, but there are no other restrictions. Very few of the men are ever out of work on account of the complete organization which obtains in the trade. During the past year about 200 men received work directly through the agency of the union.

XXXIX. THE BEEF AND MEAT DRIVERS; membership 200. Controls about 80 per cent. of the trade. The secretary keeps an out-of-work list and tries to secure the men positions. Notifications of work are sent to different cities but expenses are not paid. Men are allowed to work wherever they can find positions and no agreements are made with the employers. The union is evidently rather weak and depends for what strength it has upon the disagreeable and difficult nature of the work.

ATTITUDE OF EMPLOYERS TOWARD GENERAL EMPLOYMENT BUREAU,

By Mr. E. E. Pratt

It is rather difficult to make progress with employers of labor in an inquiry as to their attitude toward a general employment bureau, for several reasons: I experienced more or less difficulty in finding the officer who had the authority to control the policy of hiring men; the officers in authority did not, in many cases, actually hire the men and were not conversant with the actual difficulties,—frequently this function is parcelled out to the heads of departments, the superintendents of the factories usually have charge of the manual labor. In the case of large corporations, especially, was the hiring of the various classes of labor divided among many officials. The chief officers were usually favorably impressed with such a plan as that of a general labor exchange; their part in the hiring of men had to do, however, only with a small amount of clerical help in the New York offices of the company. All the manual or day labor is hired at the various factories, and as it is usually exclusively in the hands of the local superintendent such questions very seldom come to the notice of the heads of corporations or companies in the New York offices. I also found that firms located wholly in New York City, both offices and manufacturing, were inclined to treat such a proposition much more lightly than those having manufacturing plants located at some distance from the city or in the West.

Data secured in connection with another study, The Industrial Causes of Congestion in New York City, which involved a study of factories removing from New York City, show very clearly that one of the chief advantages found by manufacturers in the city is the large and abundant labor supply, not only unskilled but skilled as well. In fact, the firms which have moved from New York City to other parts of the country, and have returned here after trying to carry on a manufacturing business in a smaller center, are those which employ the most skilled labor. This would seem to indicate that the unskilled labor is content to go to the small manufacturing centers, while the most skilled labor, at least in certain lines, finds a location in New York City preeminently advantageous.

Firms with plants at various points throughout the country, especially in the West, seem very favorable to such a Bureau. The particular conditions existing at present make it rather difficult to approach an employer on this point, since such a Bureau seems quite removed from his present necessity on account of the large over-supply of labor. Many practical men are not in sympathy with any scheme the object of which is to furnish the unemployed with work or to assist them in finding it. Some brand such an enterprise as paternalistic; others say that it is an attempt to make money or to exploit the poor; others that it is unnecessary; still others that labor which cannot help itself should not be helped. But most of the men interviewed admit, after the entire situation is explained, that the opportunity exists for such an institution to do great good.

Usually the firm interviewed stated that, when the Bureau as described had a definite proposition to make it would then be considered. Others stated outright that they would be glad to coöperate with our Bureau in securing labor. In very few cases did the proposition to charge the employer a fee meet with approval. This was due, perhaps, to the fact that most of them experience very little difficulty in getting all the labor necessary. Representatives of some of the out-of-town manufacturers were, however, favorable to such a scheme of fees for services rendered. That is, manufacturers believe that if such an employment agency would relieve them of the necessity of advertising, and furnish them with help with speed and expedition, thus saving them the cost of advertising and delay, they would be willing to turn a part of this saving over to a Bureau in the shape of a fee.

A tentative proposition that an agreement should be entered into between the various manufacturers and the Employment Agency to keep the employers supplied with men at a certain rate per hundred of employees, met with approval on two or three occasions when it was proposed.

I found it very difficult to get at the proper railroad official who was at the same time sufficiently acquainted with the details to give any advice, and also had authority enough to give his opinion weight. The actual employing of the very unskilled labor is usually in the hands of the division authorities, either the division superintendent or engineer. At present the lowest grades of help are managed on the padrone system. That is, the labor is supplied by agents who not only manage and control the laborers while at work, but also keep stores and boarding houses and supply native foremen. Large numbers of these men are Italians who work for $1 or $1.25 a day and live in box cars which are provided free of charge. They buy provisions from the men who hire them (the agents or padrones) at a cost of from $1 to $1.50 a week. Shoes and other clothing are sold to them at very low prices. One superintendent with whom I talked, a man thoroughly in sympathy with this proposition, and one who says he has thought of a similar scheme for some time, pointed out the difficulties of supplying the railroads with the lower classes of labor. He spoke of the necessity for keeping to a single nationality on a particular job, the impossibility of mixing, for example, the Sicilian and the Neapolitan. But he declared that at any time an Employment Bureau such as I described could bring him as good a proposition as the Italian contractors, he would be willing to come to an agreement. Certain unskilled labor around the car yards, cleaning cars and various other low class jobs, could be turned over almost immediately to such an agency. These positions are very irregular and are held largely by Slavs. In one of the railroads there is suggestive evidence that the padrone system is in full operation, and that the officials in charge of the hiring of men hold a rather lucrative position in the matter. The officer interviewed was reluctant to give any information, but from the little he did say it was evident that the whole thing was managed through an outside agency which supplied all labor and that the railroad officials had all their dealings through this one man. They were unwilling to give out his name or allow me to see him. Another railroad official raised the point, when I mentioned a large private agency in the West, which has been very successful, that the western roads were in constant need of men but that the eastern roads, especially those entering New York City, were never in need of workmen and that usually they could get all the labor they need. One man anticipated a little difficulty in the near future if railroad improvements should commence, because large numbers of Italians have gone back to Italy, but on the other hand all that is necessary to get them again, and many more with them, is to give notice to the agents who handle this labor, and back they come. This seems to be a very neat device for getting around the contract labor law.

If then the proposed agency wishes to deal with the unskilled grades of labor, it will be necessary to organize in such a manner, and with a system so well worked out, that it can compete successfully with the padrone system. Italian officials and assistants will be indispensable, and the system will have to correspond closely to the present methods of the padrone. It seems doubtful, also, whether the eastern railroads will be willing to pay for this service, since they are evidently not paying for it now and are well satisfied. Very few opportunities are open, however, in the general railroading business outside of this general unskilled manual labor.

Coming to manufacturing establishments, The Standard Oil Company, with the free advertising which it constantly receives, declares that it can at all times get more labor than it needs. The general employment agent of that corporation was, however, very favorable and his long and large experience makes him a valuable ally. The labor in the plants is hired by the various superintendents and men are always referred to them for positions. Usually there is an over-supply. Other large, well-known companies probably have the same experience. With the less known establishments and those located at a distance from New York City, there seems to be very little doubt that a General Employment Agency would be effective and could with success charge the employers a fee. In one of two cases New York offices had been asked, during the busy season, to furnish as many as 300 men to be sent to out-of-town factories, and the labor could not be found. Many out-of-town employers make special arrangements for the transporting of prospective employees. Some will furnish tickets and then take the cost out of the employee's wages. Others simply withhold the sum of the transportation expense until the man has been in their employ long enough to insure reasonable permanency. The employers then pay for the transportation. With employers doing these things it ought to be very easy to strike satisfactory arrangements.

Perhaps a little more emphasis can be put upon the saving in advertising that a firm could effect through a general labor exchange, a part of which might be paid in fees to the Bureau. This advertising, according to one of the manufacturers' associations, sometimes amounts to a considerable item, and, furthermore, employers often find it necessary to send to quite distant localities for their labor supply, in which case it is usually necessary to forward traveling expenses.

The most important results of this inquiry then may thus be summarized:

1. That employers in the immediate vicinity of New York City do not find it difficult to secure all the labor necessary.

2. That employers outside of the largest cities (generalizing from New York's experience) do find it difficult to get labor, that they are at some expense to advertise and to furnish transportation expenses, and at some disadvantage from inability to look a man over and determine his qualifications; and that here a labor agency could find a wide field for the surplus of the city markets.

3. That the employers would receive such a proposition favorably and in a spirit of coöperation, even with a possibility of its being made a business proposition when it has once proved its real utility.

After considering the elements involved,—the labor supply, as represented by the trade unions and the unemployed, and the employers, the whole success of the enterprise will rest, in my opinion, on the coördination and coöperation of the factors, and, above all, in the most efficient, business-like, and far reaching organization.

NEW YORK MUNICIPAL LODGING HOUSE AND THE UNEMPLOYED IN NEW YORK CITY

By Mr. E. E. Pratt

The following facts and opinions were gathered and formulated in order to find out from those actively engaged in the work of handling the unemployed, what the character of the men who become the objects of charity in New York City really is, whether they would be benefitted by a general employment agency or labor exchange, and if such an agency would in any way alleviate unemployment as represented in the lodgers at the Municipal Lodging House. An endeavor also was made to find out through the Municipal Lodging House what is the status of the unemployed, at least in the men applying there.

Mr. Yorke, the superintendent of the Municipal Lodging House, when interviewed, was unwilling that any of his remarks should go beyond the immediate experience which he has had at the New York lodging house or be applied to any other class of unemployed than those whom he has himself met in their application to the city for shelter.

Unemployment in New York City is due to the congregation

here, especially during any time of depression, of the unemployed from other cities and the surrounding country. This is due in part only to the great crowd of foreigners always drifting in, since the men who apply to the lodging house for shelter are, in the majority of cases, Americans. The propositions of the principal nationalities, as given in the accompanying statistics, will show that the native Americans largely predominate. (See statistical tables attached.)

A leading cause for the concentration of the unemployed in New York City is the generally existing opinion, perhaps not unjustified, that if there is work anywhere it will be in the metropolis. Men who have tramped from city to city, from state to state hear of the great railways, subways, tunnels and buildings which New York is building, and think there should be work enough here and to spare. They even spend their last cent to come, and when no employment is forthcoming and they have walked the streets day after day until their money is spent, they turn up at the Municipal Lodging House.

When a man without employment gets "down and out" in New York City, it is pretty hard for him to get to any other place where he can find a job if there is an oversupply of labor in the city. There are often notices of men wanted in the West or in the North, or down South, but the railroad fare may be $10, it may be $25, and even then a man has no guarantee that he may not be spending his money on a fool's errand. If a man can secure a job in the North, in a cold climate, he cannot go unless he is properly clothed and shod, which many of the lodging house visitors are not. If the position offered is in the South, usually poor clothing is no excuse. It is very difficult to get a man out of New York City after he has once become entirely dependent.

It is in this respect that a generally organized employment bureau, with sub-stations throughout the country from and to which laborers might be sent, would greatly relieve the situation and assist in adjusting the supply of labor throughout the country.

Of course the men who generally go to the Municipal Lodging House would be unable to pay a fee and it would be quite impossible for them to raise money for transportation or clothes. The supplying, then, of these latter things would be quite as important as finding the job at some distant point. Could these men be expected ever to refund the money spent in their behalf? Mr. Yorke believes that in a large number of cases they could. In this matter he speaks from experience, not in loaning large amounts, but small sums which he declares are invariably returned to him after the man has been working a few weeks. These loans are not made promiscuously, but advanced to men who have found jobs and haven't money enough to pay for carfare, room-rent and meals in the meantime.

It is just at this point that a very interesting part of Mr. Yorke's work for the unemployed comes in. A lodger finds a job, but he is "broke" and pay day is usually two weeks in the future. What in the meantime? The man must have food and a place to sleep. When such a situation arises, Mr. Yorke allows the man to stay at the lodging house and get his meals there, provides him with a little lunch, and advances him carfare. Then for two weeks he is in the city's home, but in these two weeks he is put on his feet. A case in point happened as I sat in the office. A woman who had lodged at the house for several nights came in and reported that she had secured a position as laundress at $20 a month, but that the work didn't begin until the following Tuesday (this was Friday) and she would not be paid until a week from that time. What was she to do meanwhile? The superintendent told her that she might remain at the lodging house until she drew her first pay and, just here, he points out, there will be a weakness in any scheme for the employment of those out of work. He suggests that this be taken into consideration in the formation of a plan for a general Employment Bureau.

Many of the men appearing at the Municipal Lodging House have cards from employment agencies and evidently have had dealings with them. Some of them, Mr. Yorke believes, are doing a good business, but on a small scale; others are totally bad. He gave a recent instance of men sent north on railroad work. Many men went, but some who have drifted back to the Municipal Lodging House report conditions inferior to those in which a horse could live. Too often this is the case with jobs out of the city.

Many of the men do not want steady jobs, while others who do want jobs, don't know where to go and are unable to go very great distances for lack of carfare. Many men keep watch constantly of the want columns in the newspapers, but their experiences are always the same,—someone has been there ahead of them and they became discouraged and disgusted with newspaper advertisements.

Most of the lodgers in the house are unskilled; between 30 and 40 per cent. of those lodged report as skilled; usually less than 10 per cent. return themselves as clerical.

From a casual inspection of the record books of the lodging house, it is evident that the men often change their occupations. One of the questions asked each man is, what is your occupation? After answering, he is asked where and in what capacity he was last employed. In many cases a mechanic skilled in some trade would return another occupation as that last worked at. This occupational mobility did not appear to be great, but that some existed there can be do doubt. The applicant is asked the name of his last employer, who serves as a reference. A blank (see page 190) is then sent to the lodger's former employer. The answers on these blanks bring, when filled out, some very interesting information upon the character of the applicants.

The accompanying statistics show that a very small proportion of the lodgers give no references. In some cases this means that the lodger is actually unable to do so, that he is an old man, or, in some cases, an applicant for the almshouse, of whom references are not required. There is, however, no doubt that a large proportion of the men are unwilling to have it found out that they have found it necessary to ask for a night's lodging.

No. 28000

DEPARTMENT OF PUBLIC CHARITIES
OF THE CITY OF NEW YORK.

MUNICIPAL LODGING HOUSE.
398 FIRST AVENUE.

NEW YORK,............................190

To..

....

DEAR..................

M..

Nationality........................ Age............

has applied to this department for assistance in his efforts to secure employment, and states that he was employed by you in the capacity of........................ and refers to you for information as to his character and ability.

With the assurance that it will be received as confidential, will you please to furnish, as soon as possible, the information asked for in the following questions, together with such other facts in your possession concerning this applicant as should be of service in determining the question of his worthiness.

Your kind and early compliance with this request will facilitate the work of the department, and oblige,

Respectfully yours,

WM. C. YORKE,
SUPERINTENDENT.

....claims to have left your employ about........................ago.

Is this statement true? ....

Was his work satisfactory? ....

When did he leave your employ? ....

Why did he leave your employ? ....

Would you re-employ him? ....

Is he addicted to the use of intoxicating liquor? ....

Signature of Reference,..

Date,........................190

Please to give additional information on the other side of this sheet.

190

Especially during the past year (September, 1907, to September, 1908), a very large number of decent men have applied at the lodging house, and their character and appearance have been exceptionally good. There is, of course, more or less falsification in the references and returns which the men make, but Mr. Yorke believes,—and what evidence there is bears him out,—that the large majority give fairly truthful accounts of themselves, especially as regards age, nationality, occupation and length of time in the city. There can be no doubt that results are approximately accurate. The largest opportunity, and perhaps the largest amount, of falsification is in regard to references, although this item is not taken as a reference, the man being asked "who was your last employer?" The "dead heads" or the "old timers" at the business have a story so well made, that they are able to tell a false one on entering in the evening and the same story again the next morning after a bath and a good night's sleep.

In the statistics regarding references, it will be noted that very few are found to be actually bad, while those classified under "doubtful identification," "references not found," and "unknown to references," may, many of them, have been due to such causes, as a wrong street number, carelessness on the part of the employer in answering, or perhaps confusion of names by the applicant or in the records kept by the employer,—particularly in smaller establishments. "Previously investigated" were those references given by lodgers appearing on the record for the second or third night, and therefore included under other heads. "Pending" includes all from whom no reply has been received.

As I sat in the office, the mail came and we opened several letters at random, answers from references. A number of employers wrote that they had discharged the particular individual in question on account of slack work and that they would re-employ the man if conditions allowed. No unfavorable letters happened to be opened.

NEW YORK MUNICIPAL LODGING HOUSE. NATIVITY OF LODGERS BY YEARS

Nativity.	1902	Per Cent.	1903	Per Cent.	1904	Per Cent.	1905	Per Cent.	1906	Per Cent.	1907	Per Cent.
United States	26,428	54.6	29,151	55.7	38,332	54.2	28,523	54.9	22,848	55.8	28,801	53.8
Ireland	12,283	25.3	12,920	24.7	17,067	24.1	12,357	23.7	9,644	23.5	12,111	22.6
Germany	4,473	09.8	4,090	07.8	7,038	09.9	4,748	09.1	3,309	08.0	4,936	09.2
England	*	..	*	..	*	..	*	..	..	..	..	..
Scotland	..	..	..	..	..	..	..	..	..	..	..	..
Wales	2,018	04.0	2,359	04.5	2,958	04.2	2,060	04.0	2,041	04.9	3,693	06.9
Austria	..	..	..	..	..	..	..	..	239	00.5	707	01.3
Russia	..	..	..	..	..	..	..	..	121	00.2	518	00.9
Italy	..	..	..	..	..	..	..	..	74	00.1	296	00.6
France	..	..	..	..	..	..	..	..	46	00.1	191	00.4
Scandinavia	..	..	..	..	..	..	..	..	189	00.4	544	01.0
All others	3,093	06.3	3,853	07.3	5,401	07.6	4,299	08.3	2,274	05.5	1,984	03.6
Total	48,295	100.0	52,373	100.0	70,796	100.0	51,987	100.0	40,872	100.0	53,741	100.0

* England only, up to 1906; not further classified.

NEW YORK MUNICIPAL LODGING HOUSE. NATIVITY OF LODGERS BY QUARTERS 1907-1908

NATIVITY.	1907. JANUARY TO MARCH.		1907. APRIL TO JUNE.		1907. JULY TO SEPTEMBER.		1907. OCTOBER TO DECEMBER.		1908. JANUARY TO MARCH.	
	Total.	Per Cent.	Total.	Per Cent.	Total.	Per Cent.	Total.	Per Cent.	Total.	Per Cent.
United States	7,912	59.0	5,444	55.3	4,260	52.0	11,185	50.3	15,575	46.2
Ireland	2,688	20.0	2,339	23.8	2,037	24.9	5,047	22.8	7,135	21.1
England, Scotland, Wales	794	05.8	554	05.4	596	07.3	1,709	07.7	2,347	06.9
Germany	1,181	08.7	851	08.7	825	10.1	2,079	09.3	3,187	09.5
Austria	130	00.9	107	01.1	89	01.1	381	01.7	867	02.3
France	53	00.4	21	00.2	27	00.3	90	00.4	142	00.5
Russia	76	00.5	56	00.6	59	00.7	327	01.5	1,344	04.0
Scandinavia	133	00.9	92	00.9	49	00.6	270	01.2	571	01.7
Italy	49	00.3	44	00.5	37	00.5	166	00.8	472	01.4
All others	472	03.5	351	03.5	211	02.5	950	04.3	2,150	06.4
Total	13,488	100.0	9,859	100.0	8,190	100.0	22,204	100.0	33,790	100.0

NEW YORK MUNICIPAL LODGING HOUSE. TIME IN NEW YORK CITY BY YEARS

Time in City.	1902.		1903.		1904.		1905.		1906.		1907.	
	Total.	Per Cent.	Total.	Per Cent.	Total.	Per Cent.	Total.	Per Cent.	Total.	Per Cent.	Total.	Per Cent.
Under 60 days........	6,241	12.9	6,809	13.0	10,389	14.7	8,837	17.0	5,275	16.0	9,614	17.9
60 days–6 months.....	1,312	02.7	1,498	02.9	1,878	02.7	1,151	02.2	853	02.6	1,541	02.9
6 months–1 year......	759	01.6	765	01.4	1,523	01.9	815	01.6	689	02.1	923	01.9
1 year–5 years.......	2,957	06.1	3,300	06.3	5,833	08.2	4,189	08.1	2,579	07.9	4,857	08.9
5 years and over.....	19,219	39.8	20,960	40.0	27,967	39.4	20,248	38.9	12,756	38.9	20,501	38.1
Natives of the City..	17,807	36.9	19,041	36.4	23,406	33.0	16,747	32.2	10,638	32.5	16,305	30.3
Totals..............	48,295	100.0	52,373	100.0	70,796	100.0	51,987	100.0	32,790	100.0	53,741	100.0

NEW YORK MUNICIPAL LODGING HOUSE. TIME IN NEW YORK CITY BY QUARTERS 1907–1908

Time in City.	1907. January to March.		1907. April to June.		1907. July to September.		1907. October to December.		1908. January to March.	
	Total.	Per Cent.	Total.	Per Cent.	Total.	Per Cent.	Total.	Per Cent.	Total.	Per Cent.
60 days................	1,771	13.1	1,360	13.8	1,099	13.3	5,384	24.3	8,035	23.9
60 days to 6 months....	339	2.5	152	1.5	121	1.5	929	4.2	3,403	10.1
6 months to 1 year.....	203	1.5	160	1.6	112	1.4	448	2.0	1,061	3.2
1 to 5 years...........	1,424	10.6	941	9.6	639	7.8	1,853	8.3	3,121	9.3
5 years and over.......	5,061	37.5	4,084	41.4	3,564	43.5	7,792	35.1	10,425	30.8
Native................	4,690	34.8	3,162	32.1	2,655	32.5	5,798	26.1	7,745	22.7
Total.................	13,488	100.0	9,859	100.0	8,190	100.0	22,204	100.0	33,790	100.0

NEW YORK MUNICIPAL LODGING HOUSE. AGES OF LODGERS BY YEARS

Ages	1902	Per cent.	1903	Per cent.	1904	Per cent.	1905	Per cent.	1906	Per cent.	1907	Per cent.
Under 2 years	318	00.6	361	00.7	505	00.7	669	01.3	541	01.3	668	01.3
2 to 16 years	242	00.5	496	00.9	307	00.4	473	00.9	378	00.9	433	00.8
16 to 21 years	1,466	03.0	1,480	02.8	2,935	04.1	2,242	04.3	1,604	03.9	1,683	03.1
21 to 50 years	34,907	72.3	38,313	73.2	51,721	73.0	37,437	72.0	28,000	68.5	37,501	69.8
50 to 70 years	10,657	22.1	10,909	20.8	14,386	20.3	10,528	20.3	9,747	23.9	12,596	23.4
70 years and over	705	01.5	814	01.6	1,042	01.5	638	01.2	602	01.5	860	01.6
Total	48,295	100.0	52,373	100.0	70,796	100.0	51,987	100.0	40,872	100.0	53,741	100.0
Average age, men	40	..	40	..	39	..	41	..	41	..	..	..
Average age, women	45	..	44	..	44	..	42	..	44	..	..	..

NEW YORK MUNICIPAL LODGING HOUSE. AGES OF LODGERS BY QUARTERS, 1907–1908

AGES.	1907. JANUARY TO MARCH.		1907. APRIL TO JUNE.		1907. JULY TO SEPTEMBER.		1907. OCTOBER TO DECEMBER.		1908. JANUARY TO MARCH.	
	Total.	Per Cent.	Total.	Per Cent.	Total.	Per Cent.	Total.	Per Cent.	Total.	Per Cent.
2 years...............	87	00.6	172	01.8	132	01.6	277	01.2	349	01.0
2 to 16 years.........	66	00.5	97	00.9	93	01.1	177	00.8	297	00.9
16 to 21 years........	377	02.8	267	02.7	192	02.3	847	03.8	770	02.4
21 to 50 years........	9,186	68.1	6,529	66.2	5,402	66.0	16,384	73.8	27,524	81.5
50 to 70 years........	3,566	26.5	2,618	26.6	2,218	27.1	4,194	1.89	4,700	13.7
70 years and over....	206	01.5	176	01.8	153	01.9	325	01.5	150	00.5
Total.............	13,488	100.0	9,859	100.0	8,190	100.0	22,204	100.0	33,790	100.0
Average age of men...	41	..	41	..	42	..	40	..	37	..
Average age of women	44	..	43	..	45	..	41	..	39	..

NEW YORK MUNICIPAL LODGING HOUSE. RESULTS OF INVESTIGATING REFERENCES OF LODGERS, BY YEARS

Results	1902.	Per Cent.	1903.	Per Cent.	1904.	Per Cent.	1905.	Per Cent.	1906.	Per Cent.	1907.	Per Cent.
Favorable Reference	15,920	42.3	17,609	43.5	20,735	40.0	17,427	46.1	15,452	52.4	16,095	43.1
Bad	28	..	16	..	10	..	14	..	28	..	38	00.1
Doubtful Identification	1,569	04.1	1,170	02.8	1,111	02.2	1,144	03.0	935	03.2	1,123	03.0
Reference not found	2,096	05.3	1,733	04.3	1,985	03.8	1,234	03.3	1,111	03.8	1,249	03.3
Lodger unknown to reference	1,290	03.4	1,480	03.6	1,782	03.4	1,084	02.9	1,260	04.3	1,293	03.5
Previously investigated	14,620	38.7	17,329	42.7	24,362	46.9	11,781	31.2	8,385	28.4	11,194	30.0
Pending	2,329	06.2	1,255	03.1	1,918	03.7	5,100	13.5	2,341	07.9	6,340	17.0
Total	37,852	100.0	40,592	100.0	51,903	100.0	37,782	100.0	29,512	100.0	37,332	100.0
Reference to last Employer	37,852	78	40,592	77	51,903	73.3	37,782	72.7	29,512	72.2	37,332	69.3
No reference given	10,443	22	11,781	23	18,893	26.7	14,205	27.3	11,360	27.8	16,409	30.7

NEW YORK MUNICIPAL LODGING HOUSE. RESULTS OF INVESTIGATING REFERENCES OF LODGERS BY QUARTERS, 1907–1908

Results	1907. January to March.		1907. April to June.		1907. July to September.		1907. October to December.		1908. January to March.	
	Total.	Per cent.	Total.	Per cent.	Total.	Per cent.	Total.	Per cent.	Total.	Per cent.
Favorable............	4,553	43.8	3,591	49.2	3,144	50.6	4,807	35.9	7,323	37.0
Bad..................	20	00.2	8	00.1	2	..	8	..	22	00.1
Doubtful Identification..	360	03.4	211	02.9	188	03.0	364	02.8	1,036	05.3
Reference not found....	440	04.2	230	03.2	212	03.4	367	02.8	973	05.0
Unknown to reference...	403	03.9	276	03.8	225	03.6	389	02.8	1,086	05.5
Previously investigated..	3,321	31.9	2,185	29.9	1,768	28.5	3,920	29.2	6,712	33.6
Pending.............	1,304	12.6	799	10.9	677	10.9	3,560	26.5	2,627	13.5
Total.............	10,401	100.0	7,300	100.0	6,216	100.0	13,415	100.0	19,779	100.0
Gave Reference.......	10,401	77.0	7,300	74.0	6,216	76.0	13,415	61.0	19,779	58.0
No Reference.........	3,087	23.0	2,559	26.0	1,974	24.0	8,789	39.0	14,011	42.0

These tables show that the native residents, in spite of variations due to depressions and other causes unknown, are always in the largest proportion, in some years more than half; that the Irish, German, and English follow in order while other nationalities are comparatively insignificant. The very small number of Russians and Italians, as representing the new stream of immigrants into this country, indicate that the unemployed among them are taken care of by other agencies and that the national groups have not yet begun to break down. These figures may also be taken to indicate, to a small degree, that vagrancy is not so prevalent among our newly arrived immigrants. Taken as a whole, the figures seem to show that in the experience of the Municipal Lodging House the foreign element is not the greatest among the unemployed or at least among the habitually unemployed.

The statistics showing the time within the city are quite surprising when one remembers that the lodgers who have been in the city for five years or who are natives of New York, usually form considerably over one-half of the total, while the floating population, or those who have been in the city less than six months, are in small proportion but a proportion which increases during a period of depression, the meaning of which is that the unemployed in New York city is largely augmented during a great period of unemployment by those from other cities who are out of work and who think that employment can be found here if it can be found anywhere. These statistics emphasize the fact brought out elsewhere that the unemployed congregate in the large cities during periods of depression.

The age statistics are not sufficiently refined to warrant any conclusions. There is, however, a very appreciable percentage of lodgers over 50 years of age in which class are usually to be put those individuals who are unemployed through invalidity and old age, and are really hopeless paupers.

The tables concerned with the character of the lodgers should be interpreted in view of the fact presented above in explanation of the different items named.

There is a vast amount of material in the books of this institution which could be utilized to great advantage by one interested in the lodging house habituate, or the question of the unempolyed. For example, each man states his regular occupation or his trade and then gives the particular job at which he was last employed; records which, although difficult to work up, would furnish valuable statistics on occupational mobility.

CHARACTER OF LODGERS IN MUNICIPAL LODGING HOUSE

An Interview with Hon. Robert W. Hebberd

Mr. Hebberd, Commissioner of Charities, declares that the men who visit the Municipal Lodging House, with a few exceptions, are habitually vagrant and chronically unemployed, and that most of them would not work if given a chance. This statement he admits is not so true now, or in the present year, as it has been in years of greater prosperity; but nevertheless the greater proportion of them are men who are in the lower ranks of the working classes who at any time are just on the edge of unemployment and about to be thrown off at the first sign of a depression; in other words they are the inefficient and the casual.

It is not this class of men that will be aided, Mr. Hebberd believes, by a general employment bureau, because they are vagrants and in most cases so inefficient as to be undesirable in any position.

The Department of Public Charities in conjunction with the Street Cleaning Department is about to put in operation a scheme, novel in many respects, to tide the unemployed over periods of idleness. A trial of the scheme soon to be made, involves taking a number of men from the Municipal Lodging House to Blackwell's Island to break stone; they are to work there for a half day, return to the lodging house for a good dinner, and during the afternoon they are to be free to go where they wish,—theoretically to search for work. Another part of the plan contemplates putting a large number of these men at work on the streets, but at light work, merely going about with a stick and a bag, picking up papers. After a man has worked all the morning, he goes to the Street Cleaning Department, presents the evidence of his labor, and receives a card which entitles him to a dinner at the Municipal Lodging House. The commissioner is not sanguine of the success of this scheme because of the character of the men. No compulsion is to be exercised, the men will be asked to volunteer for the work and if they refuse it will make no difference in their treatment.

SUMMARY BY MR. PRATT

In summing up the results of this inquiry it appears that the largest proportion of the lodgers in the Municipal Lodging House are natives of this country, that their condition is due largely to inefficiency and in a considerable degree to the use of intoxicants; but that they are on the whole well intentioned and that the proper adjustment might possibly be made through an employment bureau by which many of them could be put at work and be enabled to earn enough for their own support.

REPORT ON THE MOBILITY OF WORKERS,
By Dr. R. Brodsky

The movement of workers from place to place and from occupation to occupation is a matter upon which one must trust for evidence rather to general observation than to definite statistical data. Such statistical information as is available for the United States covers, as a rule, so limited a number of cases that generalizations based on it are quite as likely to be misleading as to be really informing. Evidence of this nature may, however, have a limited value by way of suggesting possibilities that have been neglected by general observers, and at the same time of affording a means of verifying or of invalidating the results of general qualitative observation. With this possibility in mind, an examination as extended as time limitations would allow, has been made of the figures presented in the United States Census Reports, reports of state labor bureaus and free public employment offices, and of some special investigations bearing on the following points:

I. Internal Migration (*i. e.*, from place to place).
   1. The situation.
      (a) Short distance movement.
      (b) Long distance movement.
   2. Factors encouraging movement.
      (a) Propertylessness (particularly with reference to ownership of homes).
      (b) Regional and occupational variations. Youth and unmarried condition. Occupational variations.

II. Occupational Movement (*i. e.*, movement from occupation to occupation).
   1. Influences compelling or strongly contributing to occupational movement.
      (a) Idleness—seasonal or otherwise.
      (b) Sickness, disease and accident.
   2. Duration of service in given occupations.

I. INTERNAL MIGRATION

a. SHORT DISTANCE MOVEMENT. There is a large migration of population within limited areas, the main causes of which are economic. This migration is made up of a movement from rural areas to neighboring towns and cities, and between neighboring states. This situation is general, but it is more marked the closer the proximity to industrial centers. Boston, for instance, receives approximately 10 per cent. of the addition to its population from other towns of Massachusetts. The state of Massachusetts receives the largest proportion of native additions to its population from surrounding states, 14.3 per cent. coming in the aggregate from Maine, New Hampshire, New York, Connecticut and Rhode Island, no other state contributing as much as 1 per cent. Another illustration of this fact is to be found in the experience of the Massachusetts Free Employment Bureau which, during its first five months of operation, received 20,454 applications for places from inhabitants of Boston proper, 5,601 from 139 other Massachusetts cities and towns, 50 from other New England states, 5 from New York and 60 from all other states and countries.

b. LONG DISTANCE MOVEMENT. The distance travelled by migrants varies with the degree of industrial and commercial development of the city or section to which they go. The states having the most developed and most varied industries receive from other states the greatest number of migrants. Manufacturing and commercial states draw from agricultural states. In the interchange of people between states of these two types, there is always a large margin or balance of migrants in favor of the more industrial states. In the interchange between states of the same economic type the difference is small in either direction, *e. g.:*

New York receives from Iowa	53,878	
New York gives to Iowa	4,358	
Difference	49,520	Ratio 13 to 1
New York receives from Wisconsin	58,520	
New York gives to Wisconsin	6,331	
Difference	52,007	Ratio 9 to 1
New York receives from Pennsylvania	114,440	
New York gives to Pennsylvania	110,868	
Difference	3,572	Ratio 28 to 27
New York receives from California	5,400	
New York gives to California	4,544	
Difference	856	Ratio 6 to 5

The total number of migrants passing between New York and Pennsylvania aggregates 225,308 persons; between New York and New Jersey, 273,000; between such agricultural states as Mississippi and Louisiana, 69,463; between Iowa and Wisconsin, 57,447.

It is known that the building trades absorb many workers who migrate from country to city. Various commercial pursuits likewise draw many from rural to commercial and industrial areas. An investigation of the Philadelphia Rapid Transit Company, covering 200 successful applicants for employment, and showing that 13 per cent. were formerly farmers of native birth, suggest another line of movement from rural to surban pursuits.

2. FACTORS ENCOURAGING MOVEMENT—(a) PROPERTYLESS-NESS. The person without property, particularly of the non-home-owning type, is likely to be more mobile than the man who has local property attachments. Statistics of home-owning show a small percentage of home-owners among workers in the more industrial states or centers, a higher percentage in the less industrial sections. For instance, the percentage of home-owners in New York city is 12 per cent., in Fall River 18 per cent., in Jersey City and Connecticut 20 per cent. For workers only, the percentage would be still smaller. Fall River furnishes a particularly good illustration. It is a town of cotton operatives, who are very mobile. Local attachments are so weak with these workers that fines imposed for mistakes made in work serve to drive workers from one factory town to another. A study of 2,299 cotton operatives in Rhode Island showed only 10 per cent. of home owners. Reports of the Massachusetts Labor Bureau contain many references to the exodus of textile operatives to Canada and England. A sample entry records the migration of 100 weavers from New Bedford to Weston, Mass., where they were to be employed on a one-year contract at slightly increased wages. In an agricultural state like Kansas the proportion of home owners among employees in trade and industry is higher. For instance,

a study of 390 workers, almost all members of unions, made by the Kansas Bureau of Labor and Industry in 1907, showed 151 home-owners, a percentage of 39.

From the standpoint of occupational variations, the more skilled the occupation, the more steady the work, and the higher the pay, the larger in the main is the percentage of home-owners. In Pawtucket, R. I., for instance, an investigation showed among machinists 18 per cent. of home-owners, among workers in building trades 15 per cent., metal workers 10 per cent., weavers (an unusually mobile lot) 9 per cent., unskilled workers 7.9 per cent. The highest percentage was for city government employees (over 18 per cent.). Clerks showed a percentage almost as low as the unskilled workers, 9 per cent.

Similar conclusions may be drawn from the figures for other cities and states. For instance, reports from 99 unions in Michigan, covering 8,589 members, show the highest percentage of home-owners among the steady-working coopers (50 per cent.); the lowest among the less steady-working, and more poorly paid cigar makers (12 per cent.), printers (16 per cent.), tailors (17 per cent.), metal polishers (18 per cent.). An investigation of 4,800 workingmen in 34 towns in Michigan showed 26 per cent. of home-owners; another covering 5,399 in 39 towns of the same state showed 27 per cent. Of 4,948 employees in the vehicle industry in Michigan 21 per cent. owned their homes.

In the coal mines of Illinois, the percentage of homeowners among miners is 44 per cent., mechanics 54 per cent., unskilled workers 30 per cent.

In the electrical railway occupations, of 1,021 employees on 19 Michigan roads less than 20 per cent. owned homes. Of 1,865 employees of the Union Railroad of San Francisco, 24 per cent. owned homes.

(b) AGE AND UNMARRIED CONDITION. Young, unmarried, non-home-owning workers are more mobile than older, married workers. In all cases, unskilled laborers of the same age as skilled, show a smaller percentage of marriage. In Pawtucket, for instance, the average ages of workers and the percentage married were as follows:

	AVERAGE AGE.	MARRIED. PER CENT.
Building Trades	37	65
Machinists	33	57
Metal Workers	33	55
City Government Employees	37	64
Bookkeepers	29	47
Laborers	37	52

Among street railway employees there is a low percentage of marriage. Most street railway companies employ only men 35 years of age or under. The following figures covering street railway employees in five different cities, including one city and interurban area, illustrate the situation:

	30 YEARS AND UNDER. PER CENT.	OVER 30 YEAR PER CENT.	MARRIED. PER CENT.
Detroit	80	20	39
Scranton	80	20	36
Philadelphia	80	20	42
Pittsburg	88	12	29.9
Connecticut R.R	70	30	49

Workingmen are inclined to marry at about thirty years of age and mobility, regional as well as occupational, is in consequence larger before thirty than after that age. The statistics of the New York and Massachusetts free employment bureaus illustrate the situation with regard to the relative proportions of married and unmarried persons in skilled and unskilled pursuits. In the New York bureau, and skilled workers placed show 40 per cent. of married, the unskilled 32 per cent., servants 20 per cent., clerks, 17 per cent. In the unskilled group the occupations were as follows:

	NUMBER.	MARRIED. PER CENT.
Drivers	132	35
Coachmen	60	33
Laborers	204	31
Stablemen	40	25
Useful Men	134	18
Handy Men	45	15
Farm Hands	64	13

The figures of the Massachusetts bureau do not specify numbers of married and unmarried by occupations. There is, however, a general average of 18 per cent. of married persons among successful applicants. The fact that of all successful male applicants (3,212), 75 per cent. were unskilled and 10 per cent. clerks (85 per cent. in all), suggests the same situation as that afforded by the New York figures.

Within skilled trades the percentage of marriages increases with higher wages and greater steadiness of work.

Periodic idleness also contributes to change of residence as well as to change of occupation. The fact that of skilled workers who make use of employment bureaus the large proportion are workers in the building trades tends to confirm this conclusion. But this phase of the subject may better be treated in the next section.

II. OCCUPATIONAL MOVEMENT

1. INFLUENCES COMPELLING MOVEMENT. (a) IDLENESS, SEASONAL OR OTHERWISE.—Protracted idleness often leads a person in a skilled trade to seek other temporary employment or to change his occupation entirely. In New York City, for instance, pressers and tailors often give up their trades for employment on street cars, elevated or subway trains, for civil service or for business. The inquiry into the former occupations of applicants for positions with the Philadelphia Rapid Transit Co., showed that 40

per cent. of the applicants from skilled lines of work were previously employed in the building trades, in which seasonal periods of idleness are, of course, very prominent. The statistics of the free employment bureaus of New York and Massachussetts illustrate the same point. Of the skilled mechanics who applied for positions in the New York bureau, over 30 per cent. were skilled workers in the building trades, and in the Massachusetts bureau, over 40 per cent.

The question whether or not idleness in the skilled trades is more of a problem than in the unskilled cannot be answered here. The data obtained are too incomplete to formulate a conclusion. All we know is that the idleness in various skilled trades reappears regularly every year, while for unskilled workers there are no limits to the periods of idleness, forces that are less calculable ruling there to a larger degree than elsewhere.

The consequences of idleness as to change of occupation are very different for skilled and unskilled workers. The skilled mechanic knows his slack times and is prepared for them, while the unskilled man is uncertain of them, lives from hand to mouth and in case of temporary unemployment is prepared to take up any kind of work offered him. He changes one occupation for another. Such is not the rule with skilled workers, who are seldom found in the free employment bureaus or in other occupations than their original ones.

(b) DISEASE AND INDUSTRIAL ACCIDENTS peculiar to certain trades are further factors in forcing a movement of workers to other occupations. Considering the rapid industrial development of the United States, leading to a large amount of disease and accident in industry, the changes in occupation due to these two causes must assume considerable importance. To determine exactly the extent of their influence, to measure their effect upon permanency of occupation, to find their place among the other causes of change of residence or change of occupation, one must examine tables of sickness and accident in connection with various occupations, and such tables have not yet been worked out with any degree of uniformity for the Unietd States. It is also necessary to discover what becomes of those persons who are sick or injured but still able to work. Confining ourselves to daily observation we may conclude that the occupations of watchmen, street-car conductors, elevator men, handy and useful men are the dumping ground for those persons who have previously been employed in dangerous trades and who have suffered physical injury therein.

This conclusion is illustrated by an examination of the statistics of sickness as a cause of idleness among applicants for employment, compiled by the New York State Free Employment Bureau, by reports of the New York Bureau of Labor Statistics bearing on causes of idleness among union workers, and by a hasty examination of fifty cases of workers injured in Pittsburg industries. The Pittsburg figures show the following results: Of 24 skilled workers, 2 (machinists) retained their former trade, 8 have been out of work, and 14 changed their occupations as follows:

    3 machinists became 1 street car conductor, 1 farmer, 1 laborer.
    1 electrician became a travelling salesman.
    1 painter became a porter.
    1 carpenter became a laborer.
    1 moulder became a laborer.
    1 boilerman became a laborer.
    1 ironworker became a laborer.
    1 steam power man became a laborer.
    1 steel worker became a watchman.
    1 gasfitter became a dealer in lumber.
    2 brakemen became 1 fireman, 1 conductor.

Of 26 unskilled workers, 16 retained former occupations, 1 has been out of work, 1 moved away, 1 became a prisoner, and 7 became servants and handy men at occasional labor.

Cases coming before charitable societies illustrate the same downward tendency in which sickness, accident, the growing incapacity due to advancing age and general inefficiency promote unusual occupational versatility. The following instances from the case records of the New York Charity Organization Society are typical: a driver of 56, crippled with rheumatism, was employed as a paper-folder and as a watchman; an iron-worker found employment as conductor, motorman, and porter; a waiter had also been a watchman, a snow-shoveller, and a janitor; a shoemaker had worked as pantryman, wood-chopper, and paint-mixer; an actress of 48 became in turn house-keeper, collector and sample agent; and a boy of 20 had already been unsuccessfully a designer, embroiderer, peddler, factory hand, newspaper vender and motorman.

A study of sources of information such as these, suggests that if a skilled mechanic changes his work (not taking into account the long unemployment period) he does it because of sickness or accident. It shows, too, that then and not before, he applies to the free employment bureau and is willing to do any kind of work related to his former occupation. This also partially answers the question why free employment bureaus show so large a proportion of applications from unskilled workers and why the unions encourage the movement toward free employment bureaus. Their encouragement comes, not only because of solicitude for unskilled laborers who suffer from the machinations of private employment bureaus, but because the unions, although successful in securing positions for their efficient workers, are unable to provide employment for their own sick or injured members, and pass them on to the free employment bureaus for easier work.

3. DURATION OF LABOR IN GIVEN OCCUPATIONS.—A high percentage of home-owning, as well as a high marriage rate, indicates lack of mobility among workingmen. Unemployment, sickness or accident compel movement on the part of workers. The conclusions reached under these heads with regard to the relative mobility of skilled and unskilled workers receive further verification from an examination of certain data illustrating the period of employment in different occupations. Here again

the duration is longest among skilled workers and lowest in unskilled occupations. This, of course, is to be expected. The skilled mechanic is a specialist and he is not likely to change his manner of work unless forced to do so by circumstances. Clerks are mobile in response to a variety of opportunity, and they change frequently. Unskilled workers are largely at the mercy of forces that they cannot foresee, and by virtue of circumstances they move in response to opportunities, which often carry them downward instead of upward as in the case of clerks.

Among skilled occupations, those which have their origin in the handicrafts and have been modified to suit changed economic conditions, which are not subject to seasonal variations and which are organized, show the greatest stability. The skilled trades which do not have apprenticeship arrangements or their equivalent, which are not organized into trade unions and which offer seasonal work, show the least stability. The whole policy of trade unions, whether it be through trade agreement to check strikes and establish a uniform scale of wages for a long period over a large territory in a particular industry, or whether it be to maintain or raise the standard of living of workingmen to the highest possible point by efforts to shorten hours of labor, increase wages and secure greater responsibility from employers in cases of accident,—this policy works always in the direction of the greatest possible stability of labor. The following table, giving the average duration of employment of 4,800 workers in 34 towns in Michigan, is illustrative:

Trade.	Years Employed.
Cooper	22.7
Blacksmith	18.4
Harness-maker	17.0
Painter	19.0 (in another investigation, 9)
Moulder	17.8
Mason	16.0
Miller	16.0
Engineer	15.0
Cigarmaker	12.0
Machinist	13.0
Tailor	8.4
Barber	11.1

Trade.	Years Employed.
Butcher	10.0
Machine Helper	8.8
Woolen Mills	6.3
R. R. Work	8.3
Teamster	5.7
Factory	5.0
Laborer	4.5
Helper	4.5
Manager	13.0
Foreman	10.3
Bookkeeper	7.6
Clerk	
Salesman	9.9
Shipping Clerk	6.5

An investigation of the duration of work in the coal mines of Illinois showed the following results.

Occupation.	Number Involved.	Years of Service.								
		Five Per Cent.	Ten Per Cent.	Fifteen Per Cent.	Twenty Per Cent.	Twenty-five Per Cent.	Thirty Per Cent.	Thirty-five Per Cent.	Forty Per Cent.	Over Forty Per Cent.
Laborers	762	23.0	30.0	26.0	11.6	5.0	2.3	1.0	..	1.0
Mechanics	206	18.0	18.0	16.0	19.0	13.0	5.0	5.0	3	3.0
Miners	8,818	8.7	20.8	22.1	16.7	13.9	7.2	5.7	2	3.0
Others	473	0.2	12.2	18.0	20.0	20.0	10.0	6.0	3	3.6
Total	10,259	10.0	00.20	22.0	17.0	14.0	7.0	5.0	2	2.0

That the street railways are the dumping ground for the unemployed is illustrated by the following table:

EMPLOYED BY WASHINGTON WATER POWER CO. (1902) (107 PERSONS)

Duration of Work.	No.
Less than 1 year	40
1-2 years	19
2-3	10
3-4	6
4-5	6
Total less than 5 years	81 or 75.7 per cent.
5-9 years	13 or 12.1 per cent.
10 years and over	13 or 12.1 per cent.
Total	107

Similar results are shown in the cases of the United Railroad Company of San Francisco, and of 19 electric railways of Michigan (1,029 employes).

Little information has been obtained as to former occupations of persons changing employment. The table given above regarding accident cases bears on the matter, as do the following figures of the Philadelphia Rapid Transit Company, covering 200 successful applicants for positions:

18 per cent came from skilled industries.
20 per cent came from the commercial and professional pursuits.
58 per cent came from unskilled occupations.
4 per cent came from servant class.

SOME GENERAL CONCLUSIONS

1. Skilled workers in trades are little inclined to change their occupations unless forced to do so by circumstances beyond their control. Change of residence in response to larger opportunities of employment is not infrequent, but change of occupation in response to similar influences is an exceptional occurrence.

2. Unskilled workers show a higher occupational mobility than do the skilled. But here again it is the pressure of necessity more often than the call of larger opportunity that brings change of occupation. With reference to change of residence the figures for age, marriage and home-owning would suggest larger possibility of movement on the part of unskilled than of skilled workers; but these figures may be very misleading in this respect.

3. The clerical group is particularly mobile. With them new opportunities are more often sought and embraced than with the other two groups.

4. Any employment agency which seeks to find employment merely for those who apply for work, and which aims to accommodate applicants for helpers merely by sending workers from their list of applicants for work, will encounter a situation suggested by

the first two conclusions. Except in the case of domestic servants and of wholly unskilled workers, the activities of such a bureau would in such case be confined to the relatively inefficient residue of the skilled and unskilled groups, rather than to the more capable workers. A bureau that would promote genuine mobility among workers must find some means of reaching the mass of employees and employers in such a way as to substitute opportunity for necessity as a cause of movement.

APPENDIX VIII

Statement from Charles K. Blatchly,

SUPERINTENDENT OF THE JOINT APPLICATION BUREAU, IN REGARD TO AN EXPERIMENT IN FINDING EMPLOYMENT FOR MEN IN THE COUNTRY.

On May 21, 1908, the Joint Committee authorized me to send out letters to newspapers published in the smaller towns within a radius of fifty miles of New York City. Three hundred letters were mimeographed and sent to the editors on June 1. The letter read as follows.

During the present financial depression when thousands of men are out of work, it has been frequently stated by the press and at public meetings that if the idle men of the cities were willing to go into the country, farmers would be able to give work to these unskilled, unemployed men on their farms.

The conditions of last winter still exist, and the number of unemployed, unmarried men is still large. These men come to the office of the Joint Application Bureau in New York City and beg for work. Many of them have no home, and there are few city positions in which they can be placed. Possibly, if these facts should be brought to the attention of your readers, they might secure needed labor at reasonable wages, and so relieve distress.

We shall be glad, should any of your readers desire to communicate with us with this end in view, to send (passage prepaid at our expense, to be refunded out of their first wages) such men as we believe could fill the positions wanted. We would investigate to the best of our ability the qualifications of each man, and would try to send the best man, in each case, for the work desired.

It is almost impossible in the great majority of homeless cases, to thoroughly establish the truth of the statements made to us, so it can be readily understood that we would not wish to incur any responsibility for their conduct or honesty; we could simply do our best to ascertain the facts.

We have investigated the cases of many of the men who have applied to us, and have received favorable reports from their former employers.

May we ask you to give space in your publication—as often as you feel so disposed—to this letter, so that the opportunity of securing labor may be conveyed to your readers.

From June 1 to September 30, work was secured for 78 men and we have sent out since that time enough men to make 100.

For the 78 men we furnished transportation amounting to $222.28, of which we received as refunds $118.96, or 53.4 per cent. We received refunds on the transportation from 46 men.

The reports received were generally favorable, unsatisfactory reports being received in only 11 cases.

The larger part of these men were placed at wages paying from $10 to $15 a month, very few of them receiving more.

A large number of letters were written by this bureau to ascertain the reliability of the prospective employers.

I feel that this work was not begun early enough in the year to place the number of men that might have been placed had we sent out the letters earlier in the season. Besides there is a limited demand for farm labor within a radius of 50 miles of New York City. If we had extended the territory over which we sent our letters, I think we could easily have placed a much larger number of men.

DECEMBER 17, 1908.

APPENDIX IX

Extract from the Sixth Annual Report (1908) of Hon. Oscar S. Straus, Secretary of Commerce and Labor—Page 23

DIVISION OF INFORMATION

Section 40 of the immigration act of February 20, 1907, provided for the establishment of a Division of Information in the Bureau of Immigration and Naturalization. Its duties were defined as follows:

> It shall be the duty of said division to promote a beneficial distribution of aliens admitted into the United States among the several states and territories desiring immigration. Correspondence shall be had with the proper officials of the states and territories, and said division shall gather from all available sources useful information regarding the resources, products, and physical characteristics of each state and territory, and shall publish such information in different languages and distribute the publications among all admitted aliens who may ask for such information at the immigrant stations of the United States and to such other persons as may desire the same.

The purpose of this law, as interpreted by me, is twofold: first, to bring about a distribution of immigrants arriving in this country, thus preventing, so far as possible, the congestion in our larger Atlantic seaport cities that has attended the immigration of recent years; and second, to supply information to all of our workers, whether native, foreign-born, or alien, so that they may be constantly advised in respect to every part of the country as to what kind of labor may be in demand, the conditions surrounding it, the rate of wages, and the cost of living in the respective cities.

PROBLEM OF THE UNEMPLOYED.—It is a subject of great interest in all commercial countries how to provide work, especially in periods of industrial depression, for the unemployed. There are always two kinds of unemployed,—those who are too lazy and shiftless to work, which we need not take under consideration, and those who, without fault of their own, are unable to find work because of depression or because the labor market is oversupplied.

In a country so great as ours, with its multiplicity of industries, it is not an unusual condition that when the demand for labor is slack in one part of the country there is a demand for additional labor in other parts of the country, and when some industries slow down there is a demand for additional workers in others. This condition frequently obtains in the demand for farm laborers, and often at seasons of the year when manufacturing industries are slack. While these conditions apply less to skilled than to unskilled labor, it is also true that the problem of the unemployed affects chiefly this latter class. I regard the extension and development of the work of this division as of the very highest importance in meeting this problem, and the first requisite is to make accessible the information above referred to, and the second is to facilitate and cheapen transporattion. This may be done, perhaps without legislation, by an arrangement with the various railroad and transportation companies of the country for a labor-exchange rate. I present the subject in the hope that it will receive the consideration that so important a subject demands, and as supplying a remedy, if not a complete solution, in this country of the problem of the unemployed.

The work of the division since its organization is described in detail in the report of its chief, to which reference is made. I desire to express thanks for the hearty cooperation that the department has received from the postmaster-general and from the secretary of agriculture.

The scope of this division could be usefully extended in another direction, which I have embodied in the recommendation for the amendment of the law, proposed by the division. The emigration figures to which I have referred afford evidence that most of the immigration to this country is stimulated by false, glowing and misleading information in regard to the opportunities here, as if the country were an Eldorado where laziness is rewarded and large returns await even the slothful. When such immigrants come they find that while the rewards of labor are much greater in this country than in their own, the American laborer is more industrious, energetic, and self-reliant than elsewhere, and that while the opportunities in this country are greater the qualities necessary to benefit thereby also require an increase of effective energy, and that the same lack of qualifications which spelled failure at home are writ even larger in this country. With their delusions dispelled, they return to their countries sadder but wiser men.

Much of this kind of immigration could be stopped at its source by the dissemination of correct information throughout foreign countries from which our immigration chiefly comes. Perhaps the best medium through which this information could be disseminated from time to time is through our consuls; also the various labor organizations of the country could be of aid to the division, both in the collection and presentation of the various kinds of information referred to. I foresee great and substantial extension that can be given to the scope and work of this important division, and trust that Congress will enable the department to carry forward this work in the various directions I have outlined.

APPENDIX X

The Value of Labor Exchanges

EXTRACT FROM A PAMPHLET ON "LABOR EXCHANGES,"
By Mr. W. H. Beveridge, of London

A labor or employment exchange is an office for registering on the one hand the needs of employers for work-people, on the other hand the needs of workpeople for employment. It is a means not of making work but of putting those who want work and those who want workpeople into immediate communication. It is a market-place for labor. What is the use of a market-place for labor?

In the first place, it may be urged that there is nothing surprising in labor exchanges being thought useful. Everything else that is bought and sold,—corn, or wool, or stocks,—has its known market-place. Labor is the only thing which still finds a buyer only, or, as a rule, by being hawked from door to door. There must, on the face of it, be as much reason for abolishing this antiquated and wasteful method of hawking in regard to labor as in regard to anything else. The surprising thing is not that labor exchanges should be wanted now, but that they should not have been established long ago.

It is, however, unnecessary to rely on general arguments. As soon as the question is examined a whole series of practical reasons may be seen for regarding the organization of the labor market by a connected system of labor exchanges as the first step in any solution of the unemployed problem.

1. Labor exchanges, in some form or other, are indispensable for the abolition of casual labor. It is not possible for each individual employer to employ only regular men. It is possible for all employers to agree or to be compelled to take their irregular men from some common center. The business of that central office will then be so to distribute work as to give each man who gets any work at all a fairly regular flow of work under several employers in turn, where it cannot be regular under one employer alone.

2. Labor exchanges, though they cannot, in times of depression, make work, can reduce unemployment even in such times by abolishing all unemployment that is merely local in character. They, and they alone, can make it impossible for men to be vainly seeking work in one place, while employers are vainly seeking just those men in another.

3. Labor exchanges are necessary for any drastic treatment of vagrancy. The excuse of the habitual vagrant is that he is tramping in search of work. A national system of labor exchanges using the post office, the telephone, and the railway, will gradually relieve the habitual vagrant of the excuse and the decent workman of the necessity for going blindly on the tramp.

4. Labor exchanges are necessary to provide a test of unemployment in the mass and in the individual. They will show at all times what the problem is and where it lies. They will automatically register the beginning, depth, and ending of exceptional depression, and will thus guide the administration of any special measures that may be thought necessary. They alone will show as to any individual workman whether he is now unemployed against his will, because they alone will keep all men in immediate touch with all the employment that offers. No system of insurance against unemployment and no system of relief outside the Poor Law is safe from abuse without such a test.

5. Labor exchanges in direct connection with the elementary schools are necessary, in order to organize and guide the entry

of boys and girls into industrial life, to give each a wider choice of the work for which he or she is best fitted, to study and to influence the character of the demand for youthful workers, to accumulate for the formation of public opinion or the framing of laws information as to the careers offered by various occupations.

It is not possible here to do more than thus state in bare outline some of the services which labor exchanges may be expected to render in regard to unemployment. The first alone is dealt with at greater length in the following pages (omitted here). The "decasualisation of labor" is at once the most important point, in view of the admitted facts of the unemployed problem, and the one most needing special explanation.

APPENDIX XI

Extract from Address by Rt. Hon. Winston Churchill, M.P.,

PRESIDENT OF THE BOARD OF TRADE, AT THE ANNUAL GATHERING OF THE COUNCIL OF THE SCOTTISH LIBERAL ASSOCIATION, OCTOBER 9, 1908

We talk a great deal about the unemployed, but the evil of the under-employed is the tap-root of unemployment. There is a tendency in many trades, almost in all trades, to have a fringe of casual labor on hand, available as a surplus whenever there is a boom, flung back into the whirlpool whenever there is a slump. Employers and foremen in many trades are drawn consciously or unconsciously to distribute their work among a larger number of men than they regularly require, because this obviously increases their bargaining power with them, and supplies a convenient reserve for periods of brisk business activity. And what I desire to impress upon you, and through you upon this country, is that the casual unskilled laborer who is habitually under-employed, who is lucky to get three, or at the outside four, days' work in the week, who may often be out of a job for three or four weeks at a time, who in bad times goes under altogether, and who in good times has not hope of security and no incentive to thrift, whose whole life and the lives of his wife and children are embarked in a sort of blind, desperate, fatalistic gamble with circumstances beyond his comprehension or control,—that this poor man, this terrible and pathetic figure is not as a class the result of accident or chance, is not casual because he wishes to be casual, is not casual as the consequence of some temporary disturbance soon put right. No, the casual laborer is here because he is wanted here. He is here in answer to a perfectly well-defined demand. He is here as the result of economic causes which have been too long unregulated. He is not the natural product, he is an acticle manufactured, called into being, to suit the requirements, in the Prime Minister's telling phrase, of all industries at particular times and of particular industries at all times. I suppose no department has more means of learning about these things than the Board of Trade, which is in friendly touch at every stage all over the country with both capital and labor. I publish that fact deliberately, I invite you to consider it, I want it to soak in. It appears to me that measures to check the growth and diminish the quantity of casual labor must be an essential part of any thorough or scientific attempt to deal with unemployment, and I would not proclaim this evil to you without having reason to believe that practicable means exist by which it can be greatly diminished.

If the first vicious condition which I have mentioned to you is lack of industrial organization, if the second is the evil of casual labor, there is a third not less important,—I mean the present condition of boy labor. The whole underside of the labor market is deranged by the competition of boys or young persons who do men's work for boys' wages, and are turned off as soon as they demand men's wages for themselves. This is the evil so far as it affects the men; but how does it affect the boys, the youth of our country, the heirs of all our exertion, the inheritors of that long treasure of history and romance, of science and knowledge,—aye, of national glory,—for which so many valiant generations have fought and toiled,—the youth of Britain, how are we treating them in the twentieth century of the Christian era? Are they not being exploited? Are they not being demoralized? Are they not being thrown away? Whereas the youth of the wealthier class is all kept under strict discipline until 18 or 19, the mass of the nation runs wild after 14 years of age. No doubt at first employment is easy to obtain. There is a wide and varied field; there are a hundred odd jobs for a lad; but almost every form of employment now open to young persons affords them no opening, is of no use to them whatever, when they are grown up, and in a great number of cases the life which they lead is demoralizing and harmful. And what is the consequence? The consequence may be measured by this grim fact, that out of the unemployed applying for help under the Unemployed Workman Act, no less than 28 per cent. are between 20 and 30 years of age. That is to say, men in the first flush of their strength and manhood, already hopelessly adrift on the dark and tumultuous ocean of life. Upon this subject, I say to you deliberately that no boy or girl ought to be treated merely as cheap labor, that up to 18 years of age every boy and girl in this country should, as in the old days of apprenticeship, be learning a trade as well as earning a living.

All attempts to deal with these and similar evils involve the expenditure of money. It is no use abusing capitalists and rich people. They are neither worse nor better than any one else. They function quite naturally under the conditions in which they find themselves. When the conditions are vicious, the consequence will be evil; when the conditions are reformed, the evil will be abated. Nor do I think the wealthy people of Great Britain would be ungenerous or unwilling to respond to the plain need of this nation for a more complete or elaborate social organization. They would have a natural objection to having public money wasted or spent on keeping in artificial ease an ever-growing class of wastrels and ne'er-do-weels. No doubt there would also be a selfish element who would sullenly resist anything which touched their pocket. But I believe that if large schemes, properly prepared and scientifically conceived for dealing with the evils I have mentioned, were presented, and if it could be shown that our national life would be placed upon a far more stable and secure foundation, I believe that there would be thousands of rich people who would cheerfully make the necessary sacrifices.

APPENDIX XII

Extracts from a Letter Addressed by Mr. Cyrus L. Sulzberger to the Chairman of the New York State Commission of Immigration, in Regard to the Work of the Industrial Removal Office.

The Industrial Removal Office began in 1900 its work of endeavoring to distribute Jewish immigrants who were chiefly industrial and not agricultural workers from New York throughout the United States. Originally the attempt was made to secure from employers in the interior requisitions for the particular kind of help that they needed. It was soon found, however, that the difficulty of placing a man at a job when the man and the job were separated by many hundreds of miles was almost insuperable. After the requisition reached us it was necessary to find the man who met the required specifications, and by the time he was ready to leave a few days necessarily elapsed, so that when he reached his destination it was not infrequently found that the vacancy had been filled. It was therefore determined to reverse the order of procedure and bring the man first to the industrial center where employment was to be expected and then fit him into a position. Accordingly, local committees were organized, which may be called reception committees, whose business it was to receive the immigrant upon his arrival in the interior and care for him, pending employment being found for him. In larger places, to which a considerable number of immigrants were being sent, an employment agent was engaged whose sole business it was to find occupations for the new arrivals. Being acquainted in the various industries, this employment agent put himself in communication with the proprietors and superintendents of the industrial establishments and upon the arrival of immigrants took them in person to places where they were likely to find employment. Of course at this end it was necessary that care be taken in sending the men out, to select such places as were apt to give them occupation in their respective trades. A careful scrutiny is made by the office here of all applicants for removal and of the total number who apply less than one half are sent. Only those are selected who upon investigation give promise of making successful workers. The shiftless, the lazy, and the incompetent are carefully weeded out and refused consideration.

This is the eighth year of the activity of the Industrial Removal Office and it has sent from New York during that period 42,000 persons, of whom, roughly 60 per cent are breadwinners, and the remainder their wives and children. According to the statistical records that we have kept from year to year we find that 85 per cent of those whom we have sent away remained in the places to which we sent them, and of the remainder probably one-half located at other places away from New York. A statement made up last year, when 20,194 breadwinners of 167 different occupations had been sent away, showed them divided into the following groups:

	Number.	Per Cent.
Woodworkers	2,092	9.6
Metalworkers	1,861	9.3
Bldg. Trades	1,618	7.9
Printing and Lithography	168	.9
Needle Industry	3,967	19.8
Leather Industry	1,425	7.1
Tobacco Industry	150	.9
Men without trades	6,575	32.7
Dealers in fruit supplies	729	3.7
Farming	341	1.7
Office help, professionals, etc.	622	3.1
Miscellaneous	646	3.3

In the report of the Industrial Removal Office for the year 1906 occurs the following paragraph:

Of the total number of persons sent from New York, about 16,000 were wage-earners, the remainder being the women and the children of their families. What the activity of this organization means to the industrial development of the country can be appreciated by a consideration of the earnings of these 16,000 workers. Making every allowance for idle time and judging by the reports received from all over the country as to the wages paid the men, we are satisfied that they are annually earning a sum aggregating from $8,000,000 to $10,000,000 at a minimum, and are adding in that ratio to the productive capacity of the country. According to the U. S. Census report, wages constitute, roughly speaking, 20 per cent of the finished product, and it is therefore evident that the proteges of this office are producing not far from $50,000,000 worth of goods annually. A comparatively small part of this product is consumed at the point of production; all the remainder is necessarily transported upon the railroads of the country either for home consumption or for the swelling of our foreign commerce. Of this entire army of producers not a single individual was earning his living at the time this office sent him away.

The number of wage-earners sent away being now 50 per cent greater than it was at the time this report was written, the other figures are also subject to a like increase of 50 per cent, and it therefore follows that the amount of goods now annually produced by those sent from New York by the Industrial Removal Office must reach not far from $75,000,000.

This briefly gives the story of the work of the Industrial Removal Office, and I may say that the success of the entire work rests primarily upon the organization of what I have called the reception committees. Without such committees to receive and look after the immigrant upon his arrival in a strange town, the whole work would fail. It is upon the assurance that a friendly hand of welcome will be extended to him when he arrives at his destination, that the immigrant is willing to move on to an unknown land. New York city with its cosmopolitan population enables every newcomer to find himself in a congenial and familiar atmosphere, and it is the dread of the unknown quite as much as the attraction of New York that holds the immigrant here. If then, distribution of immigration is to proceed on a larger scale, I should say that a condition precedent would be the organization of committees or governmentally the appointment of honorary commissions. Such commissions should exist in every industrial locality, and should be composed as far as possible of representative men of the same races as the prevailing immigrants, so that Italians may find an Italian, Hungarians a Hungarian, and Jews a Jew, sympathetic with their needs and prepared to aid them with friendly advice.

A further important requirement is a very low and merely nominal transportation rate. I have observed in the sixth annual report of the Commissioner of Commerce and Labor just issued, a recommendation by him on the subject of cheaper transportation for the unemployed. He advocates a "labor exchange rate," (pages 23 and 24). There should in addition to such labor exchange rate be an immigrant rate, applying only from the seaboard but not to it, and such rates should be very much lower than the existing immigrant rate, which is 10 per cent less than the usual passenger rate. Immigrants should be carried from the seaboard at a rate of not more than a half cent per mile, and while probably the cost to the railroads might be more than they would thus recover, the ultimate result would inevitably redound to their advantage. The carrying of an immigrant occurs but once. The carrying of his products from the interior point of production to the point of consumption or exportation occurs annually. According to the United States Census reports, the average value of the product of each industrial worker of the United States is about $2,500, and as very little of this is consumed at the point of production there would be for the transportation companies goods to the value of more than $2,000 annually to be transported for every immigrant moved from New York. On this freight shipment the railroad company would speedily recoup any loss that it might sustain on the original transportation of the producer. Whether the establishment of such transportation rates and the appointment of such commissions is a matter requiring State or Federal action is a question which it is not for me to determine.

DECEMBER 14, 1908.

APPENDIX XIII
A Partial Bibliography

ON THE SUBJECT OF EMPLOYMENT BUREAUS

The literature on the general question of the unemployed is voluminous and this list, prepared with the assistance of Mrs. Helen Page Bates, does not intend to cover it, though some titles which do not deal primarily with labor registries are included because of certain chapters or paragraphs.

In the case of official publications no attempt has been made to present a complete list, but only those documents have been included which have been accessible for reference in the preparation of this report.

Abbott, Grace: "The Chicago Employment Agency and the Immigrant Worker." In American Journal of Sociology, November, 1908.

Adler, George: "Arbeitsnachweis und Arbeitsbörsen." In Handwörterbuch der Staatswissenschaften, 3d Ed., Jena, 1909, Bd. 1, pp. 1130–40.
"Arbeitsmarkt, Der," Monatschrift des Verbandes Deutscher Arbeitsnachweise, Berlin, Dr. J. Jastrow, Ed.
"Arbeitslosigkeit und Arbeitsvermittelung," Bericht über den Sozialen Congress in Frankfurt A.M. (1893)." Berlin, 1894.

Ayres, P. W.: "Free Public Employment Offices in Ohio; an Experiment in Socialistic Legislation." International Congress of Charities, 1893, pp. 124–31.

Bartram, Charles E.: "Free Public Employment Offices." National Conference of Charities and Correction, 1897, pp. 207–17.

Becci, Gabriel: "Le Placement des Ouvriers et Employés des deux Sexes et des Toutes Professions et la Loi du 14 Mars, 1904," 221 pp. O. Paris, Rousseau, 1906.

Beveridge, W. H.: "Curse of Casual Labor." In Socialist Review, June, 1908.
"Labour Exchanges." 11 pp. 1907. To be obtained from the Central (Unemployed) Body, 165 Temple Chambers, Temple Avenue, London, E. C.
"Labor Exchanges and the Unemployed." In Economic Journal, March, 1907, pp. 66–81.
"Unemployment and Its Cure: The First Step." In Contemporary Review, April, 1908, pp. 385–98.

Bliss: Cyclopedia of Social Reform, 1908. Article on "Unemployment," pp. 1234–47.
"Uselessness of Labor Colonies," pp. 1246–7.

Bliss, W. D. P.: "What is Done for the Unemployed in European Countries." United States Bureau of Labor, Bulletin 76, May, 1908, pp. 741–933.

Bogart, E. L.: "Public Employment Offices in United States and Germany." In Commons, Trade Unionism and Labor Problems, 1905, p. 603–26; also in Quarterly Journal of Economics, vol. 19, May, 1900, pp. 341–77.

Böhmert: "Zur Statistik der Arbeitslosigkeit, der Arbeitsvermittelung u. s. w." In der Zeitschrift des sächsischen Bureaus, Jahrg., 1894.

Brooks, John Graham: "Future Problem of Charity and the Unemployed." 27 pp. 1895. American Academy of Political and Social Science Publications, 122.

Burns, John: "Unemployed." 1892 (Fabian Tracts, No. 47). Bibliography, p. 19. Reprint from Nineteenth Century, December, 1892.

Byles, A. Holden: "German Labour Bureaus." In Progress, April, 1906, pp. 106–15.

Chance, Sir William: "Poor Law and the Unemployed." In Poor Law Conferences, 1905–6 pp. 134–47.

Chapman, Sydney J.: "Work and Wages." Pt. 11, Chapter on Unemployment, London, Longmans, 1908.

Clay, Arthur: "Unemployment and Legislation." In London Charity Organisation Review, May, 1905, pp. 255–67.

Conner, J. E.: "Free Public Employment Offices in United States." United States Bulletin of the Bureau of Labor, No. 68, January, 1907. pp. 1–115.

Conrad, Carl: "Die Organisation des Arbeitsnachweises in Deutschland." Leipzig, 1904.

Cormier, Crosson du: "Les Caisses Syndicales de Chomage en France et en Belgique." Paris, Chevalier. 1905.

Dawson, William H.: "Problem of the Unemployed." In Social Switzerland, 1897, pp. 130–42.
"Unemployed." In German Workman, 1906, pp. 1–86. Chap. 1, Labour Registries. Chap. 2, Munich Labour Bureaus.

Devins, John Bancroft: "Report of the Cooper Union Labor Bureau." New York Association for Improving the Condition of Poor, Report 1900, pp. 81–88.

Dewey, Davis R.: "Irregularity of Employment." American Economic Association. Publication No. 5–6, 1894, pp. 53–67.

Drage, Geoffrey: "Problem of the Unemployed." New York, Macmillan, 1894.

Eckert: "Der moderne Arbeitsnachweis," Leipzig, 1902.

Faquot, F.: "Le Chomage." 210 pp. Paris, Soc. nouvelle de librarie et d' édition, 1905.

France, Government Publications: "Ministère de Commerce et de l'Industrie—Office du Travail. Le Placement des Employés Ouvriers et Domestiques en France: son Histoire, son État Actuel." 734, pp., 1893.
"Report, 1901." 188 pp.
"Documents sur la Question du Chomage." 398 pp. 27m. Paris, Imprimerie nationale, 1896. Résumé in U. S. Department of Labor, Bul. 12, September, 1897, pp. 622–24.

Great Britain, Government Publications: "Report of Commission to Investigate Distress from Want of Employment." 3 v. F. 1895.
"Report of Select Committee on Distress from Want of Employment;" with proceedings, minutes of evidence, appendix and index. 118 pp. F. London, Eyre. 1896.

"Labour Bureaux: Report made to the President of the Local Government Board." 32 p. F. London. Darling. 1906. By Arthur Lowry, which see.

"Unemployed Workmen Act, 1905: Return as to the Proceedings of Distress Committees in England and Wales and of the Central (Unemployed) Body for London under the Unemployed Workmen Act, 1905." March 31, 1906-07. 30 pp. F. London, Wyman.

"Annual Reports of the Local Government Boards of England and Wales, of Scotland, and of Ireland, 1905 to date, for Proceedings of Distress Committees under the Unemployed Workmen Act of 1905."

"Board of Trade Report on Agencies and Methods for Dealing with the Unemployed, 1893." By D. F. Schloss, which see.

"London County Council. Lack of Employment in London:" Minutes of Proceedings at Conferences, held Feb. 13, April 3, 1903 (No. 662). 50 pp. F. London.

"Central (Unemployed) Body for London. Second Report upon the Work of the Central Body from May 12, 1906, to June 30, 1907," 149 pp. London. King, 1908.

Hall, Prescott F.: "The Effects of Immigration on Unemployment." In Immigration, 1906, pp. 135-38.

Herz, Hugo: "Arbeitsscheu und recht auf Arbeit; kritische Beiträge zur oesterreichischen Straf und sozial-gesetzgebung." 100 pp. O. Leipzig, 1902. pp. 87, Der arbeitsnachweis; pp. 100, Bibliographie.

Hobson, John A.: "Problem of the Unemployed." 1896.

International Labour Office. Bulletin No. 1, 1906. "Act Relating to State and Local Contributions to Norwegian Unemployment Societies," June 12, 1906.
"Decree of Dec. 9, 1905, Concerning Subventions for Unemployment Societies (France).

Jastrow: "Sozialpolitik und Verwaltungswissenschaft." Bd. 1, Berlin, 1902.

Kellor, Frances A.: "Out of Work." 1905. Free employment offices, p. 237-57.

Leo: "Die bestehenden Einrichtungen zur Versicherung gegen die Folgen der Arbeitslosigkeit." Teil 11: Der Stand der gemeinützigen Arbeitsvermittelung im Deutschen Reich, Berlin, 1906.

Lodwick, Libbie: "Relation of the State to the Unemployed." Iowa State Conference of Charities and Correction, 1900–03. pp. 19–25.

Long, W. H.: "Outline of Scheme for Dealing with Unemployed." Proposed at Conference of Metropolitan Guardians, October 14, 1904. Great Britain Local Government Board Report, 1904–5, pp. 154–56.

Lowry, Arthur: "Labour Bureaux: Report of Local Government Board." 32 pp. F. London, Darling, 1906.

Ludwig: "Der gewerbsmässige Arbeitsnachweis," Berlin, 1906.

Mackay, Thomas: "Relief of the Unemployed." In London Charity Organisation Review, November, 1904, pp. 260-69.
"Unemployed." In London Charity Organisation Review, January, 1894, pp. 3–6.

Malavé: "La Bourse du Travail à Paris." Brussels, 1889.

Mercer, A.: "Unemployment." In Economic Review, April 15, 1907, pp. 167–76.

Molinari: "La Bourse du Travail." In Journal des Economistes, 1888.
"Les Bourses du Travail." Paris, 1893.

Münich: Städtisches arbeitsamt. "Geschäftsberichte," 1895 to date.

New South Wales: "State Labor Bureau, Annual Reports of Director of Labor.
"Report of the Unemployed Advisory Board." 1899.

Nunn, T. Hancock: "Municipal Labour Bureaux." In Loch, Methods of Social Advance, 1904, pp. 96–106.

"Our Unemployed: and What Count Rumford Did for the Poor in Bavaria, by a Vice-president of the American Humane Education Society." 11 pp. n. d.

Plotz, Paul P.: "Securing Employment for the Idle." St. Vincent de Paul Society, International Convention, 1904, pp. 242–47.

Propert, P. S. G.: "Problem of Unemployment." In Westminster Review, August, 1907, pp. 193–200.
"Problem of Unemployment with Special Reference to the Unemployed Workmen Act, 1905." In Poor Law Conferences, 1905–6, pp. 672–87.

Reitzenstein, Friederich F.: "Der arbeitsnachweis: Seine entwickelung und gestaltung im in-und Auslande." 586 pp. Berlin, 1897.

Report of a Special Committee of the Council of the Charity Organisation Society (London), on the Relief of Distress Due to Want of Employment. November, 1904, pp. 231.

Rivière, Louis: "Mendiants et Vagabonds." Ed. 2. 239 pp. O. Paris, Lecoffre, 1902.

Russell, C. E. B.: "Manchester Boys." Chap. 26. Municipal Labour Bureaus: A Suggestion.

Schloss, D. F.: "Report to the Board of Trade (Great Britain) on Agencies and Methods for Dealing with Unemployed in Foreign Countries." 1904.

"Schriften des Verbandes deutscher Arbeitsnachweise," Munich, 1898, Leipzig, 1908.

Sellers, Edith: "Unemployment in Switzerland." In the Nineteenth Century, November, 1908.

Siegfried, Jules: Free Municipal Labor Bureau of Paris. In Social Service, April, 1904, pp. 75–76.

Singer, Rudolf: "Die Organisation des Arbeitsnachweises in Wien." Zeitschrift für Volkswirtschaft, Sozialpolitik und Verw., Jahrg. 1895.

Toynbee, H. V.: "Problem of the Unemployed." In Economic Review, July 15, 1905, pp. 291–305.

United States Industrial Commission. "Unemployment." Vol. 19, pp. 746–63, 1901.

United States Government Publications: Bulletin of the United States Bureau of Labor." Nos. 54, 68, 76. (See Bliss, Conner.)

Annual Reports of the Free Public Employment Bureaus, State and Municipal, which have been Established or Authorized in the following States: California municipal bureaus (1893); Colorado (1907); Connecticut (1901); Illinois (1899); Kansas (1901); Maryland (1902); Massachusetts (1906); Michigan (1905); Minnesota (1905); Missouri (1898); Montana municipal bureaus (1895); Nebraska (1897); New York (1896, abolished 1906); Ohio (1890); Washington municipal bureaus (1899); West Virginia (1900); Wisconsin (1899); (Some of the free employment bureaus publish weekly or bi-weekly bulletins or gazettes.)

"Massachusetts Bureau of Statistics of Labor." Report for 1893. See Wadlin. Report for 1903, pp. 131–214. Free Employment Offices in the United States and Foreign Countries.

"Bulletin 51." July–August, 1907, pp. 36–40. Free Employment Offices in Foreign Countries.

Reports and Bulletins of the State Bureaus of Labor for Current Information in Regard to Unemployment in Organized Trades.

Wadlin, Horace G.: "Unemployment." In the 24th Annual Report of the Mass. Bureau of Statistics of Labor, 1893.

Western Australia: Government Labor Bureau. "Annual Reports of Superintendent," 1898 to date.

Willoughby, William F.: "Employment Bureaus in the United States." 16 pp. Monographs on American Social Economics, No. 6, 1900.

"Measurement of Unemployment." In Yale Review, August, 1901, pp. 188–202; November, 1901, pp. 268–97.

Wright, Harold O. S.: "Sociological View of Unemployment." In Westminster Review, April, 1908, pp. 376–92.

Printed in Dunstable, United Kingdom